Computers, Thinking, and Social Studies

Computers, Thinking, and Social Studies

Gene E. Rooze
Texas Tech University
Lubbock, Texas

and

Terry Northup
McMurry College
Abilene, Texas

1989
TEACHER IDEAS PRESS
A Division of
Libraries Unlimited, Inc.
Englewood, Colorado

TEACHER IDEAS PRESS
A Division of Libraries Unlimited, Inc.
P.O. Box 3988
Englewood, Colorado 80155-3988

Library of Congress Cataloging-in-Publication Data

Rooze, Gene Edward.
    Computers, thinking, and social studies / Gene E. Rooze and Terry Northup.
        xiii, 257 p. 22x28 cm.
        Rev. and updated ed. of: Using computers to teach social studies. 1986.
        Includes bibliographical references.
        ISBN 0-87287-718-3
        1. Social sciences--Computer-assisted instruction.   2. Social sciences--Computer programs.   3. Thought and thinking--Study and teaching.   I. Northup, Terry, 1941- .   I. Rooze, Gene Edward. Using computers to teach social studies.   III. Title.
    LB1584.7.R66   1989
    300'.285536--dc20   89-20271
                                                            CIP

This book is dedicated to our wives,
Esta Mae Rooze
and
Mary Jacque Northup,
for their devoted love and support.

CONTENTS

PREFACE

This book is designed to meet the needs of a variety of professionals. Its purposes are:

- to describe how computers can be used in a variety of approaches to teaching social studies.

- to describe the nature of thinking and how it can be developed.

- to discuss how the development of thinking skills can be enhanced through the use of computers.

- to explain some of the newly emerging applications of the computer for the classroom and their effects on the teaching of social studies.

- to explore the ways a teacher can use the computer as a management tool.

- to provide a set of resources specifically for the social studies student, teacher, and supervisor at all grade levels, elementary and secondary.

The scope of the book is limited to the relationship of the computer to social studies. While it seems to be a rather narrow topic, even this cannot be covered fully. Although we touch upon a wide variety of the philosophies of social studies, we focus on the development of knowledge, thinking skills, and technology in the field. We show that computers can improve instruction in the social studies and at the same time help students prepare for their future by developing the skills necessary for the information age in which they will live.

Readers should remember that, with the rapid rate of change in the field, material related to specific computer software and its price goes out of date quickly. In addition, new software and approaches to computer programming are being developed constantly. In such a situation, it is impossible for any article or book to be up to date.

Our primary audience is social studies professionals at all levels: preservice teachers, elementary and secondary classroom teachers, supervisors, and college professors. Teachers of other subjects concerned with the development of knowledge, thinking skills, and curriculum technology will also find the book useful.

This volume has several unique features. It combines the theory and application of computer use, unlike other books that emphasize one or the other of these approaches. For example, Ahl's (1983) book, *Computers in Science and Social Studies*, is a collection of program listings. Abelson's (1983) *Using Computers in the Social Studies Classroom* is a good collection of theoretical articles about the use of computers, but it does not provide practical help for teachers. Glenn and Rawitsch's (1984) *Computing in the Social Studies Classroom* is practical but limited in depth.

Budin, Kendall, and Lengel's (1986) book *Using Computers in the Social Studies* is a brief overview of application and uses of the computer in social studies. Its emphasis is on the general use of the computer. Ehman and Glenn's (1987) *Computer-Based Education in the Social Studies* reviews the research on the application of the computer to social studies.

Where emphasis is placed on computer applications, this book focuses on databases, online database services, word processing, and spreadsheets. These may be the areas of greatest potential in social studies education. The book also presents a wide variety of resources including an annotated bibliography of books and articles and lists of print materials, software, and distributors of social studies computer software.

Social studies curriculum has been neglected by both software developers and textbook authors, as noted by Nancy Roberts (1982) in her article "Who's Last in Line for Computers? The Social Studies Teacher." While in the past few years there have been some pamphlets and articles specific to social studies, there has not been a comprehensive book that attempts to tie together theory and practice in the field. This book is an attempt to meet the need felt by social studies professionals who are either beginning or more advanced computer users. We include activities and resources for both groups.

Chapter 1 is an introductory chapter that provides an overview of three kinds of computer use: computer literacy, computer applications, and computer assisted instruction (CAI). The important role of the computer in developing thinking skills is described, and a review of current research is presented.

Chapter 2, "The Impact of the Computer on the Social Studies Curriculum," discusses the message implied by computer use, the major viewpoints regarding what social studies is, and how computers can be used to support each viewpoint.

Chapter 3, "Software Evaluation: A Crucial Element in Successfully Using Computers," explores the problems of evaluating software, describes some evaluation systems, proposes a format for use, and provides some sample evaluations using that format.

Chapter 4, "Using Thinking to Put Together the World of Information," describes why the development of thinking must be a priority in social studies classrooms, what the types of thinking skills are, how thinking in the classroom can be developed, and how computers can be used to develop thinking.

Chapter 5, "Using and Making Software: Yes, You Can," describes how to use CAI programs and how to write your own.

Chapter 6, "Integrating Software into the Curriculum to Develop Thinking," describes strategies for the use of a variety of tools to promote organization, analysis, and reporting skills.

Chapter 7, "Teacher Uses of the Computer," explains how the computer can be used as a management tool. The chapter begins with a discussion of integrated software and goes on to show ways of using the computer to grade, to create course material that develops thinking, to create learning activity packets that foster thinking, and to use special print programs.

Chapter 8, "Sources and Resources for Using Computers in Social Studies Education," provides lists of magazines and software producers, an annotated bibliography of print resources, and descriptions of more than 300 programs in social studies that can help you be a more effective teacher.

REFERENCES

Abelson, Robert. 1983. *Using Computers in the Social Studies Classroom.* Boulder, Colo.: Social Science Education Consortium.

Ahl, David. 1983. *Computers in Science and Social Studies.* Morris Plains, N.J.: Creative Computing Press.

Budin, Howard, Diane Kendall, and James Lengel. 1986. *Using Computers in the Social Studies.* New York: Teachers College Press.

Ehman, Lee H., and Allen D. Glenn. 1987. *Computer-Based Education in the Social Studies.* Bloomington, Ind.: Social Studies Development Center.

Glenn, Allen, and Don Rawitsch. 1984. *Computing in the Social Studies Classroom.* Eugene, Oreg.: International Council for Computers in Education.

Roberts, Nancy. 1982. "Who's Last in Line for Computers? The Social Studies Teacher." *Classroom Computer News* (November/December): 17-18.

1

INTRODUCTION

SETTING THE STAGE

In 1983 *Time* magazine gave its "Man of the Year" award to the computer, declaring, "The 'information revolution' that futurists have long predicted has arrived, bringing with it the promise of dramatic changes in the way people live and work, and perhaps even in the way they think. America will never be the same" ("The Computer Moves In," 3 January 1983). In a survey *Time* reporters found that 68 percent of the respondents expected that computers would raise the quality of education in the United States. Such a development would certainly be welcome in the wake of the recent attacks by critics of education.

The fact that computers are being sold like hotcakes is news to no one. Businesses and families are buying computers at a rapid rate. So are schools. In 1980 Chambers and Bork found that 54 percent of U.S. school districts were using computers for computer assisted instruction (CAI). The teachers involved felt that these programs were effective. Hassett (1984) noted in September 1984 that 86 percent of the high schools, 81 percent of the junior high schools, and 62 percent of the elementary schools had computers. Bell (1983) cites a report that claimed that by 1987 the average school would have thirty-five computers. A survey by Becker found that the average student in 1983 spent about forty-five minutes per week at a computer (Glenn and Rawitsch 1984).

One survey (*Electronic Learning*, October 1987) reported that teachers are more interested in instructional computing, money for teacher training has increased, and software budgets are higher. It also stated that between 1986 and 1987 the number of microcomputers in schools rose by 18 percent. Talmis, a research firm, surveyed schools during the 1987/1988 school year and found that there were 2.03 million microcomputers in schools (*Electronic Learning*, May/June 1988). This same report also stated that 59 percent of these are Apple computers, 16 percent are Tandy computers, 11 percent are IBM computers, and 9 percent are Commodore computers.

NEW CONDITIONS REQUIRE NEW APPROACHES

Computers are in the schools and more are coming, but what are teachers to do with them? There are three approaches. First, computers can be used to develop "computer literacy." Many feel that it is an absolute necessity for individuals to know how to use computers as we move into an increasingly technological future. Molnar (1983) claims that it is as much a social obligation for the schools to provide this knowledge as it is to provide reading skills. Most advocates of this approach stress the importance of learning to program in one or more of the computer languages. This is seen as a method of teaching problem-solving skills and structured thinking as well as programming (Bitter et al. 1985). Second, the computer can be used as a tool to acquire data, analyze and synthesize data, and communicate data in logical forms. What is being emphasized here is the use of the computer to develop thinking skills. (In chapter 4 we describe the rationale for developing thinking skills in social studies and present a list of essential skills that should be developed. In later chapters examples of how this can be done will be provided.) Third, computers can be used to deliver instruction by way of CAI. This approach uses the computer to more efficiently or more effectively help students reach learning objectives in content areas.

In this book we will explore the latter two of these uses, since both are important as a part of social studies instruction. For a moment, however, let us consider all three concepts in more depth.

Computer Literacy: What Is It?

Computer literacy is a term in search of a definition. To some it involves learning terms and techniques for constructing programs, including the development of logical thinking skills necessary to create algorithms on which the programs are based. Others see an understanding of the role of computers and information about computer careers as an essential part of computer literacy. Still others stress the ability to use the computer as a tool to perform functions such as word processing, data management, and statistical analysis. Any computer literacy program will touch upon all these in some measure, but will lean toward either programming or tool use, depending on the orientation of the curriculum designer. There is a tendency to emphasize programming at the expense of tool use in computer literacy courses, but programming knowledge may not be essential today. With the current abundance of software for almost any purpose, few users need to be programmers. This is especially true in business and industry. The software exists; employees only have to follow the directions in order to make use of it.

An example of the disagreement over the proper emphasis in computer literacy programs occurred at the Texas Computer Education Association meeting in February 1985. Art Luehrmann, the man who coined the term *computer literacy* fifteen years ago, said in a panel discussion that he knew exactly what he meant then and he means the same thing now. To him computer literacy involves knowing what a computer can and cannot do and being able to tell the computer what you want it to do—computer awareness, computer applications, and computer programming (Bitter et al. 1985). Jack Roberts, editor of *Electronic Learning*, spoke on the same panel from a very different viewpoint. Roberts said that in the past year he had seen a definite shift in the conception of computer literacy away from programming and toward applications programs such as filing, word processing, and spreadsheets. He said he believed computer literacy programs should teach students what tools are available, which are best for particular tasks, and how to use these programs (Bitter et al. 1985).

Computer literacy is usually taught in a separate course and is not a part of social studies. It is for these reasons that this book will not devote time to computer literacy in the usual sense of the word. We are treating the use of the computer as a tool as a separate approach. Tool use can be developed in any subject, not just in a computer course.

Developing Thinking Skills: The Computer's Potential

Many social studies teachers believe one of their primary goals is to teach students to acquire, analyze, and synthesize data. Increasingly, in an information society, this is what jobs require. Computers and computer programs can be used to stimulate this process. Chapter 4 will discuss the development of thinking skills. Chapters 5, 6, and 7 will describe ways that thinking can be developed via computers.

CAI: What Is Its Role?

Computer assisted instruction, hereafter referred to as CAI, uses the computer as a simulated teacher. The computer provides instructional material or questions, awaits the student's response, and then provides feedback based on the student's individual response. While CAI can never fully replace the teacher, there are some roles it can perform more efficiently and effectively.

Critics of education have accused schools of being both ineffective and inefficient, and students are not performing as well as in the past, according to some. Many see CAI as one means of solving this problem.

In CAI the computer is used as a mediating device that delivers some portion of the instruction. The next two sections discuss the effectiveness of CAI. Later in the book, the use of CAI in social studies will be considered in depth.

A Review of the Research on the Educational Uses of Computers

Most of the research on the educational uses of computers relates to CAI, since this was the earliest use of computers in education and is still the most common. The bulk of the research compares CAI and traditional approaches (Garson 1983). This is like comparing radio and television to see which one the student hears best. Television is more than a radio and has much more potential for instruction; likewise, CAI has the potential to do new and different things. Using it only to provide traditional instruction will keep it from reaching its full potential.

Another research problem involves what has been referred to as the "John Henry Effect" (Winkle and Mathews 1982). Simply stated, teachers in control groups have been observed to work extra hard in order to produce results as good as those achieved by the experimental groups. Their behavior is similar to that of the legendary John Henry, who worked himself to death trying to beat the machine designed to replace him.

Forman (1982) conducted an extensive review of the research in the field and drew the following conclusions:

1. CAI has been found to be at least equal to, and often better than, traditional instruction in terms of test results.

2. CAI achieved these equal or better results in less time than traditional instruction takes.

3. CAI develops positive attitudes in students and often improves their motivation, attention span, and attendance.

4. Reluctant learners become more active and involved with CAI.

5. Drill and practice and tutorial programs using CAI are quite effective with low-ability students.

Other reviews have reported similar results, as well as some additional ones. Lawton and Gerschner (1982) found that CAI is very effective with high-ability students and that CAI users exhibited more internal responsibility. The Los Angeles (Bell 1983) and Chicago (Chambers and Sprecher 1983) public schools found significant increases in the standardized test scores of students who used CAI. In addition, CAI is very cost effective (Adams 1989).

Becker (1988) reviewed available research on CAI. His conclusions are consistent with those mentioned above. He argues, however, that we need more research that is methodologically sound. In a review of fifty-one recent studies, only one was found to have been done well in terms of the principles of research. This one study found a positive effect for CAI but it included only a few classrooms in one school. Hardly the evidence one would want to base decisions upon.

Why Is CAI Effective?

What is there about learning with CAI that produces the results mentioned above? The material below summarizes the findings of a variety of scholars. Since the early 1980s no additional findings have been noted.

1. CAI individualizes the pace of learning, allowing the student to progress at his or her chosen speed (Forman 1982; Chambers and Sprecher 1983; Jernstedt 1983; Lawton and Gerschner 1982).

2. In programs that are designed to branch, CAI can individualize on the basis of the student's responses by advancing to different locations within the program (Forman 1982; D'Angelo 1983).

3. CAI can provide immediate feedback on a specific problem, as well as provide an up-to-date summary of progress for the entire lesson (Forman 1982; Jernstedt 1983). Lawton and Gerschner (1982) note that students liked this feature because they could get feedback in private, without embarrassment.

4. The computer also provides immediate reinforcement (Forman 1982; Chambers and Sprecher 1983). Reinforcement and feedback are similar (and in some cases almost indistinguishable). Feedback merely gives the student information regarding the correctness of his answer. Reinforcement provides a response that indicates some value. Reinforcement could consist of a computer response of "Good, Johnny" or a graphic display that communicates to Johnny that his answer was correct. Lawton and Gerschner (1982) found that students like reinforcement and the fact that the computer never forgets to provide reinforcement.

5. CAI programs can be used for review, remediation, or enrichment—that is, they are flexible and can meet a variety of needs (Forman 1982).

6. CAI involves the student actively (Forman 1982; Chambers and Sprecher 1983; Jernstedt 1983), in contrast to most large-group lessons in which students are required only to sit and (perhaps) listen, responding externally only if called upon and internally only if the lesson especially interests them. Working with a computer is like having a one-to-one tutor; the student must respond before the next idea or problem is presented. Since research supports the idea that more is learned through active than through passive participation, this is a significant feature of CAI.

7. CAI can free the teacher from some instruction and grading tasks, allowing him or her to perform those functions that require the human touch while the computer performs the mechanical tasks. The teacher can give attention to those who really need it (Forman 1982; Chambers and Sprecher 1983).

8. In most fifty-minute classes a student receives fifteen seconds of personal attention from the teacher, but a computer gives the student its undivided attention. In addition, the computer has endless patience and is precise and objective (Forman 1982; D'Angelo 1983; Lawton and Gerschner 1982).

9. Doerr (1979) and Scrogan (1988) suggest that one of the advantages of CAI is that it creates a nonthreatening, noncompetitive environment. In such an environment a student can venture an answer without negative consequences. Reflective students are not under pressure to respond immediately, as they are in a regular classroom situation.

10. Doerr (1979) also suggests that CAI makes it possible for the teacher's role to change. She sees the teacher becoming an ally rather than an adversary, acting more as a coach and encourager. Given a set of objectives, problems, and tasks that the student is to accomplish, the teacher can become a facilitator/helper, with the computer assuming the role of instructor, taskmaster, and evaluator.

11. Bracey (1988) reviewed research regarding the ratio of students to computers. He found that it is not necessary to have one computer per student. In fact, there are several advantages to small groups working together, such as greater productivity, higher test scores, elimination of sex differences on final tests, and the development of prosocial attitudes. Tom Snyder Productions is an example of a company that specifically creates software to be used by small groups.

12. David Press, a teacher and computer coordinator in New York City, suggests a final advantage, one that cannot be measured through research: "It's not something that can be tested. It's the hidden benefit that can't be recorded in the teacher's lesson plan book. But when students master the machine, they are really learning the exciting dimensions of their own potential, their own power to grow and discover and to control the world around them" (Howarth, 1983). It is at this point that the uses of the computer for CAI and as a tool merge—mastery over the machine leads to a sense of power and the realization that the machine is a tool that can unlock endless mysteries.

REFERENCES

Adams, Richard C. 1989. "Computers in School: What's the Real Use?" *NEA Today: Special Edition* (January): 26-31.

"A Report on EL's Seventh Annual Survey of the States." 1987. *Electronic Learning* (October): 39-42, 44, 83.

Becker, Henry J. 1988. "The Impact of Computers on Our Children's Learning." *Principal* (November): 64, 66, 68, 70.

Bell, Trudy. 1983. "My Computer, My Teacher." *Personal Computing* (June): 120, 122-123, 125, 127.

Bitter, Gary, Barbara Kershan, Arthur Luehrmann, James Poirot, and Jack Roberts. 1985. "Discussing Computer Literacy with Authors of Computer Literacy Textbooks." Texas Computer Education Association Annual Conference, February, Austin, Tex.

Bracey, Gerald W. 1988. "Two Studies Show Students Gain When Teaming Up." *Electronic Learning* (January): 19.

Chambers, Jack A., and Alfred Bork. 1980. "Computer Assisted Learning in U.S. Secondary/Elementary Schools." *The Computing Teacher* (September): 50-51.

Chambers, Jack A., and Jerry W. Sprecher. 1983. "Computer Assisted Instruction: Current Trends and Critical Issues." In *Run: Computer Education*, edited by Dennis O. Harper and James H. Stewart, 107-119. Monterey, Calif.: Brooks/Cole.

"The Computer Moves In." 1983. *Time* (January 3): 14-24.

D'Angelo, John. 1983. "The Microprocessor as Pencil." In *Run: Computer Education*, edited by Dennis O. Harper and James H. Stewart, 13-17. Monterey, Calif.: Brooks/Cole.

Doerr, Christine. 1979. *Microcomputers and the 3 R's*. Rochelle Park, N.J.: Hayden Book Co.

Forman, Denyse. 1982. "Search of the Literature." *The Computing Teacher* (January): 37-51.

Garson, James. 1983. "The Case Against Multiple Choice." In *Run: Computer Education*, edited by Dennis O. Harper and James H. Stewart, 120-126. Monterey, Calif.: Brooks/Cole.

Glenn, Allen, and Don Rawitsch. 1984. *Computing in the Social Studies Classroom*. Eugene, Oreg.: International Council for Computers in Education.

Hassett, James. 1984. "Computers in the Classroom." *Psychology Today* (September): 22, 24-28.

Howarth, Tony. 1983. "Taking a Stand for Computers in Education." *Personal Computing* (May): 121-123, 125, 127, 129.

Jernstedt, G. Christian. 1983. "Computer Enhanced Collaborative Learning: A New Technology for Education." *Technological Horizons in Education Journal* (May): 96-101.

Lawton, Johnny, and Vera T. Gerschner. 1982. "A Review of the Literature on Attitudes Towards Computers and Computerized Instruction." *Journal of Research and Development in Education* (November): 50-55.

Molnar, Andrew. 1983. "The Next Great Crisis in American Education: Computer Literacy." In *Run: Computer Education*, edited by Dennis O. Harper and James H. Stewart, 24-29. Monterey, Calif.: Brooks/Cole.

Naisbitt, John. 1982. *Megatrends: Ten New Directions Transforming Our Lives*. New York: Warner Books.

Scrogan, Len. 1988. "The OTA Report: New Technologies Are Making a Difference." *Classroom Computer Learning* (October): 33-34, 36-37, 39-42.

"Two Million Microcomputers Now Used in U.S. Schools." 1988. *Electronic Learning* (May/June): 16.

Winkle, Linda Wyrick, and Walter M. Mathews. 1982. "Computer Equity Comes of Age." *Phi Delta Kappan* (January): 314-315.

THE IMPACT OF THE COMPUTER ON THE SOCIAL STUDIES CURRICULUM

There are two views concerning the role of the microcomputer in education. Some believe the computer should be a mediating device that conveys knowledge to the student. Others contend the computer should itself be a focus of study.

Understanding these positions requires some historical background. Conventional wisdom holds that all knowledge passes through the teacher to the student:

knowledge ⟶ teacher ⟶ student

This model has been superseded in theory, if not in practice, by the more recent "teacher as manager" concept, which sees knowledge being transmitted through a number of mediating devices:

knowledge ⟶
teacher
simulation
textbook
film
computer software
filmstrip
videotape
programmed material
⟶ student

The teacher may transmit the knowledge firsthand or choose to use any of the mediating devices. In this model the microcomputer, like a film projector, is an instructional medium. Such a concept places the computer in a less significant role than it is often given. But it leaves the contemporary instructional model unchanged; computer assisted instruction (CAI) and computer managed instruction (CMI) become new instructional management tools for the teacher.

Computer literacy supporters see computer use as another part of the growing school curriculum. Traditionally the curriculum of the schools has been reading, writing, and arithmetic. These are essentially tool subjects. In the past century social studies and science have surfaced as part of the knowledge and values component of the curriculum. This component transmits our culture and represents the accepted disciplines of knowledge: mathematics, physical and life sciences, the social sciences, and the humanities. Computer literacy supporters see the computer as another tool, one that both processes and communicates facts and ideas. Its impact on society will be at least as important as that of printing. Its moral and ethical impact will be as important as the industrial revolution's.

Opponents of computer literacy insist that computers do not fit into the disciplines' philosophy of curriculum design. They protest that, like library skills, computer literacy is important but does not merit the status of a separate subject; promoting computer literacy as a subject would be similar to proposing that there be a subject called microwave cookery based on the fact that microwave ovens are widely used and poorly understood.

Both these positions have some merit. There is also a middle ground that sees at least four uses of the computer in education. Computers can be used as mediating devices; as tools to process, retrieve, and evaluate information; as the means to study a field; and as a means of managing instruction.

The remainder of this chapter will consider these four points. First, it will examine the effect a mediating device can have on instruction. Second, it will introduce the variety of program strategies available in computer software and look briefly at the computer as a tool. Third, it will examine a variety of views of social studies and furnish the background upon which the final section of the chapter is built. Fourth, it will discuss the use of the computer to support the various views of social studies education.

THE MEDIUM HAS A MESSAGE

The choice of instructional media affects the outcome of instruction. This section will examine the relationship of media to subject matter. First let us review the instructional interaction model.

An accepted definition of *curriculum* is: those planned experiences obtained under the auspices of the school. Those experiences involve subject matter — knowledge, skills, and values — usually called course content. This content is what schools transmit to students.

The experiences are obtained through instruction: a set of teacher actions (TA) using some mediating device (M) that allows student actions (SA), which result in an outcome. This is illustrated in the diagram below:

$$\text{Content} \longrightarrow \text{TA} + \text{M} + \text{SA} \longrightarrow \text{Resultant Outcome}$$

The point is that changing any one of these components influences the outcome of learning. The selection of a mediating device — programmed learning, textbooks, films, or CAI — *does* make a difference. It affects both teacher actions and student actions, and thus the resultant outcome.

This principle is well illustrated by considering the use of the textbook as a mediating device. There are several advantages to textbooks. First, they are fairly cheap, because they can be used repeatedly. Second, they contain information and, commonly, suggestions for student activities that can be used by teachers of varying skill levels. A beginning teacher can follow the teacher's guide verbatim and teach something. Third, textbooks allow standardization of presentation that can be built upon from year to year. Finally, they are readily available, since they are the traditional medium of instruction.

However, textbooks have several drawbacks that make them poor mediating devices. First, textbook use calls for an active teacher and passive students. Second, it often involves the memorization of facts, concepts, and principles and discourages analysis or creative thought. Third, the textbook approach can transmit the idea that knowledge is fixed—that the exploration of new knowledge and the solution of social problems should be left to the experts.

It is important, when evaluating a media device to be used in a course, to remember that it (1) makes a statement about the nature of a subject, (2) requires the use of a set of skills, and (3) transmits a set of values. Every field of knowledge has a set of ideas it attempts to transmit. These ideas are created through some means of looking at the world—methods. When one teaches the discipline to another, these methods are taught as a set of skills. In addition to this set of ideas and skills, one is taught a way of combining them to conduct further study. This method of combining becomes a set of attitudes and values. If a mediating device makes an inaccurate statement about the nature of the subject, transmits an inappropriate set of values, or requires an inappropriate set of skills, it should not be used.

Returning to the textbook example presented above, the nature of social studies presented by the textbook approach is passively descriptive. Textbook use in social studies basically requires map and study skills. (It should be remembered that the skills required to use the textbook are not necessarily the skills required to learn social studies.) The values transmitted are that social studies knowledge is fixed and generally unrelated to the life of the individual. If this is not the nature of social studies one wants to transmit, then the textbook is an improper media choice.

THE COMPUTER: A VARIETY OF MEDIATING DEVICES

When we talk of mediating devices we generally tend to envision single-purpose devices like the 16mm film projector. This conception is misleading when it is applied to the computer, because CAI makes use of several techniques for mediating instruction, as described below.

Drill and practice. Drill and practice programs are presently the most common. As the name implies, a drill and practice program presents the student with a series of questions to be answered or a problem to be solved. Such programs reinforce the learning of facts or skills.

Tutorial. The tutorial approach to CAI directly teaches facts, concepts, generalizations, or skills to students. It follows the popular direct instruction model: the program motivates, presents a model of what is to be learned, provides information, allows active participation, gives knowledge of results, and offers guidance to the student. Tutorials are increasing in number and their quality is improving.

Simulation. Simulations are based on sets of concepts and generalizations called constructs or models and are designed to describe real-world phenomena. The potential of simulation has yet to be realized in the public schools. In the past, multisession simulations were time-consuming because there were usually data to organize, and often statistically evaluate, before the next session could begin. The computer's speed has eliminated this problem and has greatly simplified and diversified the use of this instructional method.

Games. Some educational programs are designed as games, requiring a player or players, a set of rules, a contest, and a winner. They are an effective means of teaching facts or mastering skills or concepts. Often people are entranced by computerized games for hours at a time. Through such games students develop skills in planning and strategy that instructional designers find difficult to teach by traditional methods.

All of these methods of instruction use the computer's mediating capabilities—the computer delivers either information or experiences from which information can be gleaned. But the computer can also be used as a tool.

THE COMPUTER AS A TOOL

Hunter (1983) points out that until recently the tools social scientists used—computer databases, information retrieval systems, and programs for performing statistical analysis—were too expensive and complex for teachers to use in elementary or secondary classrooms. Her article identifies and describes several such tools that are now accessible for use in education. Each of these will be explained later.

Databases

A database is an organized collection of data that simplifies the retrieving and manipulation of information. One way of accessing a database uses the computer as if it were a remote terminal for a large computer. In this application the computer is connected to a telephone line through a modem, a piece of hardware that allows one to send and receive information (EPIE 1983). CompuServe and The Source are two examples of general-purpose online services that provide a broad range of general-information databases. CompuServe, for example, offers an electronic edition of the **Academic American Encyclopedia,** national newspapers for current events, and a travel section.

A second way of retrieving and manipulating information is through the use of software programs that allow the creation of a database and the use of information stored on a disk. Such programs are called database management systems. There are ways to use such systems. First, one can use commercially prepared databases and second, students can construct their own databases. Wheeler (1987) discusses two types of prepared databases. The first type, "stand-alone" programs, allow retrieval of information from a specific program and usually can not be revised. Samples of these databases are:

One World Countries Database and USA Profile, published by Active Learning Systems, 5365 Avenida Encinas, Suite J, Carlsbad, CA 92008. Developed for the Commodore 64, Apple family (128K), and the IBM PC and PC*jr.*

MECC Dataquest: The Presidents; MECC Dataquest: The Fifty States; and **MECC Dataquest: World Communities**, published by MECC, 3490 Lexington Avenue North, St. Paul, MN 55126. Developed for the Apple II family (64K).

The second type of prepared database is the "add-on," which is designed to be used with existing database managers such as **AppleWorks, Friendly Filer, pfs:File, Bank Street School Filer,** or **DCH Notebook Filer.** Examples of these databases follow:

U.S. History; U.S. Government; and **World Geography, Cultures and Economics,** published by Scholastic, Inc., 730 Broadway, New York, NY 10003. Designed for use with **pfs:File.** Developed for use with the Apple family (64K).

Heath Social Studies, published by Collamore/D.C. Heath and Co., 125 Spring Street, Lexington, MA 02173. Designed for use with **DCH Notebook Filer.** Developed for the Apple II family (64K).

As stated above, children can develop their own databases using database management systems such as **AppleWorks, Friendly Filer, pfs:File, Bank Street School Filer,** and **DCH Notebook Filer.** There has been considerable interest in this tool in the last few years. Many educators feel databases allow the development of thinking skills previously neglected. Some of the recent research reviewed by Ehman and Glenn (1987) showed that on tests of information-processing skills those students using computers outperformed other students carrying out the same structured curriculum without the computer data retrieval. We will discuss the use and preparation of databases in more detail in chapters 5 and 6.

Still another way of retrieving and manipulating data from databases is through the use of Compact Disk-Read Only Memory (CD-ROM). CD-ROM is simply a massive system of storage for the microcomputer. Using this new technology a complete encyclopedia, such as **The Electronic Encyclopedia** developed by Grolier, or database, such as the ERIC file, can be stored on one compact disk. The excitement created by this device is that it expands the potential use of databases considerably.

Electronic Spreadsheets

An electronic spreadsheet is a program that displays a screen divided into rows and columns. The intersections of the rows and columns are called cells. The program is designed to store information in these cells. This information can be in the form of words, numbers, or formulas. The value of a spreadsheet is that it can store data in tabular form. It can be used to predict outcomes based on formulas, and it can perform calculations on the rows or columns of numeric data. Uses of spreadsheets will be discussed in chapters 6 and 7.

Statistical Analysis

When most of us hear the words *statistical analysis* we close our ears, recalling hours of calculation to discover what we already suspected. Yet statistical techniques are required to teach some aspects of social studies. Hunter (1983) reports that good software and documentation are now available. The use of **TeloFacts 2** will be discussed in chapter 5.

Word and Idea Processing

Word processing is another of the important tools available for use with the microcomputer. Using a software package such as **Bank Street Writer** (produced by Scholastic, Inc., for the Apple II, IBM PC, and Atari 400 and 800) students ranging from intermediate through high school can write, revise, store, retrieve, and print essays and reports.

In addition to word processing there are a number of developments that have enhanced this initial concept. With the invention of tools for idea processing, with a program such as **ThinkTank**, published by Living Videotext, we not only have the ability to edit writing but we can create ideas, develop them, and rearrange them as they develop in our mind, and then even illustrate them graphically with programs like **Bank Street StoryBook**, published by Mindscape. We will spend more time with these ideas in chapter 6.

Integrated Software

The development of microcomputers with greater amounts of memory has allowed the development of integrated software packages that combine such tools as word processing, databases, and spreadsheets. The advantages of such software is that it allows easy transfer of one tool into another. For example, a student can develop a database in **AppleWorks**, "cut" a portion of the information out, and "paste" the resulting chart directly into a report being prepared. Only two programs existed until recently: **AppleWorks** published by Apple, the earliest program for the school and home for Apple II family users, and **Microsoft Works** published by Microsoft for Apple Macintosh users. The recent arrivals are **Easy Working** published by Spinnaker Software for Commodore, Apple II family, and the IBM PC; and **MacmillanWorks** published by Macmillan for the Commodore, Apple II family, Radio Shack, and IBM PC. The latest two entries to the market have been designed for school and classroom use.

One of the several advantages of using this type of software is the easy integration of the database, spreadsheet, and word processing. The only disadvantage is that the compacting of all three tools into one package forced the designers to limit the power of each tool. In many uses this makes very little difference, since most word processing, database management, and work with spreadsheets does not call for sophisticated software.

HyperCard and Hypertext

A recent development, that of HyperCard and other hypertext-based programs, introduces still another tool that can be used by both teachers and students. This software is assembled much like a deck of index cards, but, unlike index cards, they contain buttons which activate a cross-referencing system. Like our minds they can allow a nonsequential association of ideas. (Instead of thinking in straight lines, our minds tend to be more like spider webs, branching from one idea to another.) Hypertext programs not only allow branching, but they permit the use of a variety of forms of media. They can link text, sound, and visual input. As a tool for teachers, hypertext can be used to develop multimedia instruction (Lehrer 1989). As a tool for students, Coburn (1989) describes how one student prepared a historical report of Hannibal's trek across the Alps which included maps, pop-up footnotes, and sound.

Although HyperCard has been a tool for the Macintosh computer, it is now available on Apple IIs and IBM machines. Stacks, the name for the software that hypertext programs produce, are becoming plentiful on the general market, and programs are being produced for social studies.

CMI

Computers can be used by teachers to manage instruction. This use ranges from record-keeping devices added to individual CAI programs to separate software packages. These programs can be designed to accumulate and assign grades, maintain complete student files, group students, and even prescribe instruction. Some of these usages will be discussed in chapter 7.

POSSIBLE EFFECTS OF USING COMPUTERS*

Haney (1982) presents the conflict between subject and mediating devices as it relates to science. Haney feels the microcomputer is a natural in the science curriculum. It removes tedium and releases the mind for analysis and evaluation. But used incorrectly, it can move science away from its intended goal, that of showing the subject as a process of knowing.

The science section of table 2.1 illustrates Haney's point. *The nature of science is intended to be disciplined inquiry.* This inquiry is focused upon the natural world and one can explain this world through an analysis of physical data from which conclusions can be drawn and explanations developed.

The indiscriminate use of drill and practice software portrays science as a subject matter rather than a process of inquiry. Some information can be presented, and some skills must be taught, but a constant diet of expository presentation and unapplied skills lessons grossly misrepresents this curricular area.

---

*Tutorials and games were not mentioned by either of the authors cited in this section. Their use will be addressed in the next section.

Table 2.1

Comparative Influences of the Use of Computers in Science and Social Studies

---

SCIENCE

Advantages	**Disadvantages**
Drill and practice:	
Learn about science and practice science skills.	Science is process and not content.
Database:	
Ready access to data.	Science is observation of nature.
Increased ability to process data.	Decision making needs to be in hands of student.
Simulation:	
Can be used where real experimentation is impractical.	Danger of overuse. Experimentation is what is important.
Cheaper than lab equipment.	Savings on equipment to expense of science.

SOCIAL STUDIES

Advantages	**Disadvantages**
Drill and practice:	
Learn about social studies and practice social studies skills.	Emphasizes social studies content rather than social studies as process.
Database	
Uses data-processing skills.	Current service cost $25 to $65 per hook-up.
Students can develop their own.	Databases are time-consuming to develop.
Simulation	
Uses cause and effect.	Used as games children play without lead-up and analysis. No higher thinking and learning.
Students able to ask "what if" and can see results.	
Allows experimental situations not available previously.	

Databases are beneficial to science instruction, but too constant use might present an incorrect concept of science to the student. The use of *prepared* databases takes away some decision-making possibilities: What data are needed? How should they be organized? Prepared databases predetermine the results achieved and insert possibilities of error that may go unchallenged. Their use may promote a misconception common in the use of textbooks: It's in the database; it must be true!

While some use of simulation is recommended, cautions are in order. The purpose of simulation is to recreate the essential elements of a phenomenon, eliminating only the dangerous or distracting elements of the situation. Simulations were never intended to replace experience. With the schools' need to decrease expenditures, simulations have been promoted as equivalent to experience. Again, science is an attempt to study and understand nature. Does an experiment on the computer promote this conception? The question of purpose must be faced squarely. Does the use of simulation destroy the perception that science is the process of knowing about nature?

Roberts (1982) looks at the effects the computer can have on an understanding of the nature of social studies. We will weigh the advantages and disadvantages of computer use in the same way we analyzed computer applications to science (see table 2.1). Again we will consider: What statement does the mediating device make about the nature of the subject? What are the skills required? What values are being transmitted?

Drill and practice has always been used to teach important concepts and skills in social studies. A problem develops, however, when this teaching method is used without the subsequent application of the learned concepts or skills: content becomes fixed in a static mold. Social studies becomes a subject to be learned, not one that can be usefully applied to the student's life. The problem is not mitigated by the use of drill and practice software.

Social science, the disciplines that are the foundations of social studies, has generally been thought of as a "world of words." Actually the social sciences have become nearly as number conscious as the physical and natural sciences. Data analysis is important to solving social problems. One of the recently popular goals of social studies is "social sciencing"; this requires data analysis. In addition, the microcomputer provides access to databases previously unavailable. The use of these information-oriented databases will permit the use of the information-processing skills previously unapplied to real-world information in social studies. In addition, participating in the development of databases in the classroom will place the student in charge of organizing his or her own information. This change allowed by the computer may well make social studies a more vital part of the curriculum.

While simulation is a substitute for experience in science, it is a welcome alternative in social studies. Often the sciencing done in social studies cannot be accomplished in the real world; and the exploration of cause and effect, the asking of "what if" questions, cannot take place in the classroom either. Simulation (Roberts 1978) may be the answer for social studies. This could change the nature of social studies in the classroom and explode the "fixed-knowledge" syndrome presently transmitted.

Conclusion

The computer can revitalize social studies instruction because of the nature, skills, and values it can transmit. It should be evident that the question presented to social studies specialists is: What nature, skills, and values should be transmitted in social studies education? The answers to these questions should indicate uses of the mediating device (the computer) that will be consistent with the teacher's or specialist's philosophy.

THE ALTERNATIVE VIEWS OF SOCIAL STUDIES

Since its inception as an area of study early in this century, the overriding goal of social studies has been the training of good citizens. But the views of how best to train them have varied. Some have thought that knowledge would produce a good citizen. Others have contended that teaching the citizen to think would do the trick. Some have believed we should make society better by showing citizens how to change society. Still others have felt the need to train good citizens by teaching them to understand themselves. And still another group believed we should analyze what a citizen does and then prepare programs and instructional procedures to teach those activities.

These perspectives have all passed through periods of acceptance and periods of rejection. In some curricula, textbooks, and theoretical articles the approaches seem to merge. A careful analysis, however, discloses that one view is more prominent than the others according to the authors' bias. This chapter will consider these approaches to illustrate the possible influences of the microcomputer.

The first view is that the best way to train a citizen is to provide knowledge about our cultural heritage and teach the values of the dominant culture. Proponents of the *knowledge approach* represent opposing ends of the educational spectrum. One group, the traditionalists, promote the great literature, history, and ideas of Western civilization (Vaughn 1983). On the other end of the continuum are those who represent the academic disciplines of the social sciences (Rice 1980). The common assumption of both is that knowledge alone has value and that this knowledge produces good citizens.

Under this conception of social studies the nature of knowledge appears to be fixed. Content, in this case the information, whether it is taken from the traditional sources (political history, political geography, and the humanities) or out of the social sciences, is merely to be learned. Knowledge is contained in a locked box. The box of knowledge is to be presented to the student through descriptive textbooks, teacher lecture, and drill-type activities. Although some guided discovery is encouraged, the knowledge to be "discovered" is carefully structured.

Advocates of the *skills approach* believe that the best way to train good citizens is to teach them a set of thinking skills. This set is intended to allow students to gather and organize information from which they can draw their own conclusions. Advocates of this approach to social studies have recently divided into two camps: the thinking, decision-making skills group (Cassidy and Kurfman 1977) and the processes of the social sciences, or inquiry, group (Ryan and Ellis 1974). The first group believes that an effective citizen must have the capacity to make reasoned choices from among several alternatives. The second group believes that we need to teach the scientific approach.

The essential difference between these two groups lies in the set of skills they feel need to be taught. Both groups maintain the view that present knowledge and values are useless in a changing, technologically oriented world. We need to teach future citizens ways to process information that will allow them to select from viable alternatives. People can solve their own problems and make their decisions.

The content of the skills approach is data for reflection or inquiry drawn from real or vicarious sources. The materials used as resources for such inquiry are items like newspapers, magazines, books, films, databases, videotapes, surveys, and experience. The teaching process is inquiry oriented. Knowledge in this system is the result of inquiry and is revisable.

Social analysis represents the revisionist view of social studies. The revisionists believe that man can create a better society through change. Change should begin in the schools; the schools must carry our civilization forward. Although democratic societies are interested in maintaining some traditions and social conventions, they expect thinking individuals to make changes, promoting a better way of life for people in the society. An excellent example of this view is presented by Reardon, Scott, and Totten (1983) in their exploration of the nuclear issue. Schools have a choice of teaching *about* democracy through glib, empty generalizations or through promoting active follow-through on beliefs and concerns. Revisionists believe that students should study the issues of their society and that schools should provide children with a clear sense of the purposes of democracy and with the knowledge and skills future citizens need to change their world.

As in the skills approach, knowledge under this perspective is *created* through an analysis of what is. But in the social analysis approach there are two sets of skills: The skills of inquiry are taught as a means of determining what is and the skills of decision making are taught to establish what should be. Skills are merely a means to an end under this perspective, as opposed to *the* end under the skills approach.

There is also a subgroup within this philosophy of social studies interested in helping the individual to adapt to a world of changing technology and values (Estvan 1971). Proponents of this perspective are not interested in changing society but in adapting individuals to fit an already changing society. The school's purpose, they contend, is to help youth solve the problems that confront them today. Knowledge to this group is an awareness of current issues.

As one of society's basic socializing agencies, the school is called upon to help children cope—to help them find an identity (a sense of reality), determine purposes, and become socially productive. The skills here too are the processes of inquiry. Students study the issues important to them. This study makes the home and the school experience parallel. The community is a social studies laboratory. Emphasis is placed on social interaction and interaction skills. This subgroup differs from the main group in its focus on changing the individual as opposed to changing the society.

The *self-awareness approach* sees the purpose of social studies as creating citizens with a sense of personal identity and social responsibility (Fraenkel 1980). This is accomplished through providing individuals with knowledge about themselves, their goals, and their values. The goal of such a social studies program is to allow individuals security to fulfill themselves.

Much of the content of this curriculum focuses on the "human problem" in problem solving. It differs from the other perspectives discussed above in that it examines both the factual and the emotional aspects of the problem. It recognizes that social problems involve the personality structures of individuals. Knowledge here is knowing who I am and how I can relate successfully to others. In discovering myself, I learn of my responsibility to others.

Values are the central focus of this curriculum. Skills are important, but they are not the intended end product. Such skills as critical thinking and decision making are taught as tools, the means of solving personal and group dilemmas. Much of the learning is accomplished in a group setting where value conflicts are brought into sharp focus.

The *instructional technology approach* makes no assumption as to what specific knowledge and skills should be taught. It proposes the goal of social studies as the enhancement of citizenship. It asks the question "What is a good citizen?" and proposes the processes of scientific inquiry to find out. It dictates no prescribed set of skills, but asks "What skills do citizens need?" and proposes scientific procedures to find out. It does not require any particular teaching method, but asks "What are the best ways to teach these ideas?" Experimental procedures are used to find the answer. This approach to social studies is simply the scientific approach applied to education. Elements of this approach are present in all of the perspectives listed above. Many educators propose that it should be the foundation upon which the social studies curriculum is built.

Whenever technology is mentioned in the context of education, red flags are waved by people who fear automation and the replacement of teachers with machines. As educators we fail to realize that technology simply consists of ideas and tools that make the job of education easier (Huebner 1974). By themselves the ideas and tools have no power—they merely amplify the power of the individuals who use them. In social studies the use of instructional technology has allowed us to ask "What do good citizens need to know?" and "How can we do a better job of teaching citizens?" These questions have been asked before, of course, but instructional technology provides data-gathering and data analysis techniques needed to discover the answers. However, the answers may not support the values particular groups of social studies educators hold.

In this section we have discussed the views of social studies found in the literature (Rooze 1976). Schools have predominantly followed the knowledge and skills approaches, with smatterings of the other perspectives added as the need arose to meet public demands. In the next section we will explore the effects the computer can have on the various philosophies or natures of social studies education.

THE USE OF THE COMPUTER TO SUPPORT
THE VARYING VIEWS OF SOCIAL STUDIES

It has been stated earlier that the mediating device used in a course (1) makes a statement about the nature of a subject, (2) requires the use of a set of skills, and (3) transmits a set of values. We will now examine the effect microcomputers, used in various ways, would have on the various philosophies presented above.

Knowledge Approach

Whether the source of knowledge is from national tradition or the social sciences, the knowledge approach concentrates on transmitting fixed ideas, skills, and values to students. Skills are incidental to this philosophy; they are needed primarily to aid in the transmission of knowledge. The values are those of the dominant culture. (Even the science orientation has a set of values—an example is that of observable evidence.)

Drill and Practice

Drill and practice programs are presently very common in the social studies curriculum. As the name implies, such programs present students with a set of questions to be answered or a problem to be solved. Such programs reinforce the learning of facts or concepts.

In this application the computer works in much the same way as a workbook, except that it is interactive and provides knowledge of results very quickly. This immediate feedback is a great advantage over the time lag, usually a day, between the student's writing of the answer and the teacher's response.

An example of a drill and practice program is **Regions of the United States**, produced by Educational Activities. This program shows a student a group of states, names them, and asks the pupil to recall the name of a randomly selected state. Such programs reinforce the learning of facts by allowing students to test their knowledge against that contained in the computer program. It provides a supplement to classroom instruction.

Cohen (1982) found a plethora of geography drill programs. An example of a good drill and practice map skills program is **Unlocking the Map Code**, produced by Rand McNally. This program, designed for the Apple and Atari computers, teaches children in grades 4 through 6 the skills of identifying land and water forms, map color and symbols, direction, location, scale, and time. The students then apply their knowledge by making and flying a flight plan. Other new ways of using drill and practice are being implemented that make the recall of facts and ideas less onerous. Examples of such programs are **Interviews with History**, published by Educational Publishing Concepts, which allows students to act as reporters, interviewing famous people from six different time periods.

Alessandrini (1983) reports that one of the problems with drill and practice programs is the way they are used. The programs are intended to be used after one has received initial instruction, but students often begin using the software before such instruction is provided. The result is often confusion and frustration.

Games

Many drill and practice programs are designed as games that allow students to drill basic facts. This technique is an effective means of teaching facts or concepts. **The Medalists—States,** produced by Hartley, has several unique features that make it a useful game in the social studies classroom (see chapter 4). The game was developed to teach historical and geographical facts about the United States in grades 4 through 11. Many teachers are aware of the motivational power of this technique, but overcoming the arcade syndrome, the assumption that playing games is for fun, not learning, becomes a real challenge.

Tutorials

Eiser (1988) asks, what makes a good tutorial? She states that the power of interactive graphics and animation which amplify and explain content is one element. A second element is the ability to allow both linear programming and branching. While linear programming produces software which presents information in a fixed format, branching places control somewhat in the hands of the learner, fitting the needs of a variety of students. The third element is online evaluation, which can test at both the literal and inferential levels. Finally, record keeping allows interruptions within the program and permits the recording of student progress over time. Cohen (1983a) reported on the development of two knowledge-oriented programs which have received rather widespread acclaim: **Revolutions: Past, Present and Future**, and **Economics: What, How and For Whom**, published by Focus Media, Inc. Two more recent programs, **Constitution and Government of the United States**, and **Consumers and the Law**, by Educational Activities Inc. are also excellent tutorials.

Tutorials have been improving in the last few years and a number of publishers, including Scott, Foresman and Macmillan, are now including them as supplemental materials to their text series in teaching map skills. Nystrom has included tutorials in **Discovery**, which supplements their map skills program.

Databases

Several online services, such as The Source and CompuServe, provide factual and bibliographic databases that are available for use with microcomputers. They are fast and relatively inexpensive.

Several prepared databases are available in a variety of formats. Databases are excellent supplements to textbooks because they contain up-to-date material, and some programs, such as **World Geography, Cultures, and Economics Database**, published by Scholastic, allow user updating. Many textbook companies, including Scott, Foresman and D. C. Heath now include databases as auxiliary material for their text series.

Simulations

Simulations are based on sets of concepts and generalizations called constructs or models designed to describe real-world phenomena. They can be used to provide students with an understanding of a situation or event. In their review of geography software, Eiser and Salpeter (1987) identify several programs they list as simulations that fit the knowledge area. These include the **Spy's Adventure** series, published by Polarware, and the **Carmen Sandiego** series, published by Broderbund. Another program that has received good reviews is **Discover the World**, published by Hartley. These programs bring up an important issue that publishers and educators fail to face—calling games simulations.

Simulations are based on sets of concepts and generalizations called constructs or models intended to describe real-world phenomena. They are intended for use when the real situation is too dangerous, distracting, or intrusive. Games are not simulations. While the programs listed in the paragraph above are excellent games teaching important geographic, and in the case of **Discover the World**, historic concepts, they are not truly simulations.

One misuse of the method must be noted (Cohen 1983b). If students are only allowed to operate within the construct and are not permitted to understand the elements of the construct, the simulation simply becomes a game.

Summary

The use of the computer to teach the knowledge approach to social studies can affect the nature of social studies in two ways. First, it can provide the student with immediate knowledge of results in drill and practice programs. This is an element missing in most social studies classrooms. Second, the interaction allowed by the computer would likely make social studies more fun and possibly be more effective in teaching students the desired concepts. However, traditional media devices for drill and practice are more readily available and generally more accessible, and teachers are familiar with their use, so it is difficult to justify the computer's use.

A third possible change may come about through the use of simulations. Simulations teach constructs, combinations of concepts and generalizations, that explain the real world. No other single instructional device can run simulations as well as computers. This device will place the student in a more active role and require the teaching of the skills of problem solving and decision making, which are not at present a part of the knowledge curriculum. The question facing a proponent of the knowledge approach is whether problem solving and decision making are tolerable transgressions upon the fixed knowledge model.

Skills Approach

In the skills approach the building of skills is the important aspect. This philosophy's blind spot lies in the fact that, while many proponents masterfully build and teach a skills sequence, the skills are not applied to the real world. As mentioned earlier, some educators are proponents of the skills of social science inquiry and others prefer the use of the thinking, decision-making skills.

Saltinski (1981) takes the first perspective and sees statistical analysis as part of the K-12 curriculum. He supports his position by quoting from both the California State Department of Education curriculum guide and the Social Studies Education Framework of the National Council for the Social Studies, which state that social studies should "help students become aware of the processes by which the particular disciplines of the social sciences derive their concepts, such as observation, data gathering, classification, interpretation, inference, extrapolation, hypothesis construction, and testing and prediction" and "help students to use data from which concepts have been derived to develop and test understandings based on data." To substantiate his position, Saltinski reports the successful use of teaching and using statistics at the elementary, middle school, and senior high levels. Saltinski states, "Once statistics is justified as the 'missing dimension' in social studies, the acquisition of a microcomputer is strongly warranted."

Drill and Practice

Under the skills philosophy the computer is intended for the building of skills and, more importantly, the application of skills. Cohen (1982) found few such programs. She did find several drill packages that covered narrowly defined map skills. Several drill and practice packages are integrated into new textbook series, and drill and practice on skills is now integrated into several of the newer simulations such as the **Decisions, Decisions** series, published by Tom Snyder Productions. However, as Beyer (1986) points out, these skills must be identified for children, and the decision-making skills they are based on must be taught directly. Thinking is not a natural ability but a learned one that needs constant nurturing and pruning.

In addition, it must be pointed out that some of the programs listed under one philosophy of social education might well fit under another and fulfill an entirely different purpose. **Interviews with History**, published by Educational Publishing Concepts, is such a program. Under the skills philosophy, this program could be used to help develop the interview procedure in grades 4-8. As pointed out earlier in this chapter, results are often dependent upon actions teachers take while using the software.

Games

One of the interesting benefits of games is learning strategies to win. The development of premeditated strategies is an interesting way to teach many skills. Although most games follow drill and practice formats, there are an increasing number being developed similar to **Puzzle**

Tanks, a problem-solving program developed for the Apple family and the TRS-80 Color Computer by Sunburst Communications. It requires inductive reasoning, working backward, and record keeping.

Games such as the **Spy's Adventure** series, published by Polarware, the **Carmen Sandiego** series, published by Broderbund, and the **Crosscountry** series, published by Didatech Software, are useful for teaching mapping concepts and mapping skills; they therefore fill the purpose of both the knowledge and skills approaches to social studies. These three series of games make excellent use of graphics and are well documented. Nystrom's **Discovery** has several games in their map skills program that assist students in using maps and globes.

Tutorials

Tutorial lessons can provide basic instruction on a skill. They can be used as a supplement or even a replacement for classroom instruction. Tutorials could be an extremely useful tool to provide basic individualized instruction in those situations where children need specific skills to complete certain tasks. Cohen (1982) failed to find them in her search of social studies software.

Tutorials have been improving in the last few years and a number of publishers, including Scott, Foresman and Macmillan, are now including them as supplemental materials to their text series in teaching map skills. Nystrom has included tutorials in **Discovery**, which supplements their map skills program.

Unfortunately textual presentation often dominates tutorial software, but that trend is changing. **Introducing Maps 1** and **Introducing Maps 2** published by MicroEd make excellent use of graphics which illustrate the concepts being taught. The use of graphics in tutorials will likely increase as animation has. Some publishers, wisely, are beginning to move textual material from the computer screen and placing it in booklets where it can be more accessible. Software publishers along with many educators are seeing that the computer is just another mediating device. They seem to be using the computer as the interactive medium it is.

Software for teaching map skills exists in abundance, but there are now tutorials which teach other knowledge, skills, and values. While the greatest number focus on knowledge, such thinking skills as decision making and processing skills as interviewing have been given attention.

This is especially important with the current trend of teaching students thinking skills. As Beyer (1987) points out, being involved in the act of thinking is not the same as learning how to think. Thinking must be taught as well as the processes we use to gather information. Both thinking strategies and processing strategies must be presented in a variety of contexts. Since tutorials offer us another means of teaching thinking, it appears the time is propitious for more software such as **Decisions**, published by EMC Publishing, and **Interviews with History**, published by Educational Publishing Concepts, Inc. **Decisions** allows students to play simulations and make choices based on a decision-making model. **Interviews with History** moves into the area of teaching a processing skill: the interview technique, an important skill for gathering information. Skill learning, in a class of twenty-five students, is often impeded by the pace of one group or another. If teachers have a tutorial which reviews the skill, they have one more chance to reach the children—and one more medium is all many students will require. Branching of course allows such students to move at their own pace through a tutorial. The sections in which students know the material move rather quickly; branching in a program permits other students to move more slowly through those sections, learning what they need to know.

There are many thinking skills tools produced for reading, but if we expect students to transfer such skills to social studies, programs must be developed which apply these skills to social studies.

Record keeping is now available in such programs as **The Constitution and Government of the United States,** and **Consumers and the Law,** discussed above. The student can finish one disk at a time or even one section on a disk. One merely chooses the section of the program in which to begin and records are kept of up to fifty students. The programs rate students on application, understanding, and interpretation, which can be interpreted as skills. It should be apparent then that our classification of programs under the various approaches to social studies is dependent upon the program's predominant content. As a teacher, you may want to evaluate a program for yourself according to your teaching goal.

Databases

We have already mentioned the use of online services to access databases that would help students and teachers obtain up-to-date data for classroom use. Various databases available to computer users furnish encyclopedia, almanac, and bibliographic information. Such data would be especially useful in the application of learned skills.

Hunter (1984), basing her ideas on the teaching of information processing, thinking, and decision making, suggests that children develop their own databases. She illustrates how **pfs:File**, published by Software Publishing Corporation and designed for a variety of computers, can be used to develop databases on states, countries, and even class members. Deciding what data to gather, gathering it, organizing it effectively, and drawing conclusions from retrieved data would provide excellent skills training. This idea will be illustrated in chapter 4.

There has been much emphasis on databases in the last few years because of interest in the development of thinking skills. Weaver (1986) discussed ways of designing, building, and using databases, and described the database products available at the time of her study.

Simulations

Skills training using simulation is challenging. It allows individuals to test their decision-making power against others or against a computer program. Since applying skills is the name of the game in this philosophy, the analytic use of simulation produces excellent results.

An assessment of the analytic potential of existing simulations produces differing conclusions. Nilson (1983) feels that present simulations fail in at least two respects: they do not force players to develop and test strategies, and they do not provide experiences that allow students to practice basic skills. However, Friel (1983) more or less proves that "beauty is in the eye of the beholder." Using the often-copied **Lemonade Stand** simulation, distributed by MicroMedia, she does a masterful job of integrating several of the scientific skills: observation, data gathering, making inferences, forming hypotheses, and experimentation.

Recently a group of teachers was given the opportunity to review the program **Who'll Save Abacaxi: A Third World Simulation**, published by Focus Media. The program is an engaging one dealing with a hypothetical, yet realistic, developing country. The teachers were arranged in groups of three around President Longwe Gutpela. After determining his economic and development goals on the advice of his advisors, the president was attempting to maintain a reasonable popularity among the various factions in the nation and stay in power for five years. The discussions were animated and sometimes heated, but the acting president was able to stay in power and fulfill many of the established goals for Abacaxi. These teachers had never operated a computer, but they had read the student material and documentation that comes with the program. Like many of the newest programs, **Abacaxi** comes with a management disk that allows a teacher to track student progress.

In the last few years simulations have become more powerful in terms of the skills they produce. The Tom Snyder Production series **Decisions, Decisions** and **Simplicon**, published by Cross Cultural Software, are two more examples. Both products have received recognition for their excellence and follow the skills approach to social studies.

Simulations have also become multimediated. This illustrates the teacher-as-manager concept we discussed in chapter 2 and applies three mediating devices to transmit knowledge and involve the student in the utilization of skills. **The Golden Spike: Building America's First Transcontinental Railroad**, published by the National Geographic Society, assists in encouraging creativity, problem solving, critical thinking, and decision making (McKinney 1988-89). The advantage such multimedia programs have is their use of print, filmstrip, and computerized simulations. No one medium at present can do every task completely. In this program, the integration of the different media devices creates a useful harmony.

A problem may exist in that many educators feel that the computer should be used without the intervention of classroom instruction. This approach could cause simulations to fail. Early research in the use of the technique indicates that students must be prepared to run a simulation and, after they have run it, should discuss what they have experienced. This last step can be used to develop conclusions or to formulate testable hypotheses for a next round of play. Friel (1983) has used this method with outstanding results.

Roberts (1982) suggested that students could create their own simulations, which is now possible because of the recent creation of software that allows students to accomplish this formerly difficult task. **Simulation Construction Kit** produced by Hartley Courseware solves some of the technical problems connected with writing a simulation and allows teachers and students to concentrate on the research and design necessary to produce a simulation.

Statistical Analysis

As Hunter (1983) points out, polls and surveys are a basic tool of the social scientist. It is now possible for students to conduct and analyze their own surveys, using such tools as **TeloFacts** (published by Dilithium Software). This program assists in creating and editing questionnaires, surveys, and tests (this use is illustrated in chapter 5). Once the data has been collected, the program performs a standard statistical analysis.

A number of programs are now available that allow the use of statistical procedures in the classroom. **Hometown: A Local Area Study** (published by Active Learning Systems) allows students in early elementary through high school to conduct surveys, collect data, analyze data, and make reports based on their results. **Polls and Politics** (published by MECC) and **ASK: A Survey Kit** (by D. C. Heath) are two other examples.

Spreadsheets

The electronic spreadsheet places a means of rapid calculation in the hands of social studies teachers that will aid them in teaching thinking skills. This computer tool automates and combines the pencil, calculator, and paper worksheet into a display. Spreadsheets can be used to store and display data, predict outcomes based on data and formulas, and make calculations. Electronic spreadsheets are some of the fastest selling computer tools on the market because they allow people to make predictions and ask "what if" questions. Martorella (1984) illustrates several samples of "what if" questions that might be of interest to proponents of this view of social studies.

Summary

The use of the computer in the teaching of skills should have beneficial effects in at least four ways. First, the use of drill and practice software should aid in the teaching of skills. The popular direct instruction model of teaching skills calls for the type of interactive learning accomplished by the use of the computer. Second, the use of databases, either commercial or student generated, will serve the interests of both the scientific and the information-processing skills enthusiast. Third, simulations are a natural part of this perspective of social studies because they require the use of learned skills. Fourth, the availability of spreadsheets and tools for statistical analysis can make social studies more action oriented, allowing students to test their ideas and opinions against the ideas of others. Under the skills approach to social studies, knowledge is what is learned through inquiry. The skills transmitted are either the thinking, decision-making, or social science skills needed for inquiry. The central value taught is that knowledge can be discovered. The skills approach to social studies is changed little but enhanced greatly by the use of the computer.

Social Analysis Approach

Proponents of the social analysis approach to social studies are interested in improving society through two distinctly different avenues: citizens actively involved in change, or citizens adapted to the needs of society. Both approaches begin by looking at the world as it is, and both of them attempt to describe and implement what should be. Evidence of these positions is present in the literature promoting computer literacy. In outlining what should be known about the use and misuse of computers, Glenn and Klassen (1983) state that tomorrow's citizens should

1. understand the role of information in a highly diversified political system and the issues related to the balance between the ideals of freedom and privacy and the need for information

2. understand the individual's rights concerning information collected by government agencies

3. understand how data are collected, stored, analyzed, and used in making policy decisions

4. know how computer technology is used within government agencies

5. have an awareness of and the ability to use research techniques in the collection and processing of information utilizing the capacities of the computer

6. explore socially relevant topics such as computer crime, databanks, and systems analysis to gain an understanding of the impact of these topics on the social, economic, and political lives of the individual

7. explore their own value positions in relation to computer technology.

Continuing in a similar vein, the Cupertino Union School District (1983) holds that students should be able to

1. describe how computers affect our lives

2. recognize the legal and moral issues involved in computer use

3. describe how social scientists use computers.

On the surface, these topics seem harmless enough, even for a knowledge-type curriculum. However, the issues arising from these topics are potentially controversial. What if students don't like the role the computer is playing in their lives? Is the student to act on what he or she learns? An article by Thompson (1974) discussing a program conducted at Willowbrook High School in Villa Park, Illinois, gives the flavor of this sort of issue.

We believe at Willowbrook that one way to give students the tools to master the future is to get them to understand the technology that shapes that future: not just what technology does for us but also what it does to us. The suggestion that machines may not always be benevolent is rank heresy in the United States of course—we have worshipped our mechanized version of Baal too long to cast off his spell easily. An indictment of the machine and its works, however, does exist and we may read it if we so choose.

Hank Levin, director of the Institute for Research on Educational Finance and Governance at Stanford University, is quoted by Hollifield (1983) in support of Hollifield's contention that high technology will lower the standard of living and leave many without jobs:

> Based on our Institute's research, given the trends as they exist, given present day attitudes—yes, we're moving toward a society in which most people work at low-level tasks or have no work at all while only a select few hold interesting, skilled positions. I'm not saying we're doomed, that this is inexorable. But if we sit back and do nothing to change the present course, the high tech future isn't bright—it's frightening.

Rather than changing the technological society, many social analysts feel, we must adapt the students to the society. An interesting article that takes this view begins, "Welcome to the post-industrial revolution" ("Getting the Jump on Tomorrow's Jobs," 1983). The article goes on to describe current unemployment and the kinds of jobs people should be preparing themselves for in the next decade.

Much of the current literature concerning computers takes the view that people must adapt to the society. One example is presented by Carrozzo (1983), who writes that as educators we should be analyzing the future and building curriculum that will allow students to live successfully in it. Molnar (1982) takes an even broader view: since we live in an informational society, our nation will have to produce more high-quality scientists, knowledge workers (people who use and apply knowledge in their work), and technologically literate citizens. He states, "If we are to progress we must invest greater effort into the development of new intellectual technologies in order to amplify man's learning, analytical, and problem solving power." Obviously such change means the preparation of citizens much different from those we train today. How would the use of computers influence this philosophy?

Drill and Practice

Drill and practice is needed here only to train the student to use certain information-processing skills. But such a use would provide the student with some basic familiarity with the computer as a learning tool.

Tutorials

Tutorials could play a significant role here. Repeating sequences of skills training is extremely wasteful of teaching time. The computer is endlessly patient and repetition is something it does well.

Databases

Databases would also be very useful in this perspective, since both approaches deal with information processing and decision making.

Statistical Analysis

The use of statistical analysis tools is also important to this approach to social studies. While databases are useful, surveys of student and community attitudes would allow classes to determine predominant attitudes in their own environment. Studying the local community is an important goal in this philosophy.

Simulations

Simulation is also a useful device in both of the social analysis approaches. Since both deal with the world as it is and attempt to develop models of what should be, software programs that allow students to experience the results of their decision-making ability should be useful. Certainly, such programs as the **Decisions, Decisions** series, **Simplicon**, and **Abacaxi: A Third World Simulation** would be valuable resources under this approach.

Summary

How will the use of the computer influence the social analysis approach to social studies? It may make it the central focus of the social studies curriculum. This is true for three reasons. First, education is at a crossroads. We presently see much emphasis on skills usually defined as reading, writing, and arithmetic. But writers like Molnar are beginning to see thinking as a basic skill. Second, our economy is on a new path, as Toffler and Naisbitt point out. We must begin to make our citizens aware of the alternatives. Although many people feel powerless, power exists beyond the halls of government and the walls of corporations. And third, the nation is once again focusing its attention on the schools. Although there are those who would destroy our educational system and yoke its students to a meaningless existence, there are still those who see the promise of a better way of life for all. This promise is likely to be fulfilled through a different kind of educational program.

Self-Awareness Approach

The self-awareness approach to social studies is interested in the cognitive (intellectual, problem-solving) and the affective (social, emotional) aspects of social education. Proponents of this approach believe that citizens who have an understanding of themselves are better prepared to deal with the world.

One would not expect people espousing such a philosophy to embrace the computer. Ryba and Chapman (1983), however, see considerable promise for the device. They feel it may enhance self-concept, reduce emotional dependence, and assist students in learning self-management.

Drill and Practice

The advantages of computers come from programmed instruction and the computer's ability to provide self-pacing, immediate feedback, and small-bit learning. These features increase the student's control over his learning, and control is self-enhancing. In this respect computers have a real advantage within the self-awareness approach.

Tutorials

Computers can assist in career counseling. **System of Interactive Guidance Information,** available from Educational Testing Service, provides such guidance. Such programs allow decision making and problem solving. **Self-Exploration Series #1: Who Am I?**, published by Career Aids, Inc., is an interactive assessment system designed to allow a student to learn more about himself in the areas of money values, parent relationships, and stress management.

As indicated earlier in the teacher-as-manager model, there are alternative ways to teach knowledge and skills. The tutorial makes the computer an excellent instructional choice.

Databases

Since consumer and career awareness play an important role in this curriculum, the several databases available commercially are extremely useful. For example, CompuServe includes in one of their databases government publications relating to personal finances and consumerism.

Simulations

Skills in the self-awareness approach take on a different form—they include, for example, the ability to analyze a situation and propose alternative solutions to problems. Simulations can play significant roles in the development of such skills. Although proponents of this curriculum feel that the classroom is a laboratory for life, experimentation with another person's feelings is generally frowned upon. Simulations that allow students to play through behavioral choices can be useful, and the consequences of such choices are readily learned.

Summary

What would be the result of using the computer in the self-awareness approach to social studies? The subject would be much more interesting and likely more rewarding to the student. The skills required for understanding self and peers would be strengthened through its use. The essential value transmitted would be that life is a series of choices and that the student is responsible for the consequences of his or her choices.

Instructional Technology Approach

As a philosophy the technological approach to social studies makes no statement concerning what knowledge or set of skills should be taught. Enthusiasts are likely to say, "Tell me what you want taught and I'll show you the best way to teach it." Technologists simply ask the questions "What is a good citizen?" and "How should that citizen be taught?" Proponents of this philosophy have presented several lists of proposed learnings, which have generally been ignored. Their greatest impacts have been in the area of instructional strategies and teaching methods.

Research on the use of computers in social studies is just beginning, but it can be built on two decades of general experience (Kearsley, Hunter, and Seidel 1983) that shows that

1. computers are efficient and effective teaching devices

2. computers can be used in individualized instruction, but we still know little about the process of individualization

3. the authoring tools and techniques exist to allow us to prepare good CAI

4. good mechanisms exist to disseminate and evaluate CAI

5. we have just scratched the surface of what is possible with computers in education, and we are even further behind in social studies.

What influence will the computer have on this philosophy? It is likely that it will aid in the implementation of the teacher-as-manager model of instruction.

REFERENCES

Alessandrini, Katherine L. 1983. "How Can Educators Spell Relief? C-o-m-p-u-t-e-r." *Educational Computer Magazine* (September): 32-35.

Beyer, Barry K. 1987. *Practical Strategies for the Teaching of Thinking*. Boston: Allyn and Bacon, Inc.

Carrozzo, Guy. 1983. "Teaching the Basics with Basic Computers." *Educational Computer Magazine* (September): 54-57.

Cassidy, Edward W., and Dana G. Kurfman. 1977. "Decision Making as Purpose and Process." In *Developing Decision-Making Skills*, Forty-seventh Yearbook of the National Council for the Social Studies, edited by Dana G. Kurfman, 1-26. Arlington, Va.: NCSS.

Coburn, Janet. 1989. "Welcome to HyperSchool." *Classroom Computer Learning* (special supplement, April): S14-16.

Cohen, Mollie L. 1983a. "Computer Corner." *Social Education* (October): 456-459.

______. 1983b. "NCSS Looks at the Computer Revolution." *Social Education* (March): 186-187.

______. 1982. "Educational Software: A Taste of What's Available for Social Studies." *The Computing Teacher* (December): 11-15.

Cupertino Union School District. 1983. "K-8 Computer Literacy Curriculum." *The Computing Teacher* (March): 7-10.

Ehman, Lee H., and Allen D. Glenn. 1987. "Computer-Based Education in the Social Studies." Bloomington, Ind.: Social Studies Development Center.

Eiser, Leslie. 1988. "What Makes a Good Tutorial?" *Classroom Computer Learning* (January): 44-50.

Eiser, Leslie, and Judy Salpeter. 1987. "Where on Earth Is Washington, D.C.?" *Classroom Computer Learning* (November/December): 28-39.

EPIE and Consumers Union. 1983. "Beyond Couseware." *The Computing Teacher* (January): 37-38.

Estvan, Frank J. 1971. "Emerging Priorities for the Young." In *The Curriculum: Retrospect and Prospect*, Seventieth Yearbook of the National Society for the Study of Education, edited by Robert M. McClure, 245-259. Chicago: NSSE.

Fraenkel, Jack R. 1980. "Goals for Teaching Values and Value Analysis." *Journal of Research and Development in Education* (Winter): 93-100.

Friel, Susan. 1983. "Lemonade's the Name, Simulation's the Game." *Classroom Computer News* (February): 34-39.

"Getting the Jump on Tomorrow's Jobs." 1983. *Changing Times* (August): 26-31.

Glenn, Allen D., and Daniel L. Klassen. 1983. "Computer Technology and the Social Studies." *Educational Forum* (Winter): 209-216.

Haney, Michael R. 1982. "The Computer in Science Education: Defining the Role of Technology." *The Computing Teacher* (April): 32-35.

Hollifield, John H. 1983. "In Reality, High Tech Means Low Skills, Poor Pay." *Educational R&D Report* (Fall): 3-5.

Huebner, Dwayne. 1974. "Technology vs. Man: What Will Be the Outcome?" *Educational Leadership* (February): 393-396.

Hunter, Beverly. 1984. *My Students Use Computers.* Reston, Va.: Reston Publishing.

______. 1983. "Powerful Tools for Your Social Studies Classroom." *Classroom Computer Learning* (October): 50-57.

Kearsley, G., B. Hunter, and J. Seidel. 1983. "Two Decades of Computer Based Instruction Projects: What Have We Learned?" *T.H.E. Journal* (January): 90-94; (February): 86-89.

Lehrer, Ariella. 1989. "HyperCard K-12: What's All the Commotion?" *Classroom Computer Learning* (special supplement, April): S4-7.

Martorella, Peter H. 1984. "Calling Winners: Using Spreadsheets to Project Election Day Tallies." *Electronic Learning* (September): 56-57.

McKinney, Carl Ancil. 1988-89. "Review: The Golden Spike: Building America's First Transcontinental Railroad." *The Computing Teacher* (December/January): 37-39.

Molnar, Andrew R. 1982. "The Search for New Intellectual Technologies." *T.H.E. Journal.* (September): 104-112.

Naisbitt, John. 1982. *Megatrends: Ten New Directions Transforming Our Lives.* New York: Warner Books.

Nilson, Jeff. 1983. "The Game of Big Business." *Classroom Computer News* (February): 32-33.

Reardon, Betty, Anthony John Scott, and John Totten, eds. 1983. "Nuclear Weapons: Concepts, Issues, and Controversies." *Social Education* (November/December): 473-522.

Rice, Marion J. 1980. "Social Sciences as School Subjects: The Case for the Disciplines." *Journal of Research and Development in Education* (Winter): 123-132.

Roberts, Nancy. 1982. "Who's Last in Line for Computers? The Social Studies Teacher." *Classroom Computer News* (November/December): 17-18.

______. 1978. "Teaching Dynamic Feedback Systems Thinking: An Elementary View." *Management Science* (April): 836-843.

Rooze, Gene E. 1976. "An Analysis of the Conceptions of Social Studies Education." Lubbock, Tex.: Texas Tech University. ERIC Document Reproduction Service, ED 155 115.

Ryan, Frank L., and Arthur K. Ellis. 1974. *Instructional Implications of Inquiry.* Englewood Cliffs, N.J.: Prentice-Hall.

Ryba, Kenneth A., and James W. Chapman. 1983. "Toward Improving Learning Strategies and Personal Adjustment with Computers." *The Computing Teacher* (August): 48-53.

Saltinski, Ronald. 1981. "Microcomputers in Social Studies: An Innovative Technology for Instruction." *Educational Technology* (January): 29-32.

Thompson, Deane C. 1974. "Humanizing Technology, Heart or Hardware?" *Media and Methods* (April): 18-21.

Toffler, Alvin. 1983. *The Third Wave*. New York: Bantam Books.

Vaughn, Stephen. 1983. "History: Is It Relevant?" *The Social Studies* (March/April): 56-60.

Weaver, Dave. 1986. *Database Software for the Social Studies*. Portland, Oreg.: Northwest Regional Educational Laboratory.

Wheeler, Fay. 1987. "The New Ready-Made Databases: What They Offer Your Classroom." *Classroom Computer Learning* (March): 28-32.

3

SOFTWARE EVALUATION:
A Crucial Element in Successfully Using Computers

There is a phrase that has been associated with computers for many years—"garbage in, garbage out." This phrase, shortened to GIGO, serves as a reminder to programmers that the output of a program will only be as good as the input of data. Likewise, the quality of learning that occurs through the use of computers will be directly related to the quality of the software programs used. If teachers use programs that present and reinforce incorrect information (input), students will learn and recite that incorrect information (output)—GIGO.

Teachers are the controlling factor. If computers are used effectively it will be because teachers choose to use good programs. It is important that teachers become aware of what constitutes quality programs, learn to choose programs that fit their needs, and learn to effectively use these programs as a part of the overall social studies curriculum. It is on these first two activities, becoming aware of quality and learning to evaluate programs, that this chapter will focus.

Peter Kelman (1982) pinpointed several areas of concern when he wrote, "There has been almost no time taken to reflect seriously upon the pedagogical, psychological, philosophical, and ethical issues involved in computer-based education, not to mention time reserved for simple quality control." Indeed, computers came into the schools so fast that educators did not have time to plan for them in advance. Consequently, many problems have arisen. Often schools decided which computer to buy on the basis of advertisements or bargain prices rather than because the computer could run the needed programs. Many schools began using computers with little or no information about how to attain the best results and teachers began using them without as much training as they needed.

Another serious problem is software quality. Hassett (1984) and Bork (1984) are only two of the many experts who decry the poor quality of most software. Hassett quotes Kenneth Komoski, director of the Educational Products Information Exchange (EPIE), as saying that only 25 percent of educational software meets minimal technical and instructional standards. Worse, Komoski feels that only 3 to 4 percent of the software for education can be rated excellent.

Math, language arts, and science were the areas to which program designers flocked in the early years of computer assisted instruction. These basic subjects provided lucrative markets, because every school wanted to improve its instruction in the "basics." As these areas filled up with marketable products and profits began to decrease, software companies turned to other areas.

In social studies, the first programs to be developed were drill and practice programs. Such programs are relatively easy to create, and they filled common needs — teaching the basic facts that most teachers feel are necessary. For example, programs to teach students the capitals of the states were among the first to be created in social studies. As the market filled with such programs, manufacturers had to create programs to fit different needs in order to make sales. Now, tutorial, simulation, map, and problem-solving programs are being produced in greater numbers. In fact, hundreds of programs have been created for social studies. In chapter 6 we will provide an extensive list of social studies software. Since more is being produced nearly every day, it is impossible to create a complete list. However, this one is the most extensive yet published for social studies.

The abundance of programs is a mixed blessing — the choice is wonderful but overwhelming. Teachers can now involve students in simulations that were impossible in the past. The possibilities for individualizing instruction have also increased greatly with the wide use of computers and the massive availability of programs. Which programs will fit a teacher's needs? They all sound so good in the catalog, but can they really perform? The dilemma is compounded by the fact that the programs are quite a bit more expensive than books and many software publishers are reluctant to allow a teacher to return a program if it doesn't measure up to his or her standards.

Since software is so new on the scene, few have much experience at evaluating it, and such evaluation is an inexact science at best. A piece of software that seems useless to one person might appear very valuable to another. In fact, there is evidence that some programs teachers feel have little value can intrigue students for hours (White 1983). Also, there are many different teaching styles; a piece of software might fit one person's style but not another's. Just as all teachers do not agree on what is the best U.S. history textbook, neither will they agree on what is the best software. The fact that there is a wide variety of textbooks that sell enough copies to stay in print is evidence that there are many opinions as to what constitutes the "best" textbook.

Before beginning to discuss how software can be evaluated, it is important to clarify what the terms *software* and *program* comprise. Some think of software as only the cassette tape or diskette on which the program is recorded. However, most educational software includes a description of the program, goals for the students, ditto masters or workbook activities, and suggestions for follow-up. The term *program* refers to the commands and statements on the tape or diskette that control the computer during its operation.

DIFFERENT APPROACHES TO SELECTING SOFTWARE

Basically there are three ways to select software. First, one can just trust the ads and hope for the best. Second, one can take someone else's word for the quality of a product — that of another teacher, a review in a magazine, or a reviewing service like EPIE or Microsift. Third, the teacher or a group of teachers in a school district or a consortium of districts can, using a common format, evaluate software and share these evaluations with one another.

The first alternative, basing purchasing decisions on advertisements or salesmen's claims, is used all too often and is much less preferable than the others. In recommending the purchase of expensive software, school employees must remember they are spending the public's money and must be careful with that trust. Particularly in an era when the public wishes to reduce taxes, every penny must be spent wisely.

The second approach, accepting the opinions of experts, can also result in problems. We have all had the experience of reading or hearing a review of a movie and later, upon seeing the movie, wondering if it could have been the same film the reviewer saw. This problem of dissonant opinions exists in software reviewing as well. Whether the review appears in a respected journal such as *Social Education* or is provided by a professional reviewing service like EPIE or Microsift, the reader is being asked to trust the reviewer. Since reviewers should not be in the employ of the producer of the software, they can be relied upon more than ads and salesmen; however, reviewers are still strangers who know nothing about specific teachers' curricula, objectives, or students.

The third approach, local evaluation of software, also has problems, as well as advantages. The evaluation could be sponsored by a school district, a consortium of districts, or a subject-matter group, such as a local social studies council. This approach puts the evaluation in the hands of teachers with reasonably similar characteristics. Assuming the reviewers sign the written review, teachers interested in the program could contact them for person-to-person discussion. In this way, a good deal of information could be gained regarding the program. Also, programs could be borrowed for review. As long as copies were not made, such sharing would not violate copyright laws. As mentioned, there are some problems with this approach. Sometimes reviews of an expert are held in more esteem than those of a colleague. Also, the local group might consist of relative novices who are incapable of performing a competent review. Gaining access to software is another problem. Producers are generally unwilling to send out review copies. This is not only because of their fear of having their programs pirated but also because of the cost of maintaining records and mailing the copies. Finally, even if review copies were readily attainable, there are so many programs available that it would be impossible to review even half of them, unless a very large group of reviewers were used.

In April 1983 *The Computing Teacher* included an excellent article in its "Microgram" section outlining a seven-step strategy for acquiring software. The following elaboration of these steps should be considered in developing a thorough approach to making software decisions.

Step 1: Needs. What needs in the curriculum are not being met by the textbook or other learning materials? Are there objectives that could be better met through the use of CAI or a computer tool program? Are there topics in which computers could generate more student motivation? Have some skills that could be developed via computer been neglected for lack of materials? Many of the tutorial and simulation programs allow teachers to develop concepts and skills that were not previously possible. As software becomes even more sophisticated this will be even more true.

Step 2: Specification. Once the needs are determined, a clear set of "specs" for each needed program must be written. What type of program is most appropriate—drill and practice, educational game, tutorial, or simulation? What should be the reading level? What length of program would be best? How much money can be spent? Are support materials needed? Is the program to be used in an individualized setting? (If so, it must have very clear directions). In this step, the criteria that a program must meet are set down in detail.

Step 3: Identification. This step involves surveying advertisements, reading catalogs, and asking other teachers for programs that seem to meet the specifications. It is not yet time to make a selection, but only to identify the alternatives available.

Step 4: Evaluation. For each of the programs identified in Step 3, evaluations need to be found. These can come from a variety of sources: magazines and journals, review services, or local sources. This step involves gaining from the experience of others—how have the programs worked for them?

Step 5: Preview. If possible, the software producer should be asked for preview privileges or requested to send the program on thirty-day approval. This allows time to review the program and try it out with some students. If it does not fit the identified needs, it should be returned. Even if they don't advertise that the programs are sent on thirty-day approval, many producers will take them back if they are returned with a letter explaining why the program was not acceptable. This is especially true if the district returning the program is large and the company hopes to sell it other programs in the future.

Step 6: Purchase. If the program meets the identified needs—if it was effective in the trial use or if the reviews are unanimous in their praises—then it is time to make the purchase.

Step 7: Feedback. In this phase the effectiveness of the program is studied with several levels of pupils or with those who have a variety of learning styles. From these experiments teachers will be better able to determine which levels or types of students should use the program. If it is possible to predict in advance that a particular student will not gain from using the software, it is unwise to make him or her use it. For example, if the student does not like computers or does not learn well alone, or if the program is not on his reading level, then it would be counterproductive to make that student use it.

IDENTIFYING "QUALITY" SOFTWARE

As social studies teachers know, whenever one starts discussing what is "best" she or he has entered the realm of values, self-selected standards. Each person has his or her own unique set. What is the "best" computer? Ask that question to a group of computer-using teachers and there will likely be at least six answers. Some are adamant about a detachable keyboard. Others insist on high-resolution graphics or the new, smaller size diskettes.

Likewise, it is not reasonable to expect teachers to agree on which software programs are "best," although they would probably agree on basic criteria. For example, they would agree that software should have clear directions, be written on the students' reading level, use correct grammar, present subject matter accurately, motivate students, and allow for maximum interaction between the student and the computer. However, several different teachers might review the same program and disagree on the extent to which the program met these criteria.

Suggestions and Systems

Evaluation of software programs is essential. Without it purchasers would be acting totally in the dark. Since there is no perfect way to evaluate these programs, we must deal with what exists. What are the sources of evaluations? What are their strengths and weaknesses?

The most traditional sources of evaluations are magazines and journals. All computer-related journals, as well as many that focus on subject matter, such as *Social Education,* contain reviews of software. These are usually in narrative form and report the authors' subjective reactions to the software. While the reviews can be helpful, caution must be used in basing a decision on them. Seldom do reviewers consistently use a given set of criteria. Thus, comparison from one month to another is difficult because the same aspects are not covered. In addition, the reviewers' backgrounds are seldom described, leaving their qualifications to evaluate the programs an open question. It would be helpful to know if the reviewer has ever taught social studies at the level for which the program is designed, and how much classroom experience the reviewer has had in using computers. Finally, reviews in journals are usually short and relatively superficial. Basically, what is presented is the subjective, personal opinion of one individual—hardly the sort of evidence upon which to base a purchasing decision.

The Digest of Software Reviews is, as its name implies, a collection of reviews published in a variety of magazines. The characteristics of the software are listed, and the publisher's descriptions of the programs are included. The *Digest* provides a valuable overview, and using it is much less time-consuming than finding the individual reviews in their original sources. The fact that several reviews are provided allows the readers to weigh different opinions. If the reviewers are unanimous about a specific feature of the program, the reader may be more confident in relying on that opinion than if only one evaluation existed. If the reviews are universally positive, a district might want to preview the program. However, the disadvantages of relying on reviews remain. A final decision should probably not be made solely on three or four reviews by strangers.

The Courseware report card is another subjective approach, but it has some significant strengths as compared to reviews. *The Courseware report card* provides introductory information, a description of the program (approximately one-half page long), and an evaluation. The evaluations consist of a letter grade from A through F and short narrative paragraphs on performance, ease of use, error handling, appropriateness, documentation, and educational value/usefulness.

The evaluation sections are subjective, both in the assigning of grades and the narrative paragraphs. Again, without knowing the backgrounds of the reviewers it is difficult to trust such statements as "Students will have no trouble running the program" and "The words chosen . . . are sufficiently challenging." However, the narrative evaluations are much more helpful than reviews. The greater amount of specific information given about the programs could help an individual or committee make a sound decision regarding the potential usability of a program. In addition, the reviewers seem to be experienced in education, although their credentials are not given.

A very involved process for the evaluation of educational software is the EPIE Micro-Courseware Pro/File and Evaluation. The EPIE evaluations are produced for distribution to school districts that pay a fee for the service. (Sample evaluations of programs have appeared in *The Computing Teacher*.) The evaluations are created through a rather complex process. Evaluators come from member school systems or universities and are trained in the evaluation process. Their analyses are then synthesized by a staff person and turned into a cohesive evaluation. The several parts of these evaluations are:

- General information (author, producer, suggested grade level, and content topics)

- Analysts' summary

- Recommendations to the producer

- Other reviews of program

- Observation of student users

- Analysts' description and review

- Instructional and software design (goals, contents, methods and approaches, and evaluation and management)

As can be seen, this is a very thorough process that includes several features of the previously described approaches. Responses are always narrative rather than merely ratings, and thus provide more information for the reader. In addition, since a rigorous training process is involved, the evaluators should be more objective and less likely to make superficial observations. The disadvantage is that many districts do not choose to pay the necessary membership fees, and these evaluations are thus not available to most teachers—especially those in small districts.

The Ad Hoc Committee on Computer Courseware Evaluation Guidelines for the National Council for the Social Studies (NCSS) produced a systematic set of guidelines specifically for software in social studies (Rose et al. 1984; see figure 3.1). This set of guidelines has subsections relating to knowledge, skills, and values. Responses to questions are in the form of judgments as to whether the software places a strong emphasis, moderate emphasis, inadequate emphasis, or is not applicable in regard to a criterion. This document may be reproduced in its entirety without seeking permission from NCSS.

The NCSS system is extensive, specific to social studies, and does ask important questions. However, few of the criteria can be measured objectively. Thus the evaluation again is based on the individual judgment of the evaluator. Both the meanings of the questions and the extent to which the software meets the criteria are open to interpretation. For example, item 1.03 asks, "Does the courseware's content deal with the realities of today's world in terms of its flaws, strengths, dangers and promises?" Every four years in the national election campaigns the Democrats and the Republicans see different "realities," "flaws," "strengths," "dangers," and

(Text continues on page 38.)

SOCIAL STUDIES MICROCOMPUTER COURSEWARE EVALUATION GUIDELINES

The guidelines are organized around three areas— *Knowledge, Skills,* and *Values*—each of which contains organizational descriptors. A checklist has been included to help evaluators monitor the extent of emphasis a courseware package places on each criterion. The checklist contains four headings—Strong Emphasis (SE), Moderate Emphasis (ME), Inadequate Emphasis (IE), and Not Applicable (NA). When using the checklist, it is important to realize that the breadth of criteria in this document and the variety of courseware on the market preclude a single courseware package from meeting all the standards in these guidelines.

Knowledge

Social studies educators at all levels have rejected a curricula based exclusively on the behavioral and social sciences. Instead, they have adopted a broad-based curriculum that not only addresses the concerns of those academic disciplines but concentrates on the personal and social concerns of the student, as well as the multicultural and normative concerns of society.

SE | ME | IE | NA

Significant Characteristics

1.01 Validity
Does the courseware emphasize currently valid knowledge from one or more of the social sciences?*

1.02 Accuracy
Does the courseware present a true and comprehensive body of content, free of distortion by omission?

1.03 Reality Oriented
Does the courseware's content deal with the realities of today's world in terms of its flaws, strengths, dangers and promises?

1.04 Significance of Past and Present
Does the courseware deal with important concepts, principles and theories of modern society? Does it present significant ideas that convey the excitement of the past, present and future?

1.05 Bias
Does the courseware avoid bias and/or stereotyping with regard to gender, ethnicity, racial background, religious application or cultural group? When unfamiliar customs and institutions or different ethnic groups and cultures are dealt with, are they presented in an unbiased and objective manner?

Content Emphasis

1.11 Issue Analysis
Does the courseware engage students in analyzing and attempting to resolve social issues? Is a data base provided and does it contain information of sufficient depth and breadth for students to make realistic decisions? If not, can the data base be expanded by the teacher or student?

SE | ME | IE | NA

1.12 Pervasive and Enduring Issues
Does the courseware focus on problems and/or issues that are socially significant? Do the materials demonstrate the reciprocal relationships among the social sciences, social issues and action?

1.13 Global Perspectives
Does the courseware help students develop a global perspective? Are students assisted in recognizing the local, national and global implications of the problems being examined and their possible solutions?

1.14 Development of Society
Does the courseware develop knowledge and insights into the historical development of human society? Do the facts, concepts, principles and processes presented offer direction in organizing a study of human behavior? Does it help students understand: how modern societies develop, the role of central institutions and values of national societies and those of the world community?

1.15 Multiculturalism
Does the courseware help develop an understanding of the diversity of cultures and institutional arrangements within American society and in other societies within the global community? Does it provide a rational explanation for customs and other distinctive aspects of daily life arrangements that are explored? Does it contribute to the students' acceptance of the legitimacy of their own cultural identity as well as that of others?

1.16 Personal/Social Growth
Does the courseware help students understand their own development and capabilities as influenced by their families, peer groups, ethnic groups, media, and the society at large?

*History is included in this classification.

Skills

Social studies education should provide students with the opportunities to develop, practice, and use a variety of thought processes and skills. Students should have opportunities to probe, to extract knowledge from experience, to think and communicate their findings and conclusions, both orally and in writing. They should learn how to learn—to develop self-direction in gaining meaningful knowledge and employing it effectively. The social studies program should develop the student's ability to make rational decisions. In order to accomplish this, it is essential that students acquire skills in critical thinking, inquiry, information processing and problem solving.

(Fig. 3.1 continues on page 36.)

Fig. 3.1. Software evaluation guidelines established by NCSS. Reprinted from *Social Education*, vol. 48, no. 7 (November/December 1984): 573-76, with permission of the National Council for the Social Studies.

Fig. 3.1 — *Continued*

SE | ME | IE | NA

Intellectual Skills

2.01 Inquiry and Problem Solving
Does the courseware pose problems which require students to use the methods of inquiry? Specifically, are students given practice in: identifying and defining problems, formulating and testing hypotheses, and arriving at valid generalizations?

2.02 Critical Thinking
Does the courseware foster the development of critical thinking skills of distinguishing between fact and opinion, detecting slant and bias, determining cause and effect, and evaluating the reliability of sources?

2.03 Higher Cognitive Levels
Does the courseware help students develop and/or reinforce the thought processes of analysis, synthesis and evaluation? Do students encounter material that helps develop their understanding of the relationship between elements and how these elements fit together as a whole? Are students given opportunities to use information to construct a new communication? Are students asked to make judgments based on appropriate criteria?

2.04 Divergent Thinking
Does the courseware encourage divergent thinking which allows students to provide a variety of answers for difficult questions?

2.05 Concept Formation
Does the courseware present a broad range of illustrations, models, and examples which are appropriate for helping students image, dissect, conceptualize, define, or recognize relationships between patterns or concepts?

Decisionmaking Skills

2.11 Does the courseware develop decisionmaking skills of identifying alternatives, establishing criteria to evaluate the alternatives, evaluating the alternatives in light of criteria and making the decisions? Are students given the opportunity to retest, re-interpret and re-organize their beliefs about facts and values?

2.12 Learning Environment
Does the courseware and its accompanying materials create a social environment populated by believable characters confronting difficult circumstances and choices?

2.13 Choices
Does the courseware require the student to make choices, and are those choices then used as data for reflection?

2.14 Information Base
Does the courseware's data match the kind of data that would be accessible by citizens outside the instructional context? Is the courseware flexible enough to allow the alteration and addition of information, so that students can practice making decisions under a variety of factual and value circumstances?

2.15 Consequences
Does the courseware confront students with realistic consequences (for themselves and for others) of decisions they are required to make in using the courseware?

2.16 Assessment
Does the courseware and its accompanying materials assist the teacher and the student to assess the latter's skills and abilities in decisionmaking?

2.17 Degree of Certainty
Does the courseware provide experiences in making decisions under conditions of uncertainty? Does the courseware help the student recall the basis on which decisions were made and to make revised decisions informed by new understandings?

Information Processing Skills

2.21 Orientation Skills
Does the courseware foster the development of map and globe skills?

2.22 Chronology and Time Skills
Does the courseware provide students practice in interpreting chronology and applying time skills, i.e., sequencing events and trends, and identifying and using measures of time correctly?

2.23 Graphic Data Skills
Does the courseware help students develop skills of reading and interpreting, constructing and drawing inferences from graphs, tables and charts?

2.24 Gathering and Processing Data
Does the courseware provide opportunities for students to develop skills in locating, organizing, interpreting and presenting data?

2.25 Content Reading Skills
Does the courseware facilitate the development of the student's word attack skills and the ability to read on the literal, interpretative and applied levels?

2.26 Communication Skills
Does the courseware or its accompanying materials foster adequately developed communication skills and provide opportunities for communicating effectively orally and in writing?

Cooperation and Participation Skills

2.31 Interaction
Does the courseware and its accompanying materials require groups of students to work together? Do the learning tasks require a division of labor? Does successful completion of the tasks require shared information?

SE	ME	IE	NA	

2.32 Cooperation
Does the courseware and its accompanying materials reinforce the importance of, and provide support for, cooperation in resolving conflicts over contradictory facts and values?

2.33 Social/Political Participation
Does interaction with the courseware and its accompanying materials enhance the student's ability to participate effectively in the social and political processes of his/her school and community?

2.34 Follow-up Activities
Does the courseware or its accompanying material offer suggestions for activities that follow logically from the use of the courseware? Does the courseware allow students to experience vicariously the positive and negative consequences, the costs and benefits, the frustrations and satisfactions of taking action?

Values

The cultural pluralism characterizing American society makes value conflicts inevitable. These conflicts are particularly evident in debates about solutions to complex social problems confronting our society. Effective participation in resolving these problems requires people who have rationally developed their own value system, and are proficient at making defensible value decisions.

Social studies education should provide ample opportunities for students to rationally examine value issues in a non-indoctrinating environment. Additionally, it should promote the reflective examination of value dilemmas that underlie the personal and social issues that students confront in their everyday lives.

SE	ME	IE	NA	

Societal Orientation

3.01 Influence of Values on Behavior
Does the courseware help students develop an understanding and appreciation of the influence of beliefs and values on human behavior patterns?

3.02 Procedural Values
Does the courseware help the student identify and develop an appreciation for values that underlie substantive beliefs and procedural guarantees expressed in this nation's fundamental documents?

Valuing Processes

3.11 Beliefs
Does the courseware require the student to identify his or her own beliefs, to make choices based on those beliefs, and to understand the consequences of the choices made?

SE	ME	IE	NA	

3.12 Conjoint Reflection
Does the courseware require conjoint reflection on feelings, behaviors and beliefs?

3.13 Defensible Judgments
Does the courseware support a process of value analysis by which learners can make rational, defensible value judgments?

3.14 Feedback
Does the courseware track the process students use in making value judgments and provide useful feedback with respect to its quality and improvement?

SYSTEMS FOR EVALUATING TECHNICAL AND INSTRUCTIONAL COURSEWARE ISSUES

Computer Library Media Consortium for Classroom Evaluation of Microcomputer Courseware, 1983. San Mateo County Office of Education, 333 Main Street, Redwood City, CA 94073. Phone (415) 363-5400. (A three-page untitled evaluation reporting form.)

Dennis, J. Richard. *Evaluating Materials for Teaching with a Computer,* includes "Courseware Evaluation Worksheet." The Illinois Series on Educational Application of Computers, No. 5e, Department of Secondary Education, University of Illinois at Urbana-Champaign, 1979.

Douglas, Shirley and Gary Neights. *A Guide to Instructional Microcomputer Software,* includes "Microcomputer Software Evaluation Form." Instructional Materials Service Programs, Pennsylvania Department of Education, Box 911, 333 Market Street, Harrisburg, PA 17108. Phone (717) 783-2528.

Evaluating Instructional Computer Courseware. Materials Review and Education Center, Division of Educational Media, Department of Public Instruction, Raleigh, NC.

Evaluation Guide for Microcomputer-Based Instructional Packages. Developed by MicroSift. The Computer Technology Program, Northwest Regional Educational Laboratory. Published by International Council for Computers in Education, Dept. of Computer and Information Science, University of Oregon, 1982.

Heck, William P. et al. *Guidelines for Evaluating Computerized Instructional Materials.* The National Council for Teachers of Mathematics, Inc., Reston, VA, 1981.

Rosenstock, Robert, Norman Dodl and John Burton. *Education Microware Assessment: Criteria and Procedures for Evaluating Instructional Software.* Education Microcomputer Laboratory, Room 400, War Memorial Gym, Virginia Tech, Blacksburg, VA 24061. Phone (703) 961-5587.

Smith, Richard A. (ed.) *Guidelines for Software Evaluation,* Department of Technology, Houston Independent School District, Houston, TX (a four-page questionnaire).

"promises." What is the likelihood that any two reviewers would perceive this question in exactly the same way? Further, if it *were* similarly perceived, what is the likelihood that the reviewers would agree on the extent to which the courseware met the criterion? While there are advantages to this form, software evaluations based on it must be considered carefully due to the subjectivity of the items.

The Northup Objective Software Evaluation System

There remains a need for a reasonably objective evaluation format, one that does not require training to use, provides useful information, is easy to use, and costs nothing. Such a format — the Northup Objective Software Evaluation System (NOSES) — is shown in figure 3.2. It can be used by a district or consortium to evaluate programs already owned or ones received for review. By sharing these evaluations, teachers and districts can help each other make purchasing decisions. You may use the NOSES form without permission.

While the NOSES form is generally self-explanatory, an elaboration and examples are given below. The evaluator should avoid judgment whenever possible — the emphasis is on giving objective information for each criterion.

Most of the subsections of the *Identification Information* section are quite straightforward. In the *Program Name* and *Source* sections, the name of the program and the distributor are to be specified. Including the address of the source is helpful. In the subsection *Subject Matter Area(s)*, all possible areas should be listed. For example, a program might be appropriate for both economics and U.S. history. *Type* refers to the kind of program the software offers — for example, is it drill and practice, game, tutorial, simulation, or problem solving? In *Computer System Requirements* the necessary equipment is listed — for example, TRS-80, Model III/4, Apple II family. *Price* is an important piece of information. Since the form is to be dated at the end, the form's user should check the price in relation to the date. If the review is more than a few months old the price may have changed significantly. *Brief Description* calls for a short explanation of the program so the reader will understand its purpose.

The *Content* section also provides for essential descriptive information. *Grade Level of Subject Content* is obviously important. An outstanding program that does not fit the consumer's grade level (or range of levels) is of little use. Often the publisher's descriptive information includes information about grade levels. If the evaluator has any reason to doubt the information given, the doubt should be mentioned in this subsection. If no grade level is stated, the evaluator can make a reasonable guess and note his opinion in the evaluation — for example, "While no grade level is given by the producer, the material's content and reading level appear to be aimed at the intermediate grades." A *Description of Goals or Topics Covered* can usually be found in the documentation provided by the publisher and can be stated or summarized in the evaluation. If none are stated in the printed material supplied with the program, a listing of topics can be created by previewing the software. *Approximate Reading Level* is sometimes given in the documentation. Again, if the evaluator has any reason to doubt the stated level, this should be mentioned. Several computer programs exist that could be used to determine the reading level, and an evaluator could use one of these in the absence of other information. While evaluating *Accuracy of Information Presented* involves some subjective judgment, and may be limited by the level of knowledge of the evaluator, a trained social studies teacher should be able to spot blatant inadequacies. If there appear to be inaccuracies, the evaluator should give an example or two for illustrative purposes.

Usability is an important section, especially for teachers whose students are quite young or inexperienced in the use of computers. The subsection called *Clarity and Simplicity of Directions* is slightly subjective; however, if a teacher feels that the directions are confusing or complex, then most students are likely to find them that way too. The second subsection in this category specifies *Amount of Typing Required*. Some programs accept single-key responses and some require typed input. For young students and those without typing skills, this is a crucial criterion. Typing responses is time-consuming, especially if the student uses the "hunt and peck" approach. If students do not have typing skills or if the teacher needs a short program for enrichment, then a program that requires little typing is desirable.

NORTHUP OBJECTIVE SOFTWARE EVALUATION SYSTEM (NOSES)

Identification Information
    Program Name:
    Source:
    Subject Matter Area(s):
    Type:
    Computer System Requirements:
    Price:
    Brief Description:

Content
    Grade Level of Subject Content:
    Description of Goals or Topics Covered:
    Approximate Reading Level:
    Accuracy of Information Presented:

Usability
    Clarity and Simplicity of Directions:
    Amount of Typing Required:

Documentation
    Adequacy of Printed Instructions:
    Support Materials:
    Suggestions for Follow-up:

Educational Techniques
    Variety of Reinforcements:
    Wrong Answer Response:
        Hint:
        Explanations:
        Branching:
    Screen Report of Final Results:

Management of Student Records
    Passwords/Protection:
    Handling of Successive Scores:
    Ease of Updating:
    Retrieval:
    Report of Time Taken:

Graphics
    Variety:
    Clarity:

Other Comments

Name of Evaluator _________________________ Date __________

Fig. 3.2. NOSES software evaluation format.

The *Documentation* section is made up of three subsections. The first is slightly subjective in that it requires a judgment regarding the *Adequacy of Printed Instructions.* Are they complete? Are they clear and written at a level students can understand? *Support Materials* might be record-keeping sheets for simulation programs, ditto masters for activity sheets, or other materials that supplement the computer program. A brief description of any such materials should be included in this subsection. Finally, are there *Suggestions for Follow-up* — activities to extend the learning or provide a bibliography for further study? While many teachers will want to create their own follow-up, most would welcome suggestions for these activities. If any are given they can be noted and briefly summarized in this subsection.

Educational Techniques is an important section. A program may be very creative and have a great deal of potential, but if it is not presented in a format that communicates clearly with students it will not be effective. What happens when the student enters a response? Does the program merely accept the correct answer and move on to the next question or statement, or does it reinforce the answer with some verbal, pictorial, or audio reward? Most programs will have some type of reinforcement, but is there a *Variety of Reinforcements*? A program that responds only with "Correct, Johnny" for each right response would become boring in a very short time. Good programs' reinforcing messages will vary and may be interspersed with pictures or motion. The program's *Wrong Answer Response* is the other side of the coin. Is a *Hint* given to shape the student's next response into a more fruitful channel? Is an *Explanation* given as to why the response was incorrect? Is an explanation of the correct answer given? Is the student given the opportunity of *Branching* to a tutorial section based on his or her response before advancing to the next frame or before answering the same question another time? Programs are becoming increasingly sophisticated in the way they handle wrong answers. Students can learn much from incorrect answers if the program is designed to respond to them in a positive manner, and this is an important criterion for selection. *Screen Report of Final Results* indicates whether the student is given an indication of his or her achievement. This might be a numerical score, a score stated within a graphic, or a full-scale "bells and whistles" treatment.

Many programs have a means of recording students' scores. Describing this process is the role of the section titled *Management of Student Records.* Some programs simply request the student's name at the beginning and automatically record the score. The teacher can retrieve these scores at his or her convenience. Other programs require the teacher to input the names, and perhaps passwords, of students. Some programs will even output the information in lists on a printer in a variety of ways. One advantage of the *Passwords/Protection* system is that it prevents one student from taking the program in the name of another student and purposely scoring low in order to affect the grade of that student. Another concern involves the program's *Handling of Successive Scores.* What happens if a student attempts to take the program a second time? Will the program let him? Can he improve his score? Will both scores be recorded, or only the first one, or only the last one? Teachers will have different philosophies about the acceptability of these options, but in this subsection what is to be reported is what the program allows. What options, if any, are available to the teacher? It is up to the potential consumer, not the evaluator, to determine whether these options are appropriate. An important feature of the student management portion of the program relates to *Ease of Updating.* Is it only a minor irritation or a major project to add or delete names from the student records? The process needs to be briefly described. Similarly, what is the process for *Retrieval* of a student's records? Do disks have to be changed? Can the records be easily accessed? Can a printout be made? Can the records be printed out in a variety of formats? For example, a teacher may want the records printed out in alphabetical order for his or her own use, but for posting on the bulletin board the use of passwords would be better, as the identities of the students would be protected. *Report of Time Taken*, a feature of some programs, can be very useful. If one student completes ten simple problems correctly in two minutes, and another solves the same problems correctly in fifteen minutes, the teacher will have gained a valuable piece of data that places the students' identical 100 percent scores in a new perspective.

Finally, *Graphics* are an essential feature of computer programs. Graphics with motion really set the computer apart from printed materials. Like reinforcement, graphics require *Variety*. The same old picture or design gets boring. Is there a variety of pictures, maps, designs, and, if possible, colors? Is motion used when it would be effective? The other aspect of graphics is *Clarity*. Does the graphic get the message across accurately? Again, this is a slightly subjective category. Any judgment rendered should be backed up by a brief explanatory comment, for example, "The maps in this program are confusing because the shapes do not clearly resemble the actual outlines of states. This might be difficult for students who are not very familiar with the shapes of states."

No approach to evaluating any product or service is foolproof, but evaluations of software programs through the use of NOSES will provide valuable information to prospective users. The information that is provided will be largely based on objective information, not on the opinion of the evaluator. Observation of students using the program would provide for an even more useful evaluation. Potential purchasers of a program might want to review several evaluations of the same program, if they were available.

On the next pages are two sample evaluations using NOSES. These should help set the criteria in the reader's mind and demonstrate what the results of evaluations using this system look like.

NORTHUP OBJECTIVE SOFTWARE EVALUATION SYSTEM (NOSES)

Identification Information
> Program Name: **Satellite Down** (U.S. Version)
> Source: Focus Media
> Subject Matter Area(s): Geography
> Type: Game
> Computer System Requirements: Apple II family
> Price: $85.00 each for the U.S. and world versions
> Brief Description: The Player is a government agent who is hired to find the location of a
> > downed U.S. satellite. Using a variety of available clues, the player is to determine in
> > which state the satellite has crashed.

Content
> Grade Level of Subject Content: 7-12
> Description of Goals or Topics Covered:
> > 1.   Develop a base of factual knowledge.
> > 2.   Develop map skills including latitude and longitude.
> > 3.   Acquire reference skills.
>
> Approximate Reading Level: 6th grade
> Accuracy of Information Presented: Appears to be very accurate

Usability
> Clarity and Simplicity of Directions: Very clear—especially if prepared with student
> > materials (included).
> Amount of Typing Required: Single keys only, except for typing of the student's name and
> > the name of the states thought to be the solution to the mystery.

Documentation
> Adequacy of Printed Instructions: Very adequate
> Support Materials: The manual includes specific directions, worksheets, outline maps of
> > regions of the U.S. and a political map of the U.S.
> Suggestions for Follow-up: Nothing specific

Educational Techniques
    Variety of Reinforcements: Reinforcement is correctly identifying the location of the downed U.S. satellite. The player's score is reported in dollars and is based on determining the location with as few clues as possible.
    Wrong Answer Response: The player is told that the guess is incorrect and must continue the game.
        Hint: Clues are available from a variety of topics, such as latitude and longitude or landmarks.
        Explanations: None
        Branching: None
    Screen Report of Final Results: "Payment" is made based on the number of clues used in determining the location, and a rating, such as "excellent," is given.

Management of Student Records
    Passwords/Protection: N/A
    Handling of Successive Scores: N/A
    Ease of Updating: N/A
    Retrieval: N/A
    Report of Time Taken: N/A

Graphics
    Variety: Few graphics of any type.
    Clarity: Those that exist present a clear message.

Other Comments
    A good background of geographical knowledge is needed or references must be used. This program recommends the use of an atlas and an almanac. This program would work better if used by small groups of students who could pool their knowledge and discuss the clues.

        Name of Evaluator   Terry Northup   Date   8/88

NORTHUP OBJECTIVE SOFTWARE EVALUATION SYSTEM (NOSES)

Identification Information
    Program Name: **"And If Reelected..."**
    Source: Focus Media
    Subject Matter Area(s): Government
    Type: Simulation
    Computer System Requirements: Apple II family, IBM, Tandy 1000
    Price: $65.00
    Brief Description: Student simulates a president running for reelection. Faced with a series of decisions, the student must select the best alternatives to maintain popularity with a wide variety of special-interest groups. After each decision, specific information is given about popularity with each group.

Content
Grade Level of Subject Content: 7-12
Description of Goals or Topics Covered:
1. Predict the effects of decisions on a variety of groups.
2. Select alternatives that will maintain an overall popularity sufficient to win reelection.
3. Develop an understanding of the conflicting demands and desires of interest groups.
Approximate Reading Level: 6th grade
Accuracy of Information Presented: Appears to be very accurate; contains issues that are very current.

Usability
Clarity and Simplicity of Directions: There is confusion between "select" and "go on" — select does not mean to choose the option presented but to move to the next option. This is explained in the student workbook, which needs to be read thoroughly before attempting to play the simulation.
Amount of Typing Required: Single keys only are used to make selections.

Documentation
Adequacy of Printed Instructions: Very clear in the workbook but not on the screen; student should read workbook before attempting the program.
Support Materials: In addition to the student workbook, a teacher lesson planner and a backup disk are included.
Suggestions for Follow-up: Topics for follow-up discussion are listed.

Educational Techniques
Variety of Reinforcements: Reinforcement comes from seeing the changes in popularity with various groups. At the end the results of the election between the student and the fictional opponent are played out, state by state, as electoral ballots are counted.
Wrong Answer Response: N/A
Hint: N/A
Explanations: None
Branching: None
Screen Report of Final Results: The election results indicate whether the primary goal, reelection, was accomplished.

Management of Student Records
Passwords/Protection: N/A
Handling of Successive Scores: N/A
Ease of Updating: N/A
Retrieval: N/A
Report of Time Taken: N/A

Graphics
Variety: Charts show popularity, and the final election results are displayed state by state.
Clarity: Graphics present a clear message, are easy to read, and make good use of colors.

Other Comments
This program was a 1987 finalist for the Software Publisher's Association Awards. The program contains 130 crises of which the computer selects twelve for each simulation. There are opportunities to "stroke" each group to increase popularity as the simulation progresses.

Name of Evaluator ___Terry Northup___   Date ___8/88___

REFERENCES

Bork, Alfred. 1984. "Education and Computers: The Situation Today and Some Possible Futures." *T.H.E. Journal* (October): 92-97.

Courseware report card published since September 1982 by Courseware report card, 150 West Carob Street, Compton, CA 90220.

The Digest of Software Reviews is published monthly and sold on a subscription basis; 1341 Bulldog Lane, Suite C, Fresno, CA 93710.

EPIE, P.O. Box 839, Watermill, NY 11976.

EPIE and Consumers Union. 1983. "Beyond Courseware." *The Computing Teacher* (January): 37-38.

Hassett, James. 1984. "Computers in the Classroom." *Psychology Today* (September): 22, 24-28.

Kelman, Peter. 1982. "What If They Gave a Computer Revolution and Nobody Came?" *Classroom Computer News* (January/February): 10, 54.

"Microgram." 1983. *The Computing Teacher* (May): 33-41.

Rose, Stephen, Allan Brandhorst, Allen Glenn, James Hodges, and Charles White. 1984. "Social Studies Microcomputer Courseware Evaluation Guidelines." *Social Education* (November/December): 573-576.

White, Mary Alice. 1983. "Synthesis of Research on Electronic Learning." *Educational Leadership* (May): 11-15.

4

USING THINKING TO PUT TOGETHER THE WORLD OF INFORMATION

Thinking has been defined in several ways. Sometimes people who are daydreaming say they are thinking. Sometimes individuals jump to a quick conclusion after "thinking" about their situation. Everyone has made a decision that didn't turn out well and wished they had thought about it better. After noting that thinking is what separates man from animals, which act only on instinct, John Dewey, the first educator to explore the need to develop thinking and ways to teach it, defined thinking as "active, persistent, and careful consideration of any belief or supposed form of knowledge in the light of the grounds that support it and the further conclusions to which it tends" (1933). Today this is what we would call "critical thinking," testing supposed truth to see if it is valid. In a world that is constantly trying to "sell" us products, ideas, candidates, and a variety of other things, such thinking is necessary not only to be a good citizen but merely to survive. As the world continues to become more complex, critical thinking becomes increasingly necessary to sort out what is happening and to make the most appropriate choices in order to meet one's wants and needs. Collectively, nations that progress will be those whose citizens make the best decisions, decisions arrived at through reflection, not impulsiveness.

Dewey described the benefits for thinking clearly in 1933 and they are still valid today:

Put in positive terms, thinking enables us to direct our activities with foresight and to plan according to ends-in-view, or purposes of which we are aware. It enables us to act in deliberate and intentional fashion to attain future objects or to come into command of what is now distant and lacking. By putting the consequences of different ways and lines of action before the mind, it enables us to *know what we are about* when we act. (Dewey's italics)

To survive and thrive as individuals, a nation, or as a species we must think. It does not go too far to say that the quality of one's life is closely related to the quality of one's thoughts. This chapter will consider what constitutes thinking, how it can be taught, and how the use of computers in the classroom can help students improve the quality of their thinking.

WHY THE DEVELOPMENT OF THINKING MUST BE A
PRIORITY IN SOCIAL STUDIES CLASSROOMS

Beyer (1987) notes that thinking has long been listed as a goal of education, going back at least to the 1820s. In recent times the goal of developing thinking was reemphasized by the Education Commission of the States in 1982 when it stated that the basics of tomorrow include "evaluation and analysis skills, critical thinking, problem-solving strategies, organization and reference skills, synthesis, application, creativity, decision making given incomplete information, and communication skills through a variety of modes."

This theme was further emphasized by the National Science Board Commission on Pre-College Education in Mathematics, Science, and Technology in its report *Educating Americans for the 21st Century* (1983):

> We must return to the basics, but the basics of the 21st century are not only reading, writing, and arithmetic. They include communication and higher problem-solving skills, and scientific and technological literacy—the *thinking* tools that allow us to understand the technological world around us.... Development of students' capacities for problem-solving and critical thinking in all areas of learning is presented as a fundamental goal.

The number of students achieving higher-order thinking capability is declining rather than increasing. While the need to develop thinking is greater than ever, students are not doing as well as in the past. In 1979-1980 the National Assessment of Education Progress ("Reading, Thinking, and Writing" 1981) concluded that students

> develop very few skills for examining the nature of the ideas that they take away from their reading. Students seemed satisfied with their initial interpretations of what they had read and seemed satisfied with their initial requests to explain or defend their points of view. Few students could provide more than superficial responses to such tasks, and even the better responses showed little evidence of well-developed problem-solving strategies or critical-thinking skills.

The National Commission on Excellence in Education (*A Nation at Risk* 1983) found that nearly 40 percent of students cannot draw inferences from written materials, only 20 percent can write a persuasive essay, and only one-third can solve mathematics problems requiring several steps. Further, the dip in SAT scores, upon closer analysis, does not indicate a reduction in basic knowledge, but the items missed require complex thinking rather than simple recall and application (McTighe and Schollenberger 1985). What has dipped is not basic knowledge but thinking skills. In the 1960s and 1970s these skills were explicitly taught in social studies and other content fields. Since that time there has been a growing emphasis on accountability, which emphasizes teaching bits of knowledge that can be tested. These conclusions demonstrate that thinking skills are not being developed in schools at a time when it is crucial that they be developed.

One reason that thinking must be taught is that in an information society, individually and collectively, we will be overwhelmed by information if we do not have the skills to sort it, know when to discard some of it, make sense of it, and act upon it. Just knowing the information will not guarantee that one will be able to use it to best advantage. Learning the facts and being able to use them are two entirely different processes. In the recent past the teaching of content information to pass achievement tests or for graduation requirements has taken precedence and the teaching of information-processing skills has been relegated to a minor role. That is why the National Council for the Social Studies and more than twenty other national education groups have joined forces to promote the teaching of thinking (*Education Week*, November 6, 1985).

Thinking is not being developed in students and it must be if our society is to survive and thrive in the twenty-first century. Some teachers act as if the ability to think is genetic or that it will develop as a consequence of regular school activities. Neither is the case. It is clear that all students can learn to develop and use thinking skills, just as they can develop psychomotor skills or reading skills. Naturally, some will develop them more rapidly and to a higher level than others, but all students, given normal intelligence, can learn to think. As to thinking being a developmental phenomenon that occurs by accident, Beyer (1987), who has reviewed a massive amount of research on this subject, states clearly that thinking must be taught. He says it "is neither an incidental outcome of experience nor an automatic product of study in any particular subject matter." Thinking skills will not develop unless a direct effort is made to teach these skills; there is no evidence to the contrary. Yet, there is clear evidence that students can learn to think if they are taught in a direct and consistent way.

This should be good news to social studies teachers. In a field whose "raison d'être" is to develop citizenship, the development of thinking should be a primary goal. Unfortunately, most social studies teachers, like most other teachers, have been too busy "covering" the facts to bother with developing thinking. Over and over researchers have found that social studies tests contain over 90 percent recall questions. Why do social studies courses fail to develop thinking skills, even though these skills are essential to developing good citizens and students who are competent in subject matter?

Why Don't Social Studies Teachers Emphasize Thinking?

There appear to be several reasons why the development of thinking skills is not a focal point of social studies education.

1. Teachers are unclear about what thinking is (Phillips 1974). There are few accepted definitions of thinking and, to confuse things more, there are several different types of thinking. Thus, however one defines thinking, it is a vague, unspecific term. In these days of behavioral objectives, attempting to develop thinking seems quite nebulous. Being able to develop thinking and then measure the change in students to verify that it has been done is extremely difficult. With the current administrative emphasis on measurable results, teachers tend to avoid goals that do not easily produce such results.

2. Teachers accept the myth that students can't think unless they have learned all the facts they need to think with (Phillips 1974). As mentioned above, teaching all the facts, even all the "important" ones, is impossible. Even if it could be done, students would have forgotten many of the earlier facts before those at the end were covered. Thus, when the teacher got around to teaching students to think, the data pool would be nearly empty. It is not unusual to ask college students, who have had U.S. history four times, who won the war of 1812 and find that they don't even know who participated in the war, let alone who won it. It should be noted that in the "real world," when faced with a problem, decision makers seldom have all the facts of the issue at hand. They expect to find them. In social studies it would be beneficial to use the same approach. Start with the problem and let it define the data or facts necessary to solve the problem, make the decision, or answer the question. Facts are then learned in context of a problem, not as isolated bits of data with little or no meaning.

3. Teachers also accept the myth that highly structured content will automatically result in the development of thinking (Phillips 1974). If only students can progress through well-structured material, they will absorb these organized, logical structures and will apply them to problems and situations in school and life. It doesn't take very much experience to realize that this approach does not develop thinking in students.

4. Teaching for memorization is easy and can be measured precisely. If attempting to develop thinking is difficult and nearly impossible to measure accurately, then why not emphasize what is relatively easy to teach and measure? This approach requires only that the teacher select the facts to be learned, present them, require that they be practiced, measure to see if they have been mastered, and assign a grade. This approach offers specific objectives and yields results that can easily be converted into number or letter grades.

5. Teaching for memorization is traditional and is what the role models (college content professors) did, so it must be acceptable as a course of action. At least since the Middle Ages education has emphasized memorization. Many teachers believe that to be a learned person is to be able to quickly recall what one has learned. Since most social studies teachers have been positively influenced by one or more of these role models, they tend to teach as they have been taught.

The consequence of the five factors leads to the dominance of memorization in social studies classrooms rather than the development of thinking. Unfortunately for the students and for the nation, a vast majority of the "learned" facts are forgotten and students are left with neither a strong storehouse of facts nor a set of thinking skills that they can apply to information they encounter later, in or out of school.

Why Social Studies Should Not Emphasize Memory

Certainly some memorization is necessary in social studies. Some information is used frequently enough that it needs to be instantly available, such as the name of the nation's capital. Knowing other facts is considered essential for educated individuals and good citizens. Granting that this is the case, it is, nevertheless, not necessary to memorize thousands of isolated pieces of information. While teachers will never agree on which facts are essential, it must be realized that social studies teachers generally do require the memorization of many needless facts. Readers who think this does not apply to them might find it interesting to review tests they have given recently. If questions ask students to remember the names of political parties in Italy several hundred years ago, the names of long-forgotten popes, or even the terms of office of U.S. presidents, the test makers should reflect on what they consider important.

Why might memorization be the wrong strategy for social studies teachers to use?

1. Before the printing press, the only references one had was what resided in one's own memory. Now that there are other references, there is no reason to rely chiefly on memory. Books, microfiche, audio and video tapes, and even computers can supply a person with almost any piece of information. It is not necessary to have it all stored in one's mind.

2. With the knowledge explosion that has occurred and is continuing to occur, it is futile to attempt to accumulate all knowledge in one's head. New information and facts are being generated far faster than anyone can "learn" them. In fact, in many occupations it is folk wisdom that a person's college education will be outdated in ten years because so much information will have become obsolete.

3. Times are changing, and changing fast. What is a fact today may not be a fact tomorrow. For example, in the 1950s one of the authors had to memorize all the borderlines of all the major countries in Africa. Today those countries do not even have the same names, let alone the same borderlines. Many "facts" that students may be required to memorize are hardly worth the effort.

4. It is unnecessary — and impossible — to memorize even the facts that will remain true for a period of time. If information is not going to be used frequently and if it is relatively easy to find it in a resource, then it doesn't need to be memorized. The capitals of all the states or the terms of office of presidents are examples. If students reside in California, it is relatively unlikely that they will need to know the capitals of the New England states. If they should ever move to the East, they will be able to learn these if they need to.

5. In Ebbinghaus's classic studies on learning he demonstrated that 60 percent of what is learned is forgotten within a day and about 79 percent is forgotten within a month. Later studies have yielded similar results (Thornburg 1984). It is well known that long-term retention of memorized material is very low—5 percent or less after one year. Thus, emphasis on memorization is 95 percent *in*efficient. If memorization is this ineffective, it is time to try another approach.

6. Much of the material that is memorized is learned by rote, that is, devoid of any meaning. Students repeat a definition over and over until they can reproduce it *without thinking* on a test. Once the test is over, students forget the material because its only purpose was as a vehicle for passing the test. It was never considered to have any meaning or purpose of its own. Cognitive psychologists, such as Ausubel, Novak, and Hanesian (1978) and Bruner (1966), have said for years that to make ideas important teachers must present them in a way that students can make them a part of their cognitive structure. If students see meaning in ideas, if those ideas relate to ideas they already have or help them solve a problem, then the ideas will be retained. If the ideas are learned only to please the teacher or to pass a test, they will be quickly forgotten.

7. Memorization emphasizes what is known and presents current approaches to solving problems. This would be useful if the world of tomorrow were going to be similar to the world of today. This was the case in the Middle Ages, and even into the nineteenth century, but it certainly is not true today. As teachers, we cannot begin to imagine what our students will face in the year 2030. However, it is clear that problems will exist and that thinking, not a memorization of past persons and events, will be necessary to solve these problems. While knowing the past may prevent making the same mistakes over again, it is not a good basis for making decisions in novel situations.

The use of memorization is easy, is traditional, does not rock the boat, and is easily measurable on a short-term basis; however, it does not provide long-term benefits and certainly *does not* develop thinking skills. Teaching facts provides students with vast numbers of facts but doesn't prepare them to apply, analyze, synthesize, or evaluate these facts. The U.S. census generates facts about over 200 million Americans, but these facts are worthless unless there is some way to interpret the facts, to make sense out of them, to create explanations, and to make predictions. Facts by themselves have no value, unless one aspires to be a quiz show contestant.

The Case for Thinking

Memorization is a poor use of educational time, and there are better uses for that time. Developing thinking is one such use. Let's look at reasons why thinking should be the primary emphasis of American education, and social studies education in particular.

1. What will the world of the future be like? As previously mentioned, it is sure to be very different from today's world. We can also be sure that there will be problems—there is no telling what kind, but history demonstrates that every generation has had its problems. If change is occurring at an increasing pace, then adults of the future will have even more problems than our current generation. *Problems would not exist if current traditions, habits, and ideas were sufficient to deal with situations that arise.* The ideas of today are not sufficient for the future. The development of thinking and problem-solving skills are crucial to preparing students for the future.

2. Solving problems requires thinking. This idea has been well stated by Dunfee and Sagl (1966):

Skills of critical thinking are indispensable to the problem solving process. Although critical thinking is vital at every stage of this process from identification of the problem to decisions about its solution, the skills that require particular attention are those involving the critical analysis of information and those leading to the formulation of reliable conclusions based on that information. No effective resolution to a problem can be achieved without these special skills.

3. The objects of memorization are usually forgotten quite rapidly. In addition, even if they are remembered, they are seldom transferable or generalizable to other situations. Memorizing a specific, isolated fact is not very useful. Learning that is useful is learning that is transferable to a wide variety of situations. Thinking certainly falls into this category.

4. The skills required in an information society are those that relate to analyzing, synthesizing, and evaluating data. Thinking is a prerequisite for a successful career in such a society. This is the very reason so many business people are concerned about the state of American education.

5. A democratic society requires a citizenry that can think and solve problems. This is certainly not a new idea; however, as society faces ever new and challenging problems, citizens will more than ever need to select the best representatives and know how to influence government agencies. Naisbitt (1982) sees one of the major trends in the future to be the decentralization of government and an increase in participatory democracy. Today's students must be prepared for such roles.

6. Not only can developing thinking provide the benefits described above, but some techniques designed to teach thinking also help students learn facts in a meaningful way. Oliver and Shaver (1966) demonstrated that, using an approach designed to develop inquiry skills, students learned more facts than the control classes and remembered these facts longer.

7. Thinking skills are helpful in learning higher-level knowledge in content subjects. This is because they help learners perceive relationships between and among ideas, events, and experiences and enable them to fit these into their cognitive structures. In other words, developing understanding of content ideas can be learned through activities that require the use and development of thinking skills. The proposition is not should teachers teach content *or* thinking skills. If teachers will move away from an emphasis on rote memorization to an emphasis on developing the higher levels of Bloom's taxonomy, both content and thinking objectives can be met!

In conclusion, two things seem clear to us: Thinking skills are not being developed very consistently or well by teachers, and there is a great need for these skills to be developed as we enter the twenty-first century. This seems to be true in social studies, as well. In this chapter we hope to clarify some ideas about teaching thinking, to provide some ideas about how computers can be useful in doing this, and to list some resources for further information.

TYPES OF THINKING SKILLS

As mentioned above, thinking is a vague and ill-defined term. Beyer (1987) echoes Dewey's fifty-year-old definition of thinking when he said that thinking in its broadest sense implies finding meaning or making sense out of experience. Fortunately, Beyer goes on in his excellent book to be more specific. Thinking involves using one's mental abilities to determine one's action or to reflect on and find meaning from one's action, rather than acting purely on instinct. The ability of human beings to do this is what has allowed them to achieve superiority over other animals and to control the planet. (Some might argue that without some very quick and deep thinking, humans may also destroy the planet.)

Beyer breaks thinking down into three types. His distinctions are useful and help clear up some of the confusion about thinking. For that reason, this section will include a brief description and commentary on Beyer's types of thinking. Later, an approach that combines these into a system for social studies will be given.

Thinking Strategies

Beyer describes three types of thinking skills: thinking strategies, critical thinking, and micro-thinking skills. The first type he describes are thinking strategies. These are three very complex processes: conceptualizing, problem solving, and decision making. There are four characteristics of these that distinguish them from critical thinking and micro-thinking skills. First, thinking strategies are used to achieve a clear purpose. Second, they involve a set of steps; each step, in turn, consists of subprocesses. Third, the steps are generally followed in sequence. Fourth, each step involves the use of combinations of thinking skills.

It is clear that children use these strategies even before they enter school. Students create concepts before the end of the first year. By the time students reach school they have a set of concepts that help them understand their world. The role of the school is to help students learn to apply conceptualizing more effectively and to learn specialized subject-matter concepts.

Likewise, students solve problems and make decisions long before they receive formal training in these processes. Their attempts may be faulty, yet they do use their minds to solve problems that arise in their lives and to make decisions about which course of action they should pursue. The role of the school is to teach the model of problem solving appropriate to the subject matter, help students understand that a rational approach is more effective than an impulsive one, and to improve their ability to use these processes.

In addition to Beyer, Bruner (1966), Ausubel, Novak, and Hanesian (1978), and others, have described conceptualizing as a process through which individuals make relationships among items and events. For example, while breeds of dogs have some differences, they have more similarities with one another than they do with cows. Conceptualizing is a process of seeing the similarities of related items. Beyer notes that there are two stages in this process: identifying key attributes of the concept and applying those attributes to other potential members of the category. The process of fulfilling these stages has five steps:

1. identifying similarities of two or more items

2. determining exactly what are the common attributes

3. noting how other items do not fit all the attributes, although they may share some attributes

4. testing out these conclusions by comparing them to new examples

5. modifying conclusions about the essential attributes that define inclusion/exclusion in the category.

At this point, the person who does not know what the label is will ask what these things are called or make up a name. This is seen in children who might ask the name of animals that are fat, live in fields, and go "moo." Or, sometimes children make up names for their concepts and later find out that there is an acceptable, proper name for the classification. In any event, without the process of conceptualizing it would be very difficult to make sense out of reality. When we see similarities in items, then we know that we can deal with them in similar ways. For example, if you have a "cat" concept and know that cats like to be petted, you will know how to treat a cat.

Each individual cat will not have to be a brand new experience. Likewise, if students develop a concept of elections, then they will know that whether it is a national, state, or student council election, certain similarities will be present. Learning to apply the five-step process above will simplify conceptualizing for students.

Problem solving has been described by a variety of individuals over the years in slightly different ways, yet most people's concept of the scientific method or problem solving probably contains approximately the same steps as ours:

1. sensing that something is wrong and needs to be corrected or solved

2. stating exactly what the problem seems to be

3. listing several potential solutions

4. selecting one solution that seems to have the greatest potential for success (a hypothesis)

5. testing the chosen solution to see whether it works

6. making a tentative conclusion regarding the problem.

Problem solving, in the pure sense, is to be done scientifically and objectively, that is, without one's values and preferences affecting the selection of the alternatives that are tested. The best solution is the one that works most effectively. Such an approach involves collecting data and analyzing it to determine the best solution.

Decision making involves selecting an alternative that will meet a goal and has consequences acceptable to the decision maker. This is definitely not objective, and to arrive at the best decision requires that the decision maker consciously consider what the goal is, what values are important, and what consequences are acceptable. It can be conceptualized in the following way:

1. defining a goal

2. identifying alternative ways of achieving the goal

3. determining the positive and negative consequences that might be expected if each alternative were chosen

4. determining which alternative and set of consequences are most congruent with one's values, preferences, and abilities

5. applying the "best" alternative

6. based on the results, determining whether to apply that alternative in a similar future situation.

As was suggested, each of these three processes are complex and involve the use of many thinking skills. Yet, each is used, if even in a primitive way, by young children. At the other end of the spectrum, we can see that those who are successful in life almost always are very effective at using all three of these thinking strategies. All three are built on individual thinking skills used in combination to achieve a specific purpose.

Critical Thinking Skills

Critical thinking, as Beyer notes, is not a negative approach; that is, it does not involve being critical of a person or idea. Rather, it "means judging the authenticity, worth, or accuracy of something" (Beyer 1987). Will Brand X soap actually kill more germs than Brand Y, as claimed? Is Ford the "best built car in America"? Will the Star Wars defense shield protect us from missile attack? Is the government of Nicaragua a democratic government or a communistic one? Were the methods used in the Reconstruction period necessary to maintain democracy or were they punitive? From simple purchasing decisions to complex questions of social studies content, critical thinking—judging the authenticity, worth, or accuracy of an idea or claim—is very important in life and in social studies classrooms. These skills are essential to being a good citizen and an effective adult in our society.

Beyer lists the ten critical thinking skills that he believes are essential, noting that each one involves both analytical and evaluation skills:

1. distinguishing between verifiable facts and value claims

2. distinguishing relevant from irrelevant information, claims, or reasons

3. determining the factual accuracy of a statement

4. determining the credibility of a source

5. identifying ambiguous claims or arguments

6. identifying unstated assumptions

7. detecting bias

8. identifying logical fallacies

9. recognizing logical inconsistencies in a line of reasoning

10. determining the strength of an argument of claim.

In order to perform any of these critical thinking skills students must apply two or more of the micro-thinking skills to be discussed later. Yet, critical thinking differs from the thinking strategies because these skills are not applied in a set sequence (Beyer 1987); that is, there is no clear strategy for every critical thinking skill. Thus the critical thinking skills are an intermediate stage between the use of individual skills and the use of complex strategies, which utilize many individual skills.

Micro-Thinking Skills

These are the skills that come to mind for many teachers when thinking skills are mentioned. They are the fundamental skills that are necessary to perform critical thinking or the thinking strategies. Beyer (1987) includes the extended version of Bloom's taxonomy plus three reasoning skills. Bloom combined translation, interpretation, and extrapolation into one operation he called comprehension. Beyer prefers to list these separately for clarity, thus his list looks like this:

recall

translation

interpretation

extrapolation

application

analysis (includes comparing, contrasting, classifying, and seriating)

synthesis

evaluation

Reasoning Skills

> inductive

> deductive

> analogical

Bloom's taxonomy has been very popular during the past decade, and most teachers have likely encountered it in undergraduate classes or in teacher inservice programs. The lowest level, which takes the least thinking, is recall. Each operation upwards to evaluation requires greater skill in thinking. Unfortunately, as stated earlier, too many teachers get stuck on the recall level and do not emphasize the higher levels. Not only must teachers develop these operations, but they must move on to develop in their students critical thinking skills and also the facility to use the thinking strategies. In order to do this there must be a conscious effort to move away from recall. This does not mean that facts are ignored; it means that they are used in a different manner. If a student is asked to explain (analyze) why the South lost the battle of Vicksburg, the student will certainly have to look up certain facts in order to write an answer to the question. The facts don't have to be in the student's mind to begin with. In requiring the student to perform this task the teacher is requiring the use of the facts for a higher purpose. It is not necessary for the student to memorize exactly what forces took control of the river; it is more important to know that taking control of the river was one part of the strategy to isolate the city and put it under siege.

Beyer also believes that ability to use inductive, deductive, and analogical reasoning are essential micro-thinking skills. Inductive reasoning is the process of moving from many specifics to make a conclusion or generalization. (If each of the colonies had Committees of Correspondence, sent representatives to the Continental Congress, and picketed royal offices, then there must have been widespread dissent against King George.) Deductive reasoning is the process of going from the general to the specific. (If there was widespread dissatisfaction with the king, as represented by the signing of the Declaration of Independence, then there must have been dissent even in "moderate" colonies such as Delaware.) Analogical reasoning involves the use of analogies to arrive at conclusions. (If England was the "mother country" and the colonies were the "children," then royal officials probably wanted to protect the colonies and expected them to be thankful for the help and be obedient, just as my mother expects this of me.)

One way of simplifying this wide array of thinking skills is to integrate them into a more coherent system. The first of the two lists that follow is a list of preliminary skills. It includes micro-thinking skills and many of the critical thinking skills; these can be developed individually. The second list, which outlines an advanced set of skills, combines problem solving and decision making into one sequence. This list builds on the micro-thinking skills and integrates many of the critical thinking skills into the thinking strategies.

THINKING SKILLS—PRELIMINARY LEVEL

1. The student is able to observe situations in an objective manner and report what was observed.

2. The student is able to summarize material read or heard in class in a clear and concise way.

3. The student is able to classify objects or experiences into logical categories.

4. The student is able to compare two objects or experiences and state in which ways they are similar and in which ways they are dissimilar.

5. The student is able to imagine being someone else or being in a different situation or time period.

6. The student is able to look at a set of data or read a position statement and make inferences:

    a. The student can infer what the writer believes by reading a given statement.

    b. The student can infer what would happen given certain conditions.

7. The student is able to differentiate between statements of fact and statements of opinion.

8. Given a set of data regarding some central theme, the student is able to draw a conclusion.

9. Given a generalization, the student is able to recognize whether a new piece of data supports or refutes the generalization.

10. Given a problem, the student is able to list several plausible hypotheses regarding its solution.

11. Given a hypothesis and some data, the student is able to determine which pieces of data are relevant and which are irrelevant to the hypothesis.

12. Given a hypothesis and some data, the student can determine which data support and which refute the hypothesis.

13. Given statements of belief, the students is able to identify basic assumptions, stated or unstated.

14. The student is able to interpret and summarize data in graphs and use graphs to portray data.

15. The student is able to interpret and summarize tabular data and to use tables to portray data.

16. The student is able to interpret political cartoons:

    a. Given a political cartoon, the student can explain the symbolism used.

    b. Given a political cartoon, the student can accurately describe the cartoonist's views of the situation depicted.

17. Given data, the student is able to determine which is biased and which is not.

18. The student is able to detect illustrations of the use of propaganda techniques.

19. Given a situation and a proposed course of action, the student is able to project the probable consequences of the action.

THINKING SKILLS—ADVANCED LEVEL:
PROBLEM SOLVING/DECISION MAKING

The following is the sequence of steps of the problem-solving thinking strategy with subskills listed. In some cases all the subskills will not be utilized every time. It will be necessary to determine which apply to each problem. Since decision-making situations call for relatively quick action, it is necessary to make decisions without being able to do all the testing that is allowed in problem-solving situations. Also, decision-making situations imply that there is *no one right* decision. The decision that is made must achieve the goal but do so in a way that is consistent with the decision maker's values and that is most likely to yield consequences acceptable to the decision maker. For each step of the problem-solving model below, the decision-making subskills are listed separately.

1. The student is able to look at a situation and state what is problematic about it.

    a. The student can discern what difficulty lies at the center of a disagreement between individuals or groups.

    b. Given a goal, the student can list what impediments seem to block clear passage to the goal.

    c. Given a goal, the student can list several possible means of accomplishing the goal and realizes the problem is to select which approach to take.

    d. The student can clearly and specifically state the problem in an objective manner.

    For decision-making situations the student can clearly state the desired goal to be achieved by the decision.

2. Given a problem, the student is able to state several plausible hypotheses.

    a. The student can survey data on hand and make inferences from it as to possible solutions.

    b. The student can generate solutions to the problem and list them.

    c. The student can state hypotheses in "if, then" statements.

    d. Given that it may be impossible to test all hypotheses, the student can select one or two that are most plausible and therefore worth testing.

    e. The student can project what data or what type of data must be gathered to test the hypotheses.

    For decision-making situations the student can (a) list a wide variety of the possible alternative courses of action, (b) list the anticipated positive and negative consequences of each alternative, and (c) state his or her values and determine to what extent they are congruent with the alternatives listed.

3. The student is able to collect data appropriate to the hypothesis or hypotheses being tested.

    a. Based on the projected data needed, the student can organize a plan to collect the needed data.

    b. The student can distinguish between relevant and irrelevant data.

c.   The student can use forms of observation to collect data, such as interviews, surveys, and participant observation.

d.   The student can summarize written material into notes which can later be organized.

e.   The student can locate information in the library quickly and effectively.

For decision-making situations the student can list the alternatives in priority order from most acceptable to least acceptable.

4.   The student is able to classify and organize the data in a meaningful way and analyze it.

a.   The student is able to identify the data that is related.

b.   The student is able to discern whether a given cluster of data is consistent.

c.   The student can discriminate whether statements are based on fact or opinion.

d.   The student can identify the stated or unstated assumptions of an individual or group point of view.

e.   The student can distinguish between biased and unbiased information and determine the level to which it is biased.

f.   The student can evaluate which source of data is most reliable.

g.   The student understands his or her own values and attempts to analyze the data as objectively as possible.

For decision-making situations (a) if this is a real decision, the student applies the alternative, notes the real-life consequences, compares them to the anticipated ones, and determines to what extent the goal is achieved, or (b) if the decision is a hypothetical one, the student will be able to defend the alternative chosen to the teacher or to classmates.

5.   The student is able to draw a tentative conclusion.

a.   The student can determine whether the hypothesis is proven, disproven, or neither proven nor disproven.

b.   If the hypothesis is neither proven nor disproven, the student can suggest whether the next step is to collect other data or to restate the hypothesis.

c.   If the hypothesis is disproven, the student can use the data to propose a more plausible hypothesis.

d.   If the hypothesis is proven, the student can not only state a conclusion, but can also suggest what actions this conclusion infers.

e.   The student can explain these conclusions and inferences clearly in written or oral form.

For decision-making situations the student determines under what circumstances the same decision should be applied or whether another alternative would be preferable.

It is clear that this is a big order. Developing these skills is not the sole responsibility of social studies teachers. Yet, by virtue of our content, we can and should play a large role in developing thinking skills. Teachers don't have to choose between the teaching of content and thinking skills, because it has been found that the best way to develop thinking skills is within the context of a discipline. How this can be done will be explored in the next section.

APPROACHES TO TEACHING THINKING IN THE CLASSROOM

Beyer lists three beliefs about thinking and students that all teachers should accept. They form the basis for teaching thinking in the classroom.

1. All students think. It is clear that in their daily life, from selecting which clothes to wear to school to determining who to ask to the school dance, students think hundreds of times each day. Any action or idea that is not habitual takes thought! While habits simplify life and everyone performs many habitual acts, each of us still has to think many times each day. Thinking is not an act reserved for seniors in high school in a capstone course in Problems of Democracy, thinking is performed by every person with near normal I.Q. day in and day out from infancy.

2. All students can learn to think better than they are likely to discover on their own. Experience is a great teacher but it is a slow teacher. People might be able to learn on their own everything they need to know for their job and for life, but it would slow down the efficiency and effectiveness of society. We would still be in a backward nation! Education is designed to shortcut learning by experience, to provide learning in the right things at the right time to speed up the process. For example, without schools some people learned to read, but it was a slow, laborious process. Schools and corporate training are designed to help individuals reach maximum functioning in a short period of time. Hence, while students may learn to think well on their own, they can learn to think better and quicker if schools teach them how to think. Students, like electricity, will take the path of least resistance. Many will not choose to think unless thinking is demanded by the teacher. If teachers do not require thinking, then very little may occur.

3. The teaching of thinking is for *all* students. It is common for enrichment programs for gifted students to include development of higher-level cognitive skills. This implies that other students cannot think at these levels. Unfortunately, many teachers seem to believe that training in thinking skills should be reserved for the better students. Yet, as is clear from #1 above, even those who are less academically able think and make decisions daily. The quality of our nation's life depends on the decisions made by everyone, not just the 2 percent in the gifted class. In a country that believes in universal education, we must give our best to all students.

Beyer also stresses that classroom atmosphere is crucial to the development of thinking. The traditional conditions, with the teacher's desk in the front, with all desks in rows facing forward, and the teacher as the focus of attention is not going to produce good thinkers. This arrangement emphasizes that the teacher is the source of all right answers and students need to pay attention to the teacher rather than to use their own minds. Beyer suggests the following:

1. Seating should be arranged so that face-to-face interaction among students is encouraged.

2. The teacher's desk should be at the side or rear of the room.

3. There should be an absence of traditional workbooks that emphasize "right" answers. Rather the teacher should use open-ended questions and multiple texts or resources.

4. Activities should center around processing (using) information rather than memorizing it.

5. Students should feel free to take a risk—in putting forth an unconventional idea, challenging the views of others, and being comfortable in being challenged—and should feel free to ask questions of other students and of the teacher.

6. Teachers should encourage students to reflect on what they have studied and experienced, to reconsider conclusions, and to think about their thinking.

General Principles of Skill Development

If a teacher accepts the beliefs expressed above and develops an open atmosphere in the classroom that encourages thinking, then there are several principles of skill development that need to be considered.

1. Skills should be developed in relation to content that is relevant to the student. Skills should not be developed in isolation and divorced from the content of the subject. Students must see that thinking is something to be done in and with the content. Also, if the content is interesting to the student and if thinking can help the student understand it better, then the motivation for developing the skill will be intrinsic. In any event, in order to think one must have something to think about. The content of the course provides many things to think about. Thinking skills should be tools to help students reach objectives in the subject matter.

2. The skill that is to be taught needs to be explained and demonstrated to students by the teacher. Beyer says that the teacher should make clear the attributes of the skill or strategy and direct students' attention to the specific steps and rules that guide successful performance of the skill. As with other skills, such as finding map locations using coordinates, students need to see the skill performed, perhaps several times, to get a concept in their mind of what they are to do. A football coach would never tell young students in their first practice to go tackle someone. He would demonstrate exactly how a tackle is to be performed to be effective and safe. Even skills that seem very simple and self-evident to the teacher need to be explicitly demonstrated to students.

3. Skills are developed through a series of carefully planned lessons. "One-shot" lessons will not develop skills. The teacher must break the skill down into its subparts and develop each, or begin with a simple application of the skill and move gradually to complex applications. For example, in developing the skill of interpreting and summarizing tabular data, a series of lessons, starting with a very simple table and moving to complex tables, would be appropriate. And, once this skill is developed it cannot be assumed to be developed for all time. It must be periodically practiced. Just because you could ride a bike at age ten doesn't mean you could ride one just as well today. It would take some practice, although not as much practice to refresh the skill as it did to learn it initially. Just because students learned to read a graph in fourth grade doesn't mean that every teacher thereafter can assume that students have learned and are capable of applying this skill. Beyer notes that thinking is not learned once and for all time; thinking skills grow and develop over time as increasingly more complex situations are encountered. Also, since thinking skills don't transfer well from one subject to another, just because graphing is taught in math doesn't relieve the social studies teacher of the responsibility for teaching this skill in relation to social studies data.

4. Students must receive feedback regarding their performance of a skill as quickly as possible. In learning any new skill, whether physical or mental, people can learn bad habits as easily as good ones. If students think they are performing the skill correctly and they repeat the process several times, the performance will be ingrained. If they are wrong it will be difficult to correct their performance. It is crucial that in the first or second performance of a skill the teacher monitor each individual's performance to be sure the skill is being performed correctly. In the case of simple skills, a computer program can be helpful because feedback is instantaneous. To promote correct behavior, feedback is also required so the students will have the assurance that they are performing correctly. Sometimes teachers don't remark about correct behavior assuming that if they don't correct the students' behavior the students will know that they are performing correctly. This often is not the interpretation of students. Silence on the part of the teacher is taken to mean that the teacher is not paying attention to them. The insecure students will be confused and unsure whether they are performing correctly and may change their performance to something incorrect just because they have not received the assurance of positive feedback. Positive feedback provides the motivation to continue on in the behavior that generated the reinforcement.

5. Practice does *not* make perfect. We all have inherent limits to our abilities. Practice, if it is well designed and well directed, will help students develop skills up to their inherent limits, but not beyond them. The authors could practice shooting free throws twenty hours a day for a year and seldom make more than five out of ten because we have poor eyesight and limited physical skills. When students seem to be peaking in their performance or when no progress is observed, continuing to push students can generate discouragement, which leads to lowered confidence and lowered performance. However, if students are eager and seem motivated to continue to try to improve, the teacher should keep working with them. As in athletics, every student will not reach the same level of performance, yet all should reach a basic minimum level.

Micro and Macro Approaches to Developing Thinking Skills

There are two different ways of approaching the development of thinking skills. One, the micro approach, would teach each individual skill in isolation and assume that the student would know when and how to use several in concert when necessary. This seems to be a logical approach. Taking each skill individually allows for sequential development building from simple to complex skills. It allows the teacher to create individual skill lessons that can be scheduled in lesson plans as content is encountered that is appropriate to the skills. A sports analogy would be a basketball coach who teaches the basic skills. He might start by concentrating on dribbling for a week, then move on to passing, and eventually get to shooting. When all of these are learned, then the team can play a scrimmage to utilize all the skills.

Using the micro approach, the elementary teacher might create lessons to teach each of the preliminary skills in the list that appears earlier in this chapter. Or the secondary teacher might create lessons for each of the subparts of the advanced level processes. Using the micro approach a teacher might select several problem situations and work over and over with students on defining the problem (Step 1, Advanced Level Skills). After students seem to be able to define problems adequately, the teacher would move on to Step 2 and do repeated lessons until students could adequately state hypotheses. Moving on, the teacher would continue until all the parts of the process were covered.

Using such a limited skill makes creating a behavioral objective and a specific lesson plan quite easy, compared to trying to teach the whole process at one time. Developing the performance of individual skills is an organized and manageable approach and is the way skills are usually taught.

Someone might say, however, that just as all the parts of a 1989 Volkswagen laid out on the floor of the garage is not a 1989 Volkswagen, ability to perform independently the skills that are a part of problem solving does not mean that one can solve problems. The Volkswagen is not a Volkswagen until it is put together. Problem solving is not problem solving until the student can perform all the correct skills at the correct time to solve a problem. When using the coaching approach above, the coach often finds that in the first scrimmage some players run with the ball instead of dribbling it, some pass when no one is open, and some shoot "bricks" totally missing the basket, even though in shooting practice they do quite well. Putting it all together is harder than it seems.

Those who support the macro approach believe that skills should be taught in context. If teachers want to develop problem solvers, they should find a problem that students are motivated to attack and get them started. A teacher could ask, "What is going on here?," then lead students, as a group, to identify the problem using the subskills of Step 1 of the Advanced Level Skills. Next, the teacher would move on to Step 2, using the same problem, and continue until the problem is solved.

As the students moved through the steps toward problem solution, the teacher would be listening to student comments for clues as to when to correct misconceptions and when to digress to an explanation of how to apply the subskill. Using the basketball analogy again, the teacher would begin with a scrimmage, watch the students' performances and determine whether it would be necessary to stop for a short explanation of when to use the bounce pass. If just one or two students seem to be missing the point, the teacher could work with those students individually while the rest of the class moved on toward solution. If everyone seems to be performing well, then there is no need to restress the basics. Instruction would be on a need basis, not provided to the whole class whether they needed it or not.

The macro, or wholistic, approach has a great deal to recommend it: primarily, students are learning how to apply the whole strategy as it will have to be applied in real life. Yet, it takes an extremely talented and versatile teacher, and one who can set aside behavioral objectives for a while, to work on a process that might take several weeks before concrete results are seen.

Well, which approach is best? It is difficult to say. Different teachers have different skills and approaches. Different school districts have different curricula and rules. Different students have different preferences. For some students the macro approach might be very confusing. These students might like the security of practicing one thing until they achieved competence, before moving on. Other students might be frustrated by the micro approach, wondering what was the point of developing an individual skill. Research doesn't provide any answers. Teachers can experiment and find out what seems to work in their individual situation.

On a systemwide basis, the choice does not have to be one or the other. Perhaps a micro approach could be used in elementary schools to develop the preliminary skills, and a macro approach could be used in the middle and upper grades to develop problem-solving and decision-making strategies. One thing we can't afford to do is ignore the teaching of thinking skills until some magic approach is discovered that will work best for all teachers and all students. That day will never come.

THREE TEACHING MODES

Beyer suggests three modes of teaching introductory skills lessons: inductive, directive, and developmental. Each has different characteristics and each has different benefits and weaknesses. Which is the appropriate approach to use depends on a teacher's purposes and students. In this section each will be described briefly so that teachers can see how they would fit their individual classroom. Specific examples of these modes are contained in the chapters that follow.

The Inductive Mode

An inductive approach provides students with data and asks them to organize or process it. In doing so students discover the skill, which is refined by the teacher as the lesson progresses. Beyer suggests the following steps:

1. Introduce the new skill in the context of the subject matter being studied. Tell how the new skill can be used and how it will be helpful.

2. Ask students to execute the operation, as best they can, in a short task. This should be done using familiar content, not new content, and should be done in pairs or small groups.

3. Ask students to reflect on and talk with others about what went on in their mind as they executed the skill. What steps did they follow, what problems did they encounter?

4. Provide another task that will allow students to apply what they have learned in a similar situation.

5. Again, ask students to reflect on what they did, what rules they followed, and what degree of success they had.

An inductive approach has several advantages, as well as some potential dangers. First, students become actively involved very quickly, rather than having to listen to a long explanation or watch a demonstration. For some students this is essential; they want to be active learners. Such students are usually risk takers with strong analytical abilities. On a scale from impulsive to reflective, these students are likely to be the impulsive students, ready to plunge in, unconcerned about failure at the task. On the other hand, some students are less secure and prefer to have an explanation and a demonstration. These students are just the opposite of those described above. They are reflective, concerned about doing things right the first time. If a teacher used the inductive approach it might be more successful if students of these two different types were paired. As a teacher, you may have to determine whether more of your students fit one description or the other. Generally, most students will be somewhere in between and will be able to learn from either an inductive or a directive approach.

Another advantage of the inductive approach is that it becomes personal to students. As they grapple with the tasks and learn to figure out their own rules for applying the skill, the process becomes one that makes sense to them. They are following their own steps, not someone else's. In such cases, the "how to do it" steps are more likely to be remembered by the student. This is the beauty of the discovery approach. Those ideas we discover or figure out, even though others may have thought of them before, mean a great deal to us and they will definitely find a place in our cognitive structures.

Finally, the inductive approach is best used when the skill to be developed is a relatively simple one that won't confuse students. For example, suppose the skill is classifying objects into logical categories. Look at the list of businesses below and classify them into two or more categories.

Jim's Roofing	American Telephone and Telegraph
General Motors	Dallas Area Medical Services
The Flower Shop	U.S. Department of Agriculture
U.S. Post Office	J. J. Jones, Accountant

Is your list correct? Can you explain logically why you put each item into its category? If so, your list is correct, even though it might be very different from someone else's, whose list is also correct. Given the directions for this task, you only have to create categories and have rules for assigning items to the categories. This is a simple skill that could be initiated in an inductive mode. If a teacher wanted to introduce determining whether a hypothesis is proven, unproven, or neither proven nor unproven, an inductive approach might be confusing to many students, since this is a complex skill.

The Deductive Mode

Discovery takes a good deal of time, since students have to figure out rules and attributes for themselves. A more efficient approach, and one that appeals to the reflective students, is a deductive strategy. Beyer calls this a directive strategy because it utilizes the popular direct instruction format. He suggests that this approach be used when the skill to be introduced is complex, when students are less able than average students, or when students have no previous experience with the skill. He suggests a six-step approach.

1. Introduce the skill in the context of the subject matter and explain how being able to perform the skill will be beneficial.

2. Explain the key steps of performing the skill in sequence and any important rules or attributes that apply to the skill.

3. Demonstrate the skill, step by step, explaining each procedure.

4. Lead the students in a discussion of the procedure and discuss the attributes or rules of the skill.

5. Have the students use the skill to perform a simple task and remind them to follow the step-by-step procedure.

6. Ask students to review what they did, focusing on the steps, rules, or attributes of the procedure.

A directive approach has several advantages. First, it puts the teacher, who explains the right way to perform the skill, in control of the process. This approach also lends itself to being put into the traditional lesson plan format and is aimed at a specific behavioral objective. The results of this approach are much easier to evaluate: Can students recall the steps of the procedure and can they apply them given new data? Using the list of businesses above, in step 5 of the directive approach, students could be asked to classify the businesses as those that provide products, those that provide services, and those that provide both.

The Developmental Mode

Beyer also proposes an approach that combines elements of both the inductive and deductive, or directive strategies. This eclectic approach he calls the developmental strategy.

1. Introduce the skill just as is done in the other two approaches.

2. Give students a task that requires them to perform the skill. They can do this in pairs or small groups.

3. Students discuss what their thoughts were as they performed the task and identify steps or procedures they used. As they hear others they may gain additional insights.

4. The teacher explains any steps that students left out or misapplied and lists the steps or procedures for using the skill. Then the teacher demonstrates how to apply the skill to another set of data.

5. Once again working in pairs or small groups, students apply the modified steps or procedures to new data.

6. Students review what they have done, make any revisions necessary in the steps or procedures, and relate the skill to other skills.

This approach attempts to build on the strengths of both the inductive and directive approaches, which combined may meet the needs of both the impulsive/reflective, field independent/field sensitive, and the left brain/right brain thinkers. It combines discovery learning with learning from an expert (teacher) and may create a more complete understanding of the skill and how to apply it than would be provided by either approach used by itself.

Using these three approaches and integrating the principles of skill development should help teachers to be more successful in developing thinking skills and strategies. For further study, and in addition to the references at the end of the chapter, the following sources might be useful.

Social Education (April 1985), published by the National Council for the Social Studies, contained several articles devoted to developing critical thinking.

Educational Leadership (May 1985), published by the Association for Supervision and Curriculum Development, contained eight excellent articles related to developing thinking.

Teaching for Thinking is a book by James Raths, et al. that combines theory and many good practical suggestions for classroom application at every grade level. Originally published by Charles Merrill in 1967, it has recently been revised and is available from Teachers College Press.

Teaching for Thinking in High School Social Studies by Richard Phillips is an oldie but a goodie. It was published by Addison-Wesley in 1974.

Think Lab Jr. and *Think Lab Advanced* offer sets of individualized task cards for elementary-aged students. The teacher needs to introduce the skills first, but these activities can be used for independent practice. Using an authoring program it would be relatively simple to build a computer program for many of these activities. This would allow the student to receive rapid feedback and for the teacher to have a record of the student's performance.

Critical Thinking, Book One by Anita Harnadek includes sections on introduction to critical thinking, introduction to logic, basic concepts for critical thinking, common errors in reasoning, and other sections designed to develop logic and thinking skills. The book is oriented toward junior and senior high school and is published by Midwest Publications, P.O. Box 129, Troy, MI 48084.

Taking Sides is a series of books that present articles on both sides of educational, social, psychological, political, economic, historical, environmental, and legal issues. A guide with teaching and testing suggestions is also available from Duskin Publishing, Sluice Dock, Guilford, CT 06437.

Deciding includes a series of activities designed to help students learn to make well-informed decisions about themselves and their futures. It is published by the College Entrance Examination Board, Box 592, Princeton, NJ 08540.

Making Value Judgments: Decisions for Today has chapters titled "What Do I Value?" and "How Do I Make Decisions?" and explores twelve areas of problems that would interest most teens. This book and a teacher's guide is available from Charles Merrill, 1300 Alum Creek Drive, Columbus, OH 43216-0508.

HOW COMPUTERS CAN BE USED TO DEVELOP THINKING

It would be wonderful if computers could do all the teaching of thinking necessary in our schools. That, however, is not true now, nor will it ever be. There are some very good quality programs that can help, but nothing will ever take the place of a good teacher. Even those programs that can develop thinking skills are not independent programs; they depend on the teacher to prepare students for the programs and to follow up after students have completed them. What this section will do is suggest some ways teachers can use programs to help develop thinking skills. These suggestions will be continued in chapters 5, 6, and 7.

That computers are expected to play a part in preparing students for the future was expressed by Matsumoto (1985) when she said:

> We find, however, a surprising degree of accord among educators, educational reform proponents, demographers, futurists, economists, and employers who agree that higher-level thinking and competency with computers and related technologies are essential survival skills in the Information Society we have already entered.

If higher-level skills and computer competency are to be taught then why not "kill two birds with one stone" and use computers to develop the higher-level skills? What is necessary is better software specifically written to develop these skills and creative teachers who can use the software that exists. Since the authors wrote *Using Computers to Teach Social Studies* in 1986, the amount of software for social studies has doubled, and the improvement in the quality is amazing. There is no reason not to expect that the quality won't keep improving. Matsumoto noted that continued improvement in software depends largely on teachers. She stated: "Software will be of high quality only if educators decide on parameters for course materials, communicate their needs to software producers, and demand nothing less than the best."

It is essential that teachers be discriminating in their software purchases. Not only does this keep school districts from wasting money on poor software, but dollars are votes. Every purchase tells software companies what customers want. If schools buy only high-quality, challenging software then producers will soon begin creating that type of software. This has already happened. Three years ago when our first edition came out, there was an abundance of simplified drill and practice software. As better programs became available schools reduced their purchases of simpler programs and software companies swiftly changed course. Today there is an abundance of tutorial and simulation programs. Many of the simulation programs require the use of thinking strategies to be successful, yet there are few programs designed to teach thinking skills directly. It would not be hard to create tutorial programs that would develop these skills. Perhaps teachers have not demanded such materials.

In terms of using software that exists to develop some of the thinking skills listed earlier in this chapter, here are several suggestions.

1. It would be nice if there was a series of programs designed to develop thinking skills, from the micro skills through the thinking strategies. Unfortunately, there is either no such program or the authors have never seen it. There are some software programs that attempt to develop thinking skills, such as **Rocky's Boots** and **Gertrude's Problems**, but these are almost always in other subject matter. One program that can be justified in social studies is **The Factory**. This program provides students with a finished product made by a computer-operated machine. The student's job is to take a piece of raw material and create a set of procedures to turn the raw material into a finished product just like the model. Having created these procedures, the student can run them and see how the product turns out. If it is not like the model, then the student must figure out which steps must be modified, dropped, or added.

2. While recall is a very low-level thinking skill, it is still a skill that must be developed. Drill and practice programs are useful for developing recall. When considering purchasing drill and practice programs a teacher should ask: (1) are the facts that are being memorized important enough to spend money for the software and valuable teaching time on them? and (2) are the programs interestingly done and do they employ game or reinforcement techniques that will make students want to keep using the program until the material is memorized? If the answer is affirmative to both questions, then the teacher should purchase the program. If the program is one the teacher has not personally seen in action, it would be best to purchase the program "on approval." If, when the program is tested and it is not of good quality, it should be sent back. Teachers should spend school money as carefully as they would their own.

3. The better tutorial programs have branching systems that move the student to different parts of the program based on individual responses. Such programs use questions as a means of eliciting student responses. Many of these questions are of the recall variety, but others require application and analytical skills in order to select the correct response. When determining whether to use a tutorial program, the teacher should go through the program and evaluate the level of questions, using Bloom's taxonomy. Are there sufficient questions at the application level and above to challenge students to think rather than merely recall questions? If so, the program will help develop thinking skills regardless of the content.

4. Simulation programs always involve thinking skills to one degree or another. Strategies must be developed to achieve the goal, whether getting the wagon to Oregon or winning the presidential election. In simulation games, as in life, chance factors, in addition to the planned strategy, play a part and affect the outcome. It is the chance factors that make the game play differently each time. Some students will play **Oregon Trail** over and over, not only trying to get to Oregon, but trying to devise a strategy to get there as soon as possible. When deciding to use a simulation game to develop thinking skills, a teacher should consider factors such as: levels of thinking, the closeness of the simulation to reality, and whether the game has enough levels or variety to challenge students of all learning levels. Successful simulation games are those that meet the criteria above and that students love to play. The more they play the more they will develop the skills required in the simulation.

5. Tool programs hold the most potential for developing higher-level skills and thinking strategies. Whether one uses spreadsheet or database programs, students must use analytical, data collection, and classification skills to successfully achieve the objective. Both types of programs can be used easily to teach students to create hypotheses, test hypotheses, and develop tentative conclusions, all advanced level skills. Chapters 5 and 6 discuss examples of how this can be done. The only limitation is the teacher's imagination.

6. Using authoring systems, explained in chapter 5, is a way that individual teachers can create their own software to meet the skill development needs in their own classes. These programs are not complex, and a teacher can feel comfortable using them after just six to ten hours of concentrated practice. Basically they allow the teacher to create drill and practice or tutorial programs for their own purposes.

7. Some unique new programs with exciting potential are being developed. The **Simulation Construction Kit**, which won the 1987 Award of Excellence from *Classroom Computer Learning*, is an example. This program contains a simulation with extensive documentation that allows students to learn how it was constructed. Then, using the master disk, students can create their own simulation using research, and can produce flow charts, predict consequences, create graphics, and evaluate responses of those who use the program. Programs that are created can be saved and copied for use with other students.

If a simulation program develops thinking skills, just imagine the skills that will be developed when students become the simulation makers! This allows students to make a simulation about any topic covered in their social studies course. A teacher could use the interested capable students to create simulations for other students. No more waiting for software companies to produce what you want, do it yourself.

CONCLUSION

In this chapter we have discussed ways in which teachers can help students put together the world of information through the development of thinking skills. We have discussed why thinking must be a priority in social studies classrooms, emphasized that thinking is the most productive way of training citizens for the future, and introduced three levels of thinking skills. Detailed strategies were developed to illustrate approaches to thinking. We also explored some general ideas of how computers can be used to develop the thinking processes and suggested some resources to be used. The following chapters will provide specific suggestions for classroom applications.

REFERENCES

Ausubel, David, Joseph Novak, and Helen Hanesian. 1978. *Educational Psychology: A Cognitive View*, 2nd ed. New York: Holt, Rinehart, and Winston.

Beyer, Barry. 1987. *Practical Strategies for the Teaching of Thinking*. Boston: Allyn and Bacon.

Bloom, Benjamin S., ed. 1956. *Taxonomy of Educational Objectives: Handbook I: Cognitive Domain*. New York: David McKay.

Bruner, Jerome. 1966. *Toward a Theory of Instruction*. Cambridge, Mass.: Belknap Press.

Dewey, John. 1933. *How We Think*. Boston: D. C. Heath.

Dunfee, Maxine, and Helen Sagl. 1966. *Social Studies Through Problem Solving*. New York: Holt, Rinehart, and Winston.

"Education Groups Join Forces to Improve Students' Thinking Skills." 1985. *Education Week* (November 6): 4.

Matsumoto, Carolee. 1985. "The Potential of Computers for Teaching Thinking." In *Developing Minds*, edited by Arthur L. Costa, 249-254. Washington, D.C.: Association for Supervision and Curriculum Development.

McTighe, Jay, and Jan Schollenberger. 1985. "Why Teach Thinking: A Statement of Rationale." In *Developing Minds*, edited by Arthur L. Costa, 3-6. Washington, D.C.: Association for Supervision and Curriculum Development.

Naisbitt, John. 1982. *Megatrends: Ten New Directions Transforming Our Lives*. New York: Warner Books.

National Assessment of Education Progress. 1981. "Reading, Thinking, and Writing." In *1979-80 National Assessment of Reading and Literature*. Denver, Colo.

The National Science Board Commission on Pre-College Education in Mathematics, Science, and Technology. 1983. *Educating Americans for the 21st Century*. Washington, D.C.

National Commission on Excellence in Education. 1983. *A Nation At Risk: The Imperative for Educational Reform*. Washington, D.C.

Oliver, Donald, and James Shaver. 1966. *Teaching Public Issues in the High School*. Boston: Houghton Mifflin.

Phillips, Richard C. 1974. *Teaching for Thinking in High School Social Studies*. Reading, Mass.: Addison-Wesley.

Rooze, Gene E., and Terry Northup. 1986. *Using Computers to Teach Social Studies*. Littleton, Colo.: Libraries Unlimited.

Thornburg, Hershel D. 1984. *Introduction to Educational Psychology*. St. Paul, Minn.: West Publishing Company.

5

USING AND MAKING COMPUTER SOFTWARE:
Yes, You Can

The purpose of this chapter is to illustrate how easy and valuable it is to use computer programs in the social studies classroom. The programs to be discussed have extensive documentation written for beginning computer users. If the programs can be adapted, instructions for the adaptations are provided. Those programs that require advance preparation can be mastered with a few hours of practice using the printed material and software.

Each of the programs discussed can be applied to a variety of settings, allowing teachers and students to perform tasks generally considered too time-consuming or difficult for most classroom situations. The programs are time-savers, skill builders, and motivators. They facilitate both teaching and learning and allow educators to enter into the world of cooperative learning — teachers and students learning together, an important environment for the development of thinking.

USING COMPUTER ASSISTED INSTRUCTION

A Drill and Practice Program

Drill and practice programs can be very effective *after* the material they deal with has been introduced and developed. Teachers frequently make the mistake of assigning drill and practice programs to students without providing any prior learning activities. If students are assigned a program for which they are not prepared, all they can do is input random responses, and they will become frustrated at their lack of success. Thus, the teacher must provide an introduction to the material, use developmental activities, and provide for individual or group practice. In the following demonstration of this procedure, we will use a fairly common type of program, one that gives students practice in naming states and their capitals, states and their borders, and lakes, rivers, mountains, and interesting sites.

Title: **United States Geography**

Grade Level: 4-8

Source: Concept Educational Software
  P.O. Box 6184
  Allentown, PA 18001

System Requirements: TRS-80, Model III or 4, with one disk drive and 48K.
  A printer is not necessary.

Skills Required:
  Familiarity with the keyboard and ability to type the names of states.
  Once the disk is initially loaded and the date entered, the disk will
  load the program with a single keystroke entry.

The program **States and Their Capitals** provides an outline map of the United States with one of the states highlighted. There are two options—naming the state's capital with no help, or choosing from three major cities listed for the state. The student is to type the name of the capital correctly (using upper- and lowercase letters). Obviously, for younger students or those with less ability, the teacher would want to use the option that provides the names of the major cities. For example, when the state highlighted is Alabama, the program lists the cities of Montgomery, Mobile, and Birmingham. This choice helps students learn the correct spelling of the city names in addition to giving them an easier task. **States and Their Borders** and **Lakes, Rivers, Mountains, and Interesting Sites** are also included on the disk.

In preparation for using this program, a teacher might do the following:

1. Discuss with students the concept *capital*. What activities occur in a capital that make it different from other cities?

2. Identify the capital of the state in which the students live and show pictures of that city, including the capitol building.

3. Show a map that uses a special symbol for capitals. (Any road atlas will have such a symbol.) Have students locate their capital on the map; then have them locate the capitals of three neighboring states.

4. Provide an outline map of one region of the country and a list of capitals of those states. Assign students to find the location of the capitals in the atlas and place them correctly on their outline maps. This could be a small group activity. Then review the names and locations with students.

5. Proceed through each region of the United States as in number 4.

After such activities students in pairs or threes can go through the drill and practice program to see how high they can score. At the end of the program a score is given based on the number of capitals correctly named on the first try and on the second try. Then a percentage score is given.

If the teacher wishes, each student can be tested using the **United States Geography** program. Although the program does not have a student management system, the students could be instructed to tell the teacher when they are finished so the teacher can record the score, or a student sitting in the vicinity of the computer could be used as a monitor.

Teachers should preview any programs they plan to use with students. There might be errors that need to be corrected or quirks of which the teacher needs to be aware. In **United States Geography**, for example, input answers are not counted correct unless they begin with an uppercase letter and are followed by lowercase letters. However, when the program is loaded the computer is set in uppercase letters. Unless the operator takes the machine out of the "all caps" mode, all answers will be input in uppercase letters and will be counted wrong. The teacher must show students how to do this and remind them to do it when they begin the program.

Using a Simulation

Simulations are based on a set of concepts and generalizations called constructs or models and are designed to describe real-world phenomena. Simulations can help students understand cause and effect, observe, gather data, hypothesize, and form generalizations. The full potential of simulations has yet to be realized in the public schools because in the past running them was time-consuming. The computer's speed has eliminated this problem. White (1984) reviews several simulations intended for use in the social studies classroom.

The most popular of the recent simulations has been the **Decisions, Decisions** series as evidenced by the reviews of McCauley (1987), Vlahakis (1987), Olds (1987), and Brady (1988). Each program incorporates historical events and situations into a simulation in which students make important historical and political decisions. At the start of each simulation, the students establish their priorities; later they base their decisions on these priorities and are judged on how well they meet their goals. Whenever a decision is needed the computer presents four advisers on the screen. The students read this advice, discuss it, and then make their own decision. Most decisions are seldom clear-cut, and of course each decision is going to make some group angry or, at least, less than satisfied. The simulations can be completed as whole group activities or in small cooperative groups (Brady 1988). Activities are designed in such a manner to allow continued lessons. One-computer classrooms are well served by such programs.

In mid-1988 the series included seven programs: **Colonization: Exploring the New World; Urbanization: The Growth of Cities; Immigration: Maintaining the Open Door; Revolutionary Wars: Choosing Sides; Budget Process: A Question of Balance; Television: A Study of Media Ethics; and Foreign Policy: The Burdens of World Power.** The programs are designed for Grades 5-12 and are available separately. **Colonization, Immigration, Revolutionary Wars,** and **Urbanization** are available as the **American History Pack.**

Title: **Decisions, Decisions Urbanization: The Growth of Cities**

Grade Level: 5-8

Source: Tom Snyder Productions
     90 Sherman Street
     Cambridge, MA 02140

System Requirements: Apple II family (64K), IBM PC, or Tandy 1000.

Skills Required:
     Ability to turn on the computer and load software.

Management Procedures:
     Individuals or groups of three to five.

     Single classroom computer easily managed since play may be continued for several interrupted sessions.

This program is easily learned by the instructor and the participants. The very useful teacher's guide included in the support material recommends that the entire class go through the program to get a feel for what each group must do. Then the teacher can form teams of three to five students and the simulation can be run competitively between groups. The students are also furnished a Student Reference Book which instructs them on several concepts required to understand and win in the politics of urbanization.

As indicated in the general description above, the team must set its priorities for their city, Alpine:

1. Maintaining the quality of life

2. Improving the economic situation for all

3. Getting reelected as mayor

4. Keeping the town's expenses low

Then they select the appropriate course of action based on their priorities and the advice of Malaco, a small mining company that wants the town, or a neighboring city, to do things their way. Of course the local Save Alpine Committee (SAC) has its own set of special interests, which surely must be considered together with the views of the town as a whole. And the candidate's reelection as mayor must be considered!

Lessons for the simulation, including a postanalysis for large-group and small-group procedures, are included in the documentation that comes with the software package. Remember that this analysis is necessary if one is to teach the construct upon which the simulation, a model designed to explain real world phenomena, is going to be understood. City councils are alive and well and living in this computer program.

However, if one is to teach the processes of thinking the program must be taken one step further. Although **Decisions, Decisions Urbanization: The Growth of Cities** is based on the decision-making strategy, the actual strategy is never disclosed in the simulation. If students are going to learn thinking strategies, they must be made explicitly aware of the model, as we discussed in chapter 4:

1. Define the goal

2. Identify alternatives

3. Analyze the alternatives

4. Rank the alternatives

5. Analyze the consequences of the best alternatives

6. Choose the "best" alternative

The thinking process of decision making must be taught; thinking is not a natural process! It can be taught in a number of ways: through direct instruction, through a developmental approach, or through inductive learning. It seems as though the developmental approach would be the most effective here. After the simulation has been played a time or two, Beyer (1987) suggests the following procedure:

1. *Introduce the skill.* The teacher introduces the thinking operation, in the context of the simulation being taught.

2. *Execute the skill.* The students execute the operation as best they can without teacher instruction or guidance. In this simulation the skill is already integrated.

3. *Reflect on what was done.* The students review the simulation and identify places where they encountered difficulties.

4. *Explain/demonstrate.* The teacher explains and demonstrates those procedures or rules that can be used to resolve the difficulties students encountered.

5. *Apply the skill to another round of play.* The students, with teacher guidance, then apply the operation again, incorporating what has been discussed and explained about it.

6. *Review the skill.* The students and teacher reflect on and review how the operation can be executed and how attributes of the strategy make it easier to play the game and then how the thinking strategy can be applied to real life.

Following up the use of this simulation with the teaching of the steps of decision making, as listed above, shows the actual procedure involved in decision making. Decision making is not a capricious process. Students not only go away with an understanding of how democratic communities make decisions, they are equipped with a thinking strategy that can serve them for life.

Using and Adapting a Game

Some educational programs are designed as games. Games that require a player or players, a set of rules, and a contest can be effective for teaching facts or mastering skills and concepts. Clement (1981) holds that educators would do well to gain an understanding of "what it is that will keep people entranced by computerized games for hours at a time." Very often they are using thinking skills and developing strategies that instructional designers would find difficult to emulate by traditional methods. It is the educators job to identify and make the students aware of the thinking skills and game strategies that they are using.

Using a Game

The game **The Medalists — States** has several unique features that make it useful in the social studies classroom — it keeps track of student scores, and the teacher or students can add facts to reinforce classroom activities.

Title: **The Medalists — States**

Grade Level: 4-11

Source: Hartley Courseware, Inc.
133 Bridge
Dimondale, MI 48821

System Requirements: An Apple II with at least 48K RAM, Applesoft in ROM,
and a single disk drive (DOS 3.2 or 3.3).
A printer is optional.

Skills Required:
Ability to turn on computer and load software. The program is loaded
automatically.

Management Procedures:
Individuals or groups of three.

The game was developed to teach facts about the states and has been used successfully in grades 4 through 11. (It is one of a series of separate Medalists programs that includes **Presidents, Continents, Black Americans,** and **Women in History**.) At the beginning of the game the student can choose to study the clues (facts) about the states or play the game. The player may also choose to play against himself or herself or compete with others. If the "clues" option is selected, different states can be reviewed one at a time. If the "play" option is selected, the player is given a randomly selected state to identify and one free clue. If unsuccessful in identifying the state with the free clue, the player must select from four additional clues that cost five, ten, twenty-five, and fifty points respectively. The player with the lowest score wins the game. There is also an "others" option, which allows players to compete for bronze, silver, and gold medals. The names of previous "medalists," those who have produced the lowest scores, are presented in one of the title frames at the beginning of the game.

The program has great appeal for students. One of this book's authors, giving the game a trial run, quickly became bored with the state facts he had never attempted to learn and promptly laid the program aside. However, his daughter, a fifth grader, was very interested in becoming a "Gold Medalist." She played the program off and on for nearly four hours and won the "medal" over two graduate students who had played the game previously. The fact that some programs appeal to children and not to teachers or other adults should be considered when selecting software.

Adapting a Game

The Medalists—States provides a "teacher's menu" that offers the capability of checking and deleting student scores, viewing/changing the clue list, changing design options (clues and point values), and printing the clues presented. The Print List of Clues option on the menu, for example, yields a list of clues such as that shown in figure 5.1.

Alternative Use of a Program

The Medalists—States program can also be used to develop research skills such as searching for information in an encyclopedia. After showing students in grades 4 through 6 how to use the encyclopedia index, set the encyclopedia cart near the computer and put a team to work on the program. It will select a state randomly and present clues that will send the students scurrying through the pages to become medalists.

Games such as the **Spy's Adventure** series, published by Polarware, and the **Carmen Sandiego** series, published by Broderbund, are good for the development of research skills. Another program that has received good reviews is **Discover the World**, published by Hartley; the **Crosscountry** series, published by Didatech Software, can accomplish a similar goal with state maps and atlases.

File: IN   (INDIANA)   (16 Facts & Clues)

#	Points	Clue
1	50	This state's postal abbreviation is IN.
2	25	This state is bordered by Michigan, Illinois, Kentucky, and Ohio.
3	10	Major industries in this state include steel, metal products, and manufacturing.
4	5	The official bird of this state is the Cardinal.
5	5	This state's official flower is the Peony.
6	5	This state entered the union in 1816.
7	50	The capital city is Indianapolis.
8	10	This state's nickname is the 'Hoosier State.'
9	10	This state is east of the Mississippi River.
10	5	The Wabash and Ohio Rivers touch this state.
11	25	Large cities in this state include Fort Wayne, Gary, and Evansville.
12	5	President Harrison was a governor of this state before it was a state.
13	5	The Pacers play here.
14	10	The Indy 500 race is run in this state.
15	10	This state was not one of the thirteen original colonies.
16	50	#2165093 (picture)

```
 5 Point Clues  =   6
10 Point Clues  =   5
25 Point Clues  =   2
50 Point Clues  =   3
                   ___
Total Clues        16
```

Fig. 5.1. List of clues for **The Medalists—States**. Reprinted with permission of Hartley Courseware, Inc.

USING TOOL PROGRAMS

Using TeloFacts to Assess the Growth of Group Skills

One of the stages of growth for classroom groups as identified by Stanford (1977) is the establishment of group norms. In this stage it is important for students to know their responsibility to the group. Thus, one of the objectives of the intermediate social studies program is to develop the student's ability to work in groups. Understanding the processes, such as surveys, that social scientists use is another intermediate-level objective. One means of accomplishing both objectives is to develop a survey of attitudes concerning the roles of a group participant and to focus the group's attention on the surveying process being used. **TeloFacts** enables teacher and class to create and edit questionnaires, surveys, and tests. It organizes, stores, and protects data and assists in the collection of data; it performs standard analyses, including finding means, medians, and standard deviations; it analyzes individual items and prints results in a report format; and it performs complex subanalyses, such as sorting data to answer questions like "How do the answers from the eighth-grade group compare to the answers from the sixth-grade group?"

Title: **TeloFacts 2**

Grade Level: 9-12

Author: T. G. Lewis

Source: dilithium Software
      921 Southwest Washington Street, Suite 870
      Portland, OR 97205

System Requirements: Apple II+ or IIe (a forty- or eighty-column screen)
      64K of RAM
      At least one disk drive
      Printer required

Skills and Preparation Required:
      Some familiarity with the computer keyboard.

      Ability to turn the computer on and load software. The program is menu driven; it automatically lists the things it can do on a screen and tells you what to do next.

      Four to six hours working with the tutorial in the manual.

Management Procedures:
      Class or groups.

The survey whose questions form part of figure 5.2 was designed to assess a class's attitude toward the role of the group leader. It was intended to gauge the growth of cooperation among the students in the class and to help them appreciate the need for attitudinal changes. The quesionnaire was designed by Lippitt, Fox, and Schaible (1969, 18-19) and was revised, scored, and analyzed using **TeloFacts 2**. The instructions in the "Tutorial" section of the user's manual, "How to Use TeloFacts," were followed in the survey preparation.

Teachers and students can use **TeloFacts 2** to develop their own surveys concerning attitudes in the classroom, school, or neighborhood on current issues and trends. After the finished survey is printed out it can be duplicated and administered to the class. Once the response data have been entered, they can be displayed on the screen or printed on paper in various ways. For example, answers can be displayed by respondent or by question. The analysis of the data can be formatted into tables or reports (see figure 5.2). **TeloFacts 2** allows a much more sophisticated analysis than the one shown in figure 5.2, which is simply one illustration of the use of a tool.

(Text continues on page 80.)

```
                    GROUP LEADER SURVEY
                    All   Respondents


1. The chairman should listen to the members of a committee.
    A.      Strongly agree
    B.      Agree
    C.      Neither agree or disagree
    D.      Disagree
    E.      Strongly disagree

   # A's   # B's   # C's   # D's   # E's   Base    No Ansr Average     Median
   % A's   % B's   % C's   % D's   % E's   100.0%          Std Dev
   =====   =====   =====   =====   =====   =====   =====   =========   =========
       9       6       1       0       0      16       0     4.500       5.000
    56.3    37.5     6.3     0.0     0.0   100.0             0.612

2. When you are the chairperson of a committee, the only sure way of getting
   things done is to do them yourself.
    A.      Strongly agree
    B.      Agree
    C.      Neither agree nor disagree
    D.      Disagree
    E.      Strongly disagree

   # A's   # B's   # C's   # D's   # E's   Base    No Ansr Average     Median
   % A's   % B's   % C's   % D's   % E's   100.0%          Std Dev
   =====   =====   =====   =====   =====   =====   =====   =========   =========
       0       7       3       5       1      16       0     3.000       3.000
     0.0    43.8    18.8    31.3     6.3   100.0             1.000

3. When individual members of a committee help in making a decision, they are
   more willing to do the work.
    A.      Strongly agree
    B.      Agree
    C.      Neither agree nor disagree
    D.      Disagree
    E.      Strongly disagree

   # A's   # B's   # C's   # D's   # E's   Base    No Ansr Average     Median
   % A's   % B's   % C's   % D's   % E's   100.0%          Std Dev
   =====   =====   =====   =====   =====   =====   =====   =========   =========
       5      11       0       0       0      16       0     4.312       4.000
    31.3    68.8     0.0     0.0     0.0   100.0             0.463
```

(Figure 5.2 continues on page 78.)

Fig. 5.2—*Continued*

```
                       GROUP LEADER SURVEY
                        All   Respondents


4. If a committee has been selected to make a decision, the members should not
   seek outside help.
   A.    Strongly agree
   B.    Agree
   C.    Neither agree or disagree
   D.    Disagree
   E.    Strongly disagree

   # A's  # B's  # C's  # D's  # E's  Base   No Ansr Average    Median
   % A's  % B's  % C's  % D's  % E's  100.0%         Std Dev
   =====  =====  =====  =====  =====  =====  =====   =========  =========
      1      3      3      9      0      16      0       2.750      2.000
     6.3   18.8   18.8   56.3    0.0  100.0               0.968

5. It's a waste of time for someone to make a list of all the jobs that have
   to be done.
   A.    Strongly agree
   B.    Agree
   C.    Neither agree nor disagree
   D.    Disagree
   E.    Strongly disagree

   # A's  # B's  # C's  # D's  # E's  Base   No Ansr Average    Median
   % A's  % B's  % C's  % D's  % E's  100.0%         Std Dev
   =====  =====  =====  =====  =====  =====  =====   =========  =========
      1      2      3      8      2      16      0       2.500      2.000
     6.3   12.5   18.8   50.0   12.5  100.0               1.060

6. Without the cooperation of most members, the chairman will have a difficult
   job getting anything done.
   A.    Strongly agree
   B.    Agree
   C.    Neither agree nor disagree
   D.    Disagree
   E.    Strongly disagree

   # A's  # B's  # C's  # D's  # E's  Base   No Ansr Average    Median
   % A's  % B's  % C's  % D's  % E's  100.0%         Std Dev
   =====  =====  =====  =====  =====  =====  =====   =========  =========
      6     10      0      0      0      16      0       4.375      4.000
    37.5   62.5    0.0    0.0    0.0  100.0               0.484
```

```
                    GROUP LEADER SURVEY
                    All   Respondents


7. When you are outnumbered, you should go along with what the other members
   of a committee want to do.
   A.    Strongly agree
   B.    Agree
   C.    Neither agree nor disagree
   D.    Disagree
   E.    Strongly disagree

   # A's  # B's  # C's  # D's  # E's  Base   No Ansr Average      Median
   % A's  % B's  % C's  % D's  % E's  100.0%         Std Dev
   =====  =====  =====  =====  =====  =====  =====   =========    =========
       1      6      3      5      1     16      0      3.062        3.000
     6.3   37.5   18.8   31.3    6.3  100.0                1.087

8. After a decision has been made by voting, it should not be brought up again
   for discussion.
   A.    Strongly agree
   B.    Agree
   C.    Neither agree nor disagree
   D.    Disagree
   E.    Strongly disagree

   # A's  # B's  # C's  # D's  # E's  Base   No Ansr Average      Median
   % A's  % B's  % C's  % D's  % E's  100.0%         Std Dev
   =====  =====  =====  =====  =====  =====  =====   =========    =========
       2      6      2      5      1     16      0      3.187        3.000
    12.5   37.5   12.5   31.3    6.3  100.0                1.184

9. In a very successful committee or group, all the members are in agreement
   with one another.
   A.    Strongly agree
   B.    Agree
   C.    Neither agree not disagree
   D.    Disagree
   E.    Strongly disagree

   # A's  # B's  # C's  # D's  # E's  Base   No Ansr Average      Median
   % A's  % B's  % C's  % D's  % E's  100.0%         Std Dev
   =====  =====  =====  =====  =====  =====  =====   =========    =========
       4      6      1      4      1     16      0      3.500        4.000
    25.0   37.5    6.3   25.0    6.3  100.0                1.274
```

Fig. 5.2. Sample of data analysis using **TeloFacts 2**. Adapted from Project Book 6, *Deciding and Doing*, of the *Social Science Laboratory Units* by R. Lippitt, R. Fox, and L. Schaible. © 1969, Science Research Associates, Inc. Reprinted by permission of the publisher.

Similar results can be obtained using the **ASK: A Survey Kit** published by D. C. Heath. This program prints just the frequency counts, percentages, and a type of histogram. The program will also print the descriptive statistics for the items, and prepare cross tabulations and scatter diagrams. **Survey Taker** produced by Scholastic offers an alternative for younger learners.

Using *TimeLiner* to Assist Students in the Development of Time and Sequence Conceptions

Some of the most difficult conceptions for learners to obtain are those of time and sequence of events in history. A useful tool for assisting teachers in the development of timelines for teaching aids and for aiding students in the development of timelines is **TimeLiner** reviewed by both Vlahakis (1987) and Olds (1987). In addition, Vlahakis (1988) gives another example of how to use **TimeLiner** in the classroom.

Title: **TimeLiner**

Grade Level: Kindergarten and above

Authors: Tom Snyder and David Kaemmer

Source: Tom Snyder Productions, Inc.
90 Sherman St.
Cambridge, MD 02138

System Requirements: Apple family, one disk drive and a dot matrix printer. (IBM or IBM compatible computers and printers)

Skills Required:
Ability to turn on computer and load software.

Some familiarity with the keyboard.

Ability to read and follow simple procedures in manual.

(Which can be simplified and abstracted for young children.)

Management Procedures:
Individual or small groups.

As social studies professionals we have promoted the use of the timeline as a visual tool, but like many teachers we have found timelines time-consuming to construct for ourselves and frustrating for students to develop. **TimeLiner** allows the production of day, week, year or many-year timelines quickly and easily. As an instructor, it is convenient to take information one has gathered, or finds in a textbook, place it into a computer and get a professional-looking product that can then be displayed above a chalkboard or in a learning center.

TimeLiner allows students to overcome some of the difficulties they encounter: properly spacing events along a span of time, correctly sequencing events without having to start the whole timeline over again, and making their products look professional. In addition to the ease of initial production, both teachers and students gain the advantage of being able to add to the original timeline as the semester develops.

Another interesting feature of this program is that timelines can be merged to allow the comparison of events. As the information is being placed in the computer for timelines that are going to be merged, one must remember to produce one set of events in all capitals, one in capitals and small letters, and possibly begin each of a third set of entries with an asterisk. Of course the problem created by merging timelines can also be corrected by coloring the resulting boxes, but preplanning is preferred.

The importance of timelines to the thinking of students is that they allow visual cues with which the learner can separate events in time. Timelines are useful because they allow students to place events linearly. Young children, who have little time dimension, especially need concrete symbolization. The following is one activity that is useful in the development of personal timelines.

1. Before class cut a 36-inch cord for each child in the class and sort ten paper clips for each student (masking tape can be used).

2. Obtain a roll of masking tape for taping each end of the cord to the back of a pair of chairs or seats.

3. Divide the students into pairs.

4. Distribute ten cards to each student.

5. Have each student write the ten most important events in their life, one to a card. Have the students place a year date on each event.

6. After the children have completed their events cards have them hang their cards on the cords stretched between chairs or seats.

7. Have the students discuss their timeline in pairs and then in groups of four answering the following questions:

    a. How are the timelines alike?

    b. How are the timelines different?

    c. How can you account for the similarities and differences?

8. Now talk about these questions as a whole class allowing each group of four to report their findings. Have the students as a class answer the following question:

    a. What can we conclude about the similarities and differences of people's lives in this area?

Now the children are ready to work with timelines, because they have experienced a concrete example on which a symbolic experience can be built. It is now time to move to a similar experience with **TimeLiner.**

Using the data above, have the pairs of students place their data on the computer. Remember to have one student place his information in all capitals and the other student in small letters. It is good to have the students place dates on the events since **TimeLiner** places decade markings on the baseline. Of course this is standard procedure in timeline development. Now, have the students discuss the advantages and disadvantages of using the computer program as opposed to their string timelines.

Perhaps you are concerned about using the same content in two activities. I would like to make an important point here. There is sound reasoning behind such a procedure, often overlooked by conscientious professionals. *While one is teaching a new skill, one should not change content* (Beyer 1987). The focus of the activity should be on the teaching of the computing tool, not on the teaching of content.

Using Story Tree to Enliven Social Studies Writing

A number of social studies goals are fulfilled through writing, including the ability to report information and communicate ideas. Generally such activities are dreaded by the students; obtaining written work is a real motivational challenge to the teacher. One way to solve this social studies dilemma is to use **Story Tree.**

Title: **Story Tree**

Grade Level: Intermediate and above

Author: George Brackett

Source: Scholastic, Inc.
730 Broadway
New York, NY 10003

System Requirements: Apple IIe or II+ with 48K, or Apple II with 64K
Applesoft in ROM
At least one disk drive.

Skills and Preparation Required:
Some familiarity with the computer keyboard.

Ability to turn the computer on and load software; the program is menu driven.

Two hours working with the tutorial in the manual.

Management Procedures:
Class or small groups.

Story Tree is an easy-to-use program for reading, preparing, and printing interactive stories (the term *story* is used broadly here to include creative stories, poems, book reviews, and other reports). Interactive stories give students choices about what they want to happen next. The following example is from Carter (1984):

You hear noises. You go to the door and slowly open it. As you slip into the hallway you see a man with a package struggling with two other men at the end of the hall. He calls out for help. . . .

The choices are:
1. Call the police from the study.
2. Help the man with the package.

This choice of endings is called branching.

The **Story Tree** software package contains a complete manual, tutorial, teacher's guide, curriculum ideas, and **Story Tree** "shells," which are flowchart outlines that users can follow to develop stories, poems, book reviews, word definitions, or multiple-choice learning games. A simple word processing program is included. A disk management utility helps the user copy, erase, rename, or make a new disk.

Young writers can create stories with plot choices for their readers. Placing make-a-choice points as he or she wishes, the writer creates at least two plots for each point. The writer may choose to branch the story himself or branch the story randomly, placing chance in charge of the ending. The writer can also choose to have a combination of choice and chance, which adds an interesting dimension.

One way to begin using **Story Tree** is to read or print the branching stories contained in the program. In addition, students might enjoy reading a few branching stories from such book series as "Twistaplot" (Scholastic) or "Choose Your Own Adventure" (Bantam). Some of the books in the Bantam series are *The Cave of Time* by Edward Packard, *Journey under the Sea* by R. A. Montgomery, *By Balloon to the Sahara* by D. Terman, *Mystery of the Maya* by R. A. Montgomery, and *Inside UFO 54-40* by Edward Packard. These books have a range of interest levels listed on the back of the title page. *Inside UFO 54-40,* for example, is intended for ages ten and up. Both **Microzine** and **Microzine Jr.** (Handler 1989) published by Scholastic contain Twistaplot stories which may also be used to stimulate young writer's imaginations. As an aside, these disks contain several useful computer programs applicable to social studies. After the children get the idea, the class can develop a group branching story, accomplishing a variety of goals. Some examples of goals and how to achieve them follow.

Exploring Consequences

One of the favorite books of early intermediate youngsters is *Tales of a Fourth Grade Nothing* by Judy Blume. In one episode Fudge, the main character's two-and-one-half-year-old brother, toddles into the living room carrying Peter's turtle in its bowl. The family is being visited by Mr. Yarby, a cranky client of Peter's father, and his wife. Mrs. Yarby is deathly afraid of reptiles. Here is an excellent opportunity for the class or small groups to explore the various characters' feelings and actions, and their consequences.

The students can explore alternatives to the family's handling of Mrs. Yarby's reaction to the turtle. They can then respond to the question, "And then what might happen?" Such exercises allow children to explore the feelings-action-consequence chains important in understanding their own behavior and that of their friends. Using **Story Tree**, the students can set up branched stories that contain these chains.

Teachers often use lack of keyboarding skills as an excuse for not allowing students to use computers—yet many well-known writers use the hunt-and-peck method on the typewriter. As soon as possible children should be allowed to gain some knowledge of the keyboard. Keyboarding comes easily when the communication of ideas becomes important.

This teaching sequence could provide the foundation for two sound social studies approaches. The first approach emphasizes important skills instruction: information gathering, group organization of ideas, group writing and editing, individual writing and editing, and sharing. This is the way writing skills are successfully taught. The second approach emphasizes the recognition of feelings and attitudes, a goal of the self-awareness approach to social studies discussed in chapter 2. Is it all right to "hate" your brother at times? Do all mothers and fathers become angry? This approach also demonstrates that all actions have consequences. Some consequences can be avoided by alternative behaviors.

Examining Points of View

One of the interesting examples provided by Brackett on **Story Tree**'s demonstration disk is the story of Bigfoot. The story is branched into four areas: "Footprint Sightings," "Reported Sightings," "What Indians and Tibetans Say," and "What Scientists Say." Brackett illustrates the idea of points of view simply, presenting each report factually without using loaded words or belittling any view. The author also presents an exemplary list of references.

Critical thinking is one of the identified goals of social studies education. Beyer (1985) defines critical thinking as the process of determining authenticity, accuracy, and worth of information of knowledge claims. This is a difficult skill to teach someone unless one uses models that help students analyze information. One useful model is based on Scriven's (1976) criteria for judging the validity of an argument on the basis of points of view:

1. Clarify the meaning of important words.

2. Identify stated and implied conclusions.

3. Identify the structure of the argument.

4. Identify and critique the author's inferences.

5. Seek other possible conclusions.

6. Evaluate the argument in view of your analysis.

Middle school youngsters are intrigued and puzzled by seemingly unexplained phenomena such as the Bermuda Triangle or the "ghost lights" of Marfa, Texas, which are often written about in local newspapers and popular magazines. Another phenomenon that continues to interest many is UFOs. Students could develop brief descriptions of interesting sightings and summaries of U.S. Air Force investigations of such sightings. One letter describing such a sighting is published in the "Document of the Month" section of *Social Education* (Alexander 1984). There are interesting unexplained events in history like Virginia Dare and the Lost Colony. Hume (1979) wrote an interesting article on a lost Virginia settlement. Belenko's (1984) description of an incident, "What Really Happened to KAL Flight 007?," could be used. Students could look at the United States' official view, the USSR's official view, and the views that exist now. The Bigfoot model is a branched article based on what is reported, what legends say, and what scientists say. Strengths and weaknesses of arguments can be identified using Scriven's model, presented above. Such an approach allows students to analyze a variety of data that are often used to arrive at differing conclusions. One could also explore such issues as:

Spies and spying	Orwellian society
Nuclear weapons	Human beginnings
Crime in America	Selling through young adult and children's TV programs
Disposing of nuclear wastes	

The social studies skills approach should be evident here. Gathering information, organizing it, drawing conclusions, evaluating the conclusions, and arriving at defendable positions are all important skills. Equally important is the critical evaluation of the ideas of others.

In addition, Henney (1988), reporting on a project in language arts using **Story Tree**, found that students

1. integrated language arts skills into a meaningful context

2. recognized the importance of story sequence, cause and effect, main ideas, alternative plots, story grammar, plot development, sentence and paragraph formation, and transitions

3. gained a lot of practice in spelling, capitalization, punctuation, and word usage

4. broadened their understanding of specific concepts

5. used higher-order thinking skills such as analysis, synthesis, and evaluation.

Exploring Values

The availability of the computer has created many societal issues that students using computer software face. Hannah and Matus (1984) focus on several: tapping into protected databases, copying protected software, adapting copyrighted software, and stealing programming ideas. The authors suggest the development of relevant scenarios for class discussion.

Similar scenarios could be developed by teams of students on the basis of some of their own experiences with computers and computer software, using **Story Tree** to develop branched stories. Group participation will allow the students' cases to be more carefully developed as the positions of all the participants are explicated. A simple questioning strategy will help students develop such a focus. This set of questions can be used by the teacher in large group instruction or presented as guide questions for group work.

1. What happened?

2. How does _________ feel about it?

3. Why do you think he or she feels that way?

4. Has something like this happened to you or someone you know?

5. How did you or they feel?

6. Why do you think you or they felt that way?

7. What does this tell you about what you or they value?

8. What does this tell you about the way you or they might behave?

9. How do you feel about that?

The discussion that ensues takes place without judgment on the part of the teacher. The class or small group explores the value positions of the various characters. Such an approach makes students see each side of the situation clearly. Readers of the results could provide a check on the authoring team's rationality. The ethical issues are truly explored.

CREATING DATABASES

The microcomputer allows teachers and students to easily create databases for their classes. What is a database? Deakin (1984) states that the word embraces such a wide concept that the definition varies depending on the equipment used. For example, the term does not imply the same thing to mainframe computer operators as to microcomputer users. Since our concern is with microcomputers, the following definition and explanations apply to these machines. A database is an organized collection of data to which new data can be added, from which they can be deleted, and in which data can be manipulated and retrieved using a variety of criteria. When databases are created and maintained by computer, rapid access to and retrieval of the data is an added benefit. Parisi (1985) claims that database development and management are fast becoming necessary skills for citizenship.

The file cabinet is often used as an example of a database. The user of the file cabinet decides what information to store in it, creates section headings that are used to label dividers, and puts specific information into folders that are stored in the appropriate section. Data in filing cabinets are more accessible if the organization of the files is logical, specific, and consistent. The same is true for databases stored in computers.

Several programs can be used to create databases. Referred to as data management or electronic filing programs, they can be used without any knowledge of programming. The user can create files of information related to a central topic. Each file includes two or more items or subheadings. For example, a class could create a database on states in the United States. The information on each state would be a file, and within each file could be included information on population, capital city, major industries, and any other relevant topic. The body of information entered for each item is called a record. Once the data is entered, it can be retrieved in a variety of formats quite easily.

Introducing Database Programs with AppleWorks

The database management system is an excellent computer tool for social studies since two of our goals are to teach students to process information and to develop thinking skills. These microcomputer software packages allow one to organize, store, update, and retrieve information. In discussing the use of databases, Hunter (1985) states that teachers and students can use databases to discover commonalities and differences among individuals, groups, events, or things; analyze relationships; look for trends; test and refine hypotheses; organize and share information; keep lists up to date; and arrange information in useful ways. Parker (1986) suggests that children can use this tool to enter information into databases, retrieve factual information, organize lists, determine information needed to test hypotheses, reorganize and synthesize data to find relationships, discriminate relevant and irrelevant information, and draw logical conclusions. In addition, students can be taught to evaluate the conclusions they have drawn from information collected. But as Hunter (1987) points out, we cannot expect this tool to teach these thinking skills, any more than we expect a pencil to teach a child to write. We must create interactive environments in which students learn these skills. Watson and Strudler (1988-89) and Vlahakis (1988) provide guidelines and examples for using databases in the classroom. There are several database programs on the market. Another popular database program is AppleWorks, one of the integrated programs discussed earlier.

Title: **AppleWorks**

Grade Level: Intermediate and above

Source: Apple Computer, Inc.
       20525 Mariana Avenue
       Cupertino, CA 95014

System Requirements: Apple family (128K)

Skills Required:
       Basic computer operating skills. The teacher, with a manual, needs one to two hours operating the database.

       Students can be directed to operate the database using task cards, with teacher supervision.

Management Procedures:
       Students should work in groups of three to five assisting one another.

As we discussed in the instructional interaction model in chapter 2, the type of interaction the student has with a database affects the resultant outcome. Using a database as an instructional device requires a set of teacher actions—the things the teacher must do in a lesson sequence—and a set of student actions—the things youngsters must do to have success in the learning sequence. For students to process information with this media device, they must learn the tool. But to learn how to use this tool as a device to facilitate thinking, they must learn the thinking skills involved. To accomplish these tasks, this section will first discuss teaching the tool and then discuss the teaching of thinking skills.

Elementary and middle school students should begin with concrete databases, because, as Parker states, although many students at these levels can operate computer databases, few understand how they operate. The suggested procedure is:

Step 1:   Motivate children concerning the usefulness of a database.

Step 2:   Provide a concrete model of a database.
          Use templates (blank forms) which students complete.

Step 3:   Search the data (completed forms) to answer questions.

Step 4:   Critique the simulated database file.
          What are the weaknesses in form (template)?
          What might be added?

Hannah (1987a, 1987b) has produced material that we have revised to use this procedure (see Favorites form, figure 5.3).

Distribute the Favorites form to all the students and have them fill in the data. Have the class divide into small groups of three to five students. Have each group, using only the forms of that group's members, discuss the collected information by performing the following tasks:

1.   Have the students arrange their papers alphabetically by last name.

2.   Have the students arrange their papers according to how far they live from the school (greatest distance to the least).

3.   Have them determine if someone in the group likes the same fast food, musical instrument, etc.

4.   Have the students identify the similarities they find in their group.

5.   Have them identify the differences they see.

Discuss with the group the idea that they are using only three to five forms and that the task becomes more difficult as the number of forms (records) increases. Illustrate this fact by having one group attempt to arrange all the records alphabetically. This activity motivates, provides the students with a concrete model of a database, and presents some information on the use of a set of *records* called *files*. (One might not choose to use these database concepts here; it would depend on the level of the group.) Having had some real experience, students are now prepared to begin working on and understanding database management systems. Now it is time to transfer the simulated database to the computer, illustrate the power of this tool, and motivate students to make effective use of it.

In the last several years there have been a number of teaching strategies introduced that allow more effective instruction. Since many of us were taught these strategies in stand-up, large-group situations, we quite naturally teach children in the same way. These situations have led to two separate problems. First, as teachers we fail to see that the strategies can be used as instructional design tools—to design learning centers, games, and learning activity packets. Second, we fail to see that the thinking skills the lessons teach need to be emphasized if we are going to teach thinking. If we are teaching thinking, we must focus the student's attention on the thinking processes we are using, making youngsters aware of the thinking skills that are integrated in our teaching episodes, and calling the concepts by name. As Beyer points out, being involved in the act of thinking is not the same as learning how to think. Hannah's articles meet the criteria of using direct instruction as an instructional design tool to prepare coordinated learning activities (learning centers) and introduce a game that uses a database and teaches thinking (direct instruction will be developed fully in chapter 6).

FAVORITES

Fill in your last name and first name. After that, list your favorite for each category. After you have finished, the answers will be placed into a database on the computer.

Last name: _______________________

First name: _______________________

Distance you live from school: _________

Musical group: _______________________

Musical instrument: _______________________

Male singer: _______________________

Female singer: _______________________

Song: _______________________

Fast food rest.: _______________________

Food dish: _______________________

Fruit: _______________________

Ice cream: _______________________

Movie: _______________________

Sport: _______________________

Male athlete: _______________________

Female athlete: _______________________

Color (favorite): _______________________

Vacation spot: _______________________

TV soap opera: _______________________

Car: _______________________

Computer: _______________________

Soft drink: _______________________

Athletic shoe: _______________________

Designer label: _______________________

Actor: _______________________

Actress: _______________________

Holiday: _______________________

Collection: _______________________

Hobby: _______________________

Fig. 5.3. Form used as part of a motivating activity to provide students with a concrete model of a database. Adapted from Larry Hannah, "The Data Base: Getting to Know You." Reprinted with permission from *The Computing Teacher* (August/September 1987). Published by the International Council for Computers in Education.

The following is a procedure for teaching students to use a database.

1. Set up a center that contains an Apple computer, the AppleWorks program, and two formatted data disks (keeping a backup copy of the data disk in your file).

2. Enter into the computer the data that the class has prepared using the Favorites data form in figure 5.3. Often a student or group of students can do this for you. *Remember the form must be proofread for consistency of spelling.*

3. Using the task cards copied from figures 5.4 through 5.7, have the same groups of three to five search the prepared Favorites data file using the directions on the task cards.

After the entire class has completed the center, it's time to play the game described in figure 5.8.

Direct instruction is an excellent way to teach the development and use of databases. But neither the strategy nor the activities cited teach thinking, which Beyer (1987) defines as the mental process through which individuals make sense of experience. The actual teaching of thinking requires that the children learn the skills of analysis, synthesis, and evaluation. Beyer indicates that teachers can teach a thinking skill deductively, inductively, or developmentally. Since the children have been introduced to these skills through playing the game, the inductive approach seems most appropriate.

1. *Introduce the skills.* The teacher introduces the new thinking operation in the context of the subject matter being taught, which is using the Favorites database to answer the questions in the task above. In this case the skill is analyzing the question asked and making a judgment as to which search technique is best to determine the answer. Make sure the students are aware of the skills by name: analysis and evaluation.

2. *Execute the skills.* The students execute the operation as best they can without teacher instruction or guidance. Gaining the use of the skills above requires some trial and error, so playing the game again will allow the development of the skills. We have had no difficulty in maintaining interest in the groups we have taught. The purpose of this lesson is skill development. The content is of little importance.

3. *Reflect on what was done.* The students then review what they have learned in the operation and identify places where they encountered difficulties. Again, analysis and evaluation should be discussed. The techniques students have used to arrive at answers are often surprising. Some students have amazing insight; this should be shared. The teacher, or in many cases the other students, explain and demonstrate ways database procedures can be used to resolve the difficulties encountered. Some searching strategies are more effective than others; again, analysis and evaluation are being used to assess each student's skills.

4. *Apply the skill to new data.* Students should be encouraged, with teacher guidance, to revise the database to include information that interests them. After such revisions have been made, apply the operation again, incorporating what has been discussed and explained.

5. *Review the skill.* The students and teacher reflect on and review how the operations can be executed and how techniques given by students and the teacher make it easier to use databases.

(Text continues on page 95.)

ARRANGING RECORDS

1. You can arrange all the records in an *AppleWorks* database file based on the information in a single category (e.g. LName). The category can be arranged in any one of four ways: (1) from A to Z; (2) from Z to A; (3) from smallest number to largest; and from largest to smallest.

2. To arrange the records, use the following procedure:

   a. Place the cursor in the category you want to sort.

      —use **TAB** to move right

      —use ⌘ -**TAB** to move left

   b. Press ⌘ -**A** for Arrange;

   c. Select the option you want by typing the number of the choice you want and then **RETURN**, or by pressing the ↓ key until your choice is highlighted and then **RETURN**.

3. Try arranging the categories using different ⌘ -**A** options. ⌘ -Z allows you to switch between multirecords and single records.

4. Complete the following:

   a. What is the most frequently used first letter in last names?

      ___________________.

   b. Who lives the least distance from your school?

      ___________________.

   c. Which students live approximately the same distance you do from your school?

      _______________   _______________

Fig. 5.4. Task card for teaching the arranging of records. Adapted from Larry Hannah, "Teaching Data Base Search Strategies." Reprinted with permission from *The Computing Teacher* (June 1987). Published by the International Council for Computers in Education.

FINDING RECORDS

1. You can locate specific information in files by using a **Find** search. For example you might want to find all of the files in which strawberry is listed as a favorite.

2. To conduct a **"Find"** search use the following steps:

    a. Press ⌘ -**F** for Find.

    b. The message "Type comparison information:" will appear at the bottom of the screen. ⌘ -Y erases everything to the right of the cursor.

    c. Let's assume that you want to find all of the records that include "Strawberry." Type Strawberry and press **RETURN**.

    d. Some records may be displayed. One could be a favorite fruit and the second might be favorate ice cream. Check each of the records by using the ↓ to move to the appropriate line and then ⌘ -**Z** to zoom in on the individual record.

3. Answer the following questions:

    a. Who likes your favorite soap opera? ____

    b. Whose favorite musical instrument is the saxophone? _______________________________

    ____

    c. You have found a fabulous sale of your favorite athletic shoe. List other students in the group who might appreciate being notified?

    ____

    ____

Fig. 5.5. Task card for teaching the finding of records. Adapted from Larry Hannah, "Teaching Data Base Search Strategies." Reprinted with permission from *The Computing Teacher* (June 1987). Published by the International Council for Computers in Education.

USING RECORD—SELECTION RULES

1. Record selection allows you to ask the database to display only those records that meet certain rules. Doing a search this way lets you make quick, precise searches.

2. Let's assume that you want to locate all records that have the same fast food restaurant and favorite holiday. Follow the steps below.

   a. Press ⌘ -**R** for Record selection. A list of all categories will be displayed.

   b. Decide on the first category you want to be the basis for the selection of files (Fast food rest.).

   c. Select the category by typing its number (**8**) and then pressing **RETURN**, or press the ↓ key until your choice is highlighted and then **RETURN**.

   d. A list of operations will be displayed.

      1.   equals
      2.   is greater than
      3.   is less than
      4.   is equal to
      5.   is blank
      6.   is not blank
      7.   contains
      8.   begins with
      9.   ends with
      10. does not contain
      11. does not begin with
      12. does not end with

   e. Choose your operation (i.e., **1** [equals] using the same procedure as listed in **c.** above.

   f. Type the comparison information (**MacDonald's**).

   g. Now you will be asked to specify the relationship of the first comparison to the next selection condition.

      1.   and
      2.   or
      3.   through

   h. Choose the proper connector (**1** [and]).

   i. Choose the next category (Holiday) and its number.

   j. Type the next operation (**1** [equals]).

   k. Type in the comparison information (**Christmas**).

   l. Press **ESC** to begin the actual search. All records that meet both criteria will be displayed.

3. Follow the steps below to end a search and return to "All records."

   a. Press ⌘ -**R**.

   b. The message "Select all records? No Yes" will appear at the bottom of the screen.

   c. Press **Y** to return to all records.

   d. Complete the **GET ACQUAINTED ACTIVITY**.

Fig. 5.6. Task card for teaching the use of record selection rules. Adapted from Larry Hannah "Teaching Data Base Search Strategies." Reprinted with permission from *The Computing Teacher* (June 1987). Published by the International Council for Computers in Education.

INDIVIDUAL ACTIVITY

Choose three categories from the list. Sort through those categories to find people who share all three favorites. If no one shares all three, find one who shares two. After you have found that person, have her/him sign this form at the bottom.

Category 1: ____

Your Response: ____

People who shared that response:

_________________________________   _________________________________

_________________________________   _________________________________

Category 2: ____

Your Response: ____

People who shared that response:

_________________________________   _________________________________

_________________________________   _________________________________

Category 3: ____

Your Response: ____

People who shared that response:

_________________________________   _________________________________

_________________________________   _________________________________

Signatures of persons who shared two or three responses:

_________________________________   _________________________________

_________________________________   _________________________________

Fig. 5.7. Task card to integrate the skills of using databases. Larry Hannah, "The Data Base: Getting to Know You." Reprinted with permission from *The Computing Teacher* (August/September 1987). Published by the International Council for Computers in Education.

RULES AND PROCEDURES FOR DATABASE:
GETTING TO KNOW YOU

1. Have students complete the "Favorites" database template in a previous session.

2. Create three teams counting off by threes.

3. Each team takes roles as contestants and judges.

4. Two teams are allowed to begin the game as contestants.

5. The third team becomes the first set of judges.

6. Play begins when the emcee (teacher) poses a question such as "Name a fast food restaurant."

7. The first team to answer the question gains control and is able to supply four answers.

8. Each time an answer is given, the judges arrange the database to find how many students gave that answer. That number of points is given to the team.

9. Then the second team is allowed to give four responses to the same question.

10. No answers may be repeated.

11. Disputes will be handled by the judging team, which may also ask for more specific answers to questions.

Fig. 5.8. Rules and procedures for playing the "Getting to Know You" game. Larry Hannah, "The Data Base: Getting to Know You." Reprinted with permission from *The Computing Teacher* (August/September 1987). Published by the International Council for Computers in Education.

The purpose of this presentation has been to illustrate ways we can teach both the tool and the thinking skills. We first explored an effective way the database management system could be taught. Please notice that these lessons were entirely separate. Don't mix instructional goals.

We then illustrated how the thinking skills imbedded in the use of the database can be disclosed and taught. It must be remembered that it is important for us to teach children how to process information, but a more significant goal is to teach them the skills of thinking, which are often imbedded in our teaching strategies or in our mediating devices.

Another example of a database lesson might have students creating a database on presidents. The first step would be to determine what categories of information they wished to include. (It is wise to include a number of categories initially so that at a later time information can be retrieved without further research. If the categories created are based only on the information needed today, the database may not be adequate to answer questions that arise during tomorrow's class.) For a database on presidents, some categories are obvious: name, home state, age when elected, political party, profession, and political experience. Some critical thinking would be necessary to create other categories. A brainstorming session could be helpful at this point. Some possibilities might be education, military experience, religion, economic status as a child, significant accomplishments in office, and which interest groups supported his candidacy. Thinking skills will be best developed if the teacher lets the students brainstorm and create the categories they feel will be useful. If they select the "wrong" categories, the categories can be changed later, and the students will have learned to think the categories through more thoroughly in future database lessons.

Using pfs:File

Databases can be created by using **pfs:File**, a program designed to be used on several popular personal computers.

Title: **pfs:File** — TRS-80 Model III Version (other versions are available)

Grade Level: Intermediate and above

Authors: John Page and Don Williams

Source: Radio Shack stores

System Requirements: TRS-80 Model III or 4

Skills Required:
> Basic computer operating skills; ability to organize data. The teacher needs to practice with the program in advance and make a simplified set of directions for students.

Management Procedures:
> Students should be in groups of two to four to facilitate the collection and input of information.

The screen display for a database on presidents might resemble figure 5.9. Once the record structure is designed, students must collect the information about each president and enter it into the computer. During this phase students will have to use research skills already developed or learn them during the process of creating the database. Some of the information will be easy to find, while some of it will take some searching and interpretation. An example of the printout for Thomas Jefferson appears in figure 5.10.

PRESIDENTS

Name: Term of Office:

State of Birth: Residence when Elected:

Age when Elected: Highest Education:

Profession: Religion:

Military Experience:

Political Experience:

Economic Status when Young:

Political Party:

Interest Group Support:

Accomplishments:

Fig. 5.9. Database template for studying the presidents.

PRESIDENTS

Name: Thomas Jefferson   Term of Office: 1801-1809

State of Birth: Virginia   Residence when Elected: Virginia

Age when Elected: 58   Highest Education: College

Profession: Planter, surveyor, architect   Religion: Deist

Military Experience: None

Political Experience: Congressman, secretary of state, state legislator, governor, foreign minister

Economic Status when Young: Wealthy

Political Party: Democratic Republican

Interest Group Support: Farmers, workers, southerners

Accomplishments: Cut the budget, accomplished the Louisiana Purchase, reduced taxes, argued for free public education

Fig. 5.10. Sample record for presidents database.

The final stage is to determine the questions or hypotheses to be tested by use of the database. (Some might argue that the hypotheses should come before the selection of categories. Certainly some hypotheses should be considered at that point. However, by limiting the creation of categories to the hypotheses in mind at that time could lead to a very limited set of categories. As students engage in the process of collecting data, they will see other possible hypotheses, which can be added to the original ones.) A simple use of the database under consideration would be to ask the program to list all the presidents who were older than 55 when elected. The **pfs:File** program would search the files and print the names of those who fit this criterion. The program can also search the database to select those who fit several criteria. The possible combinations are enormous. Some interesting ones are:

Which presidents served in both the House and the Senate?

Which had military experience and also served in Congress?

Which were college educated and younger than 55 when elected?

Which were supported by labor unions and were from an upper-class background?

Which had no military background but served as president during wartime?

The Value of Databases

The creation and use of databases will appeal to most teachers who espouse the skills approach to social studies, particularly those who emphasize the development of social science processes. The use of databases can develop a wide range of skills, including locating, organizing, and interpreting information, synthesizing and summarizing data, and creating hypotheses. In addition, students can learn to reach conclusions based on data, learn what generalizations are and that they have exceptions, and learn that a computer is a tool to help solve problems. In short, students can learn that social studies is not necessarily a set of facts in a book to be memorized, but rather is a process for finding answers to questions. This is exactly the type of preparation that is necessary to live in a future that is rapidly changing and in which there will be problems to handle and situations to face that parents and teachers today cannot even imagine.

Topics around which databases could be built are unlimited. The list below suggests only a few. Creative teachers will conceive many others.

Inventors	Indian Tribes
Explorers	Cities in Our State
Famous Blacks	Jobs in Our Community
Famous Women	Corporations
Frontier Life	States/Countries
Community Resources	World Leaders
State Governments	Losing Candidates for President

Electronic filing programs are a powerful, flexible teaching tool. In only a couple of hours a teacher can learn to use one and teach it to students. Only by using it can a teacher really see its potential.

USING ONLINE DATABASE SERVICES

One of the exciting new areas of computer use is the capacity to communicate with other computers over phone lines. The number of databases accessible to computers has grown from 300 in 1975 to about 1500 in 1983 (Edelhart and Davies 1983). A microcomputer in a school or home can connect with remote mainframe computer installations to make possible online access to vast information resources. Instant access to encyclopedias, several big-city newspapers, U.S. government publications, and the like can invigorate the study of social issues by providing data not readily available in most schools. Some companies provide individuals access to a wide variety of databases. These companies are called online services. The use of these services is another aspect of using the computer as a tool to improve teaching.

Equipment Needed for Using Online Services

In order to use online services some hardware and software are needed. The first requirement is a phone modem. This device connects the computer to a telephone and makes it possible to communicate between two computers. The price for a modem ranges from $59 to $399 and even higher. There are two commonly used speeds, 300 baud and 1200 baud, on which information is transmitted. The 300-baud rate is slower, but the modem and rates for the online service are cheaper. While the 1200-baud modem and connect charges are higher, if the service is used frequently it is worth the extra cost. For example, one online service, CompuServe, charges just over twice as much at night, and only $2.50 per hour more during the day, for the time a 1200-baud system is connected than for a 300-baud system. However, the 1200-baud system can receive information four times faster. Thus the cost of using 1200 baud will only be about one half as much as 300 baud at night and even less during the day.

In order to connect a computer to an online database service, phone lines must be used to communicate with the service through a telecommunications network. Currently there are three major networks: Telenet, Tymnet, and Uninet. These networks provide the connection between a user's computer and that of the online service, such as CompuServe, The Source, or Dialog. In some cases it is possible to access the same online service through two or even three of these networks. If multiple access to a service is possible, the user can save money by selecting the one with the closest phone number. Most medium-sized to large cities have a local number that can be used to connect to the network. In smaller towns, a long distance call to the nearest city with a phone connection to the network is necessary. Online services provide the user with a phone number of a network they prefer or the one closest to the user. In most cases the telecommunications network is transparent—the user is unaware of its presence.

Finally, a software package is necessary to enable the microcomputer to transmit the ASCII code necessary to communicate through the telecommunications networks (Edelhart and Davies 1983). Again, prices vary on the basis of how complex and useful the software is. For the TRS-80 computer, such a software package can cost as little as $49.95 and includes one hour of free time on CompuServe. This hour is necessary to become familiar with the system so that information can be obtained with as little wasted time as possible.

How an Online Database Service Works

Databases can be classified in several ways. Edelhart and Davies (1983) suggest two systems that are helpful. The first is classification by data type. Data may be numeric, representational, alphanumeric, or bibliographic. Numeric data is data in the form of numbers. This type of data is often used for in-house information, such as the amount of sales for a quarter. Data in representational form show structural models. An alphanumeric database includes written materials such as newspapers and encyclopedias. Naturally, this type would be quite useful for students. Finally, bibliographic databases include information on articles in bibliographic or abstract form—that is, the full text is not included. The second type of classification is by purpose. This is a simpler scheme than the first, as there are only two categories: reference and source. Reference databases are the same as the bibliographic category mentioned above and can be used to obtain bibliographies and lists of software, for example. Source databases provide the full text of a document.

There are, of course, many databases for many purposes. Here will be provided an example of a general-purpose online service, CompuServe*, that provides several types of databases potentially useful to social studies teachers. (Later in this chapter some other online services will be cited that may also be of interest to teachers.) CompuServe costs $12.50 per hour for 300 baud and $15 for 1200 baud during the daytime, and $6 per hour for 300 baud and $12.50 for 1200 baud after 6 p.m. Some databases within the CompuServe service cost additional amounts. Most of these bill the user monthly through CompuServe; others require a separate subscription. Examples of these will be noted later.

When the software package is purchased, the user is given an I.D. number and a password. After the user connects with the system by calling the CompuServe phone number in the nearest city, a menu appears on the screen. CompuServe is menu driven—that is, after a selection is made on the first menu, another menu is given with more specific categories, then another more specific menu, and so on until the user selects a specific article or piece of information.

For example, the first menu encountered in CompuServe is this:

1   Home Services
2   Business & Financial
3   Personal Computing
4   Services for Professionals
5   The Electronic Mall™
6   User Information
7   Index

The user then selects one of these general categories. Home services is one that is useful for teachers. It reads as follows:

1   News/Weather/Sports
2   Reference Library
3   Communications
4   Home Shopping/Banking
5   Discussion Forums
6   Games
7   Education
8   Home Management
9   Travel
10 Entertainment

Going down one more level in the menus, if Reference Library is selected, the following menu appears:

*CompuServe is a registered trademark of CompuServe Incorporated.

1   Academic Amer. Encyclopedia

2   U.S. Government Publications

3   New Tech Times (PBS)

4   Human Sexuality

5   Family Healthcare

$6   The Electronic Gourmet

7   New Car Showroom

$ indicates surcharged service

The Academic American Encyclopedia contains 30,000 articles and more than 10,000,000 words. It is available on a subscription basis and costs $49.95 per year.

Let's assume that the user selected U.S. Government Publications. The next menu that appears is:

1   Government Publications Catalog and Ordering Information

2   Current Information/Federal Register Highlights

3   Valuable Consumer Information Articles from Government
    Publications

If selection 3 is made, then another menu appears. It looks like this:

Select the topic you are in interested in from
Government Publications

1   Personal Finance

2   Health and Fitness

3   Automotive Topics

4   Food Preparation and Storage

5   Parent and Child

6   Energy Conservation

7   Consumer Notes

Finally, if the user selects Energy Conservation, he or she gets to the last menu, which reads:

1   Firewood for Your Fireplace

2   Low Cost-No Cost Energy Savers

At this point the user selects one of the articles or returns to the previous menu. If an article is selected, a condensed version of it begins appearing on the screen.

After a little use, one can become familiar with the system and jump directly to a menu that provides the desired choice. This saves time and money. However, the series of menus provides beginners with a road map so that they can't get lost.

The amount of information contained in the CompuServe system is staggering. The menus above merely followed a linear path to one end point. Literally thousands of other paths are available. Once the specific information the user desires is located it can be printed out or, to save money, loaded into the computer's memory and printed after the user disconnects from CompuServe.

Scrogan (1987) reviews two new services of interest to teachers. Dialog has created a special program for schools called *Dialog's Classroom Instruction Program* designed to help students learn about and use online databases. Consisting of fifty general databases of interest to junior and senior high school students, it utilizes a simplified command structure. The package includes student workbooks ($8 each), a teacher's guide ($20), software ($45), and limited connect charges ($15 per hour) with no monthly fee. The other service is Einstein from Addison-Wesley. This service includes ninety databases and limits charges to $4.50 per search plus the phone charges. This service has been well received by social studies teachers, according to Scrogan.

Dodge and Dodge (1987) and Goldberg (1988) have written articles on telecommunications for the more advanced users. These are good articles for computer users who have the understanding to benefit from them.

Some Concerns

While such systems make a great deal of information available, use of online services by schools does present some problems. In addition to the initial cost for equipment and software, there is the cost of telephone connections to the system, as well as the system's per-hour charges. How will these be billed? The school will need a system to account for the charges. Also, there must be a phone available near the computer. It is not likely that a school would be willing to put a phone in each room that has a computer. A more likely solution would be to locate the telecommunications hookup in the learning resources center. This, of course, leads to the problem of access. Will a teacher or students be able to use the system when they need to or will they have to wait in line?

While these kinds of problems present some administrative difficulties, the advantages of online services make it worth trying to overcome the problems. It is not possible for us, as authors, to suggest solutions, since these will vary from school to school. However, teachers and school administrators need to be aware that the problems exist.

Online Service Resources

Among the many online services, CompuServe, Dialog, Einstein, and The Source seem to be the most useful to social studies teachers. These four services contain information related to social studies course goals, provide access to a wide variety of databases, are reasonably easy to access, use a reading level that is appropriate for many students, and provide substantial excerpts or full texts of articles and information. Of the four, Dialog is the largest; it is also the most difficult to use and the most expensive. Each potential user needs to study the options carefully to determine which one best fits his or her needs. The addresses and phone numbers of the four services reviewed in this discussion follow.

Einstein
Addison-Wesley Information Services Division
2725 Sand Hill Road
Menlo Park, CA 94205
(415) 854-0300

CompuServe
5000 Arlington Center Boulevard
Columbus, OH 43220
(800) 848-8199

Dialog Information Services
3460 Hillview Avenue
Palo Alto, CA 94304
(800) 227-1927

The Source
1616 Anderson Road
McLean, VA 22102
(703) 734-7500

Other online services that might be of interest to teachers include:

BRS (Bibliographic Retrieval Service)
1200 Route 7
Latham, NY 12110
(800) 883-4707
Includes ERIC and has less expensive evening rates.

Dow Jones News Retrieval
P.O. Box 300
Princeton, NJ 08540
(800) 257-5114
Includes a full-text encyclopedia, the *Wall Street Journal*, and other economic information.

SDC/Orbit
2500 Colorado Avenue
Santa Monica, CA 90406
(800) 421-7229
Includes eighty databases, but manuals cost $100 and one day of training costs $100.

There are also magazines and books that deal with online services, for example:

Magazines

> *Link Up*
> 3938 Meadowbrook Road
> Minneapolis, MN 55426
> A one-year (twelve-issue) subscription costs $23.95.

> *Online Today*
> P.O. Box 639
> Columbus, OH 43216
> A one-year (twelve-issue) subscription costs $18.00 (for CompuServe users only).

Books

> *Database Directory, 1984-1985*. White Plains, N.Y.: Knowledge Industry Publications, 1984.

> *Datapro Complete Guide to Dialup Databases*. Delran, N.J.: Delran Research Corporation, 1985.

> Edelhart, Mike, and Owen Davies. *Omni Online Database Directory*. New York: Macmillan, 1983.

> Fenichel, Carol. *Online Searching: A Primer*, 2nd edition. Medford, N.J.: Learned Information, 1984.

> Palmer, Roger C. *Online Reference and Information Retrieval*. Littleton, Colo.: Libraries Unlimited, 1983.

CD-ROM

CD-ROM stands for Compact Disk-Read Only Memory. The heart of the system is a 12-centimeter (4.72-inch) plastic disk that holds the equivalent of 1500 floppy disks of data, or 250,000 printed pages. Even with this vast amount of data, any item is accessible in two to three seconds. According to Tanner and Bane (1988), Tandy has made a breakthrough discovery that will lead, by 1990, to compact disks that can be written on, rather than just read. This will allow for CAI lessons, perhaps up to 1500 of them, to be stored on one disk. Salpeter (1988) presents a good introductory article for a person interested in this new technology.

A variety of disk readers are available for IBM, Apple, and Macintosh computers. Prices range from $600 to $1500. The reader is connected to a microcomputer that displays the selected material from the disk.

A wide range of disks is available. For fast access to research data, the entire ERIC system is on three disks. Another product is the *Microsoft Bookshelf* which includes *Roget's Thesaurus*, the *Chicago Manual of Style, Bartlett's Familiar Quotations*, the *American Heritage Dictionary*, a world almanac, and two other resources, on one disk. This program is memory-resident so it can be used conveniently with a word processor, taking only a keystroke to alternate from one to the other.

Other programs of interest to social studies teachers include: the *Grolier Electronic Encyclopedia, Facts on File News Digest, The Map Cabinet, Fact Past*, and census information. For more information, a monthly magazine titled *CD-ROM Review* is published. The subscription rate is $34.97 (12 issues). Contact:

IDG/Communications
80 Elm Street
Peterborough, NH 03458.

AUTHORING SYSTEMS

Certainly most teachers do not have the time, and maybe not the skills, to become sophisticated at computer programming. Authoring systems allow teachers to create CAI programs without having to use traditional programming techniques. On the basis of input from the user, the authoring system constructs a program to present the lesson. It is a tremendous shortcut, saving many hours of programming time and allowing for the creation of CAI programs by teachers with modest computer skills. Authoring systems can be learned in a few hours. The basic requirement is the ability to develop sequential lessons, an ability that most teachers have. Once a lesson has been created, it can easily be updated or modified in response to the students' performance or feedback from them.

Authoring systems allow the teacher to create lessons to fit specific curricular or student needs. Off-the-shelf software does not always meet such needs and is often not adaptable to a variety of instructional levels. Authoring systems free the teacher from reliance on software companies and greatly reduce the cost of software. The use of such systems also allows the teacher to create programs that fit his or her objectives and are aimed at the ability level of the students.

There are several authoring systems, and at least one for every major brand of microcomputer. Several will be described in the "Authoring Resources" section of this chapter. In this section, the features of **Author I** by Radio Shack, created for the TRS-80, will be described to give the reader a general idea of how authoring systems work, what type of curricular design the teacher must do before attempting to create a lesson, and what type of student records will be available to the teacher as a result of the program.

Title: **Author I**

Source: Radio Shack stores

System Requirements: TRS-80 Model I or III or 4 with 32K or 48K RAM.

Skills and Preparation Required:
> Basic keyboard skills.
>
> Knowledge of how to design individualized instructional lessons.
>
> Three to four hours of practice with the program.

Author I consists of four independent but interrelated modules. The "Author" module is used to create the lesson, the "Teach" module is used to present the lesson to students, the "Student" module is used to set up and maintain student scores, and the "Print/Verify" module is used to print a hard copy of the lesson or score files. Each module must be loaded separately when the user changes functions. The "Author" module will be described in detail, since it demonstrates how a teacher can create a lesson. The features of the other modules will be briefly described to give a picture of what is possible with such a system.

The first menu that appears on the screen at the beginning of the "Author" module allows the user to (1) add pages, (2) review and edit pages, (3) save the lesson on a disk, or (4) return to the operating system (leave the module). In creating a lesson, the user would select the *add pages* option, which allows him or her to create four types of pages: text, question, control, and glossary. Each of these types is explained below.

A text page has room for eleven lines of material, with fifty-eight spaces on each line. These lines may be used for descriptive text material, questions, graphics, or a combination of these. The **Author I** system has 100 ready-made graphic symbols (including a smiling face, a pointing finger [for emphasis], phonetic symbols, and a stick figure) plus the capacity to provide user-made line drawings. (Although the graphic symbols appear on the screen, they do not print out on a paper copy of the lesson. Neither do the line drawings.) Figures 5.11 through 5.13 illustrate a text page used as a title screen, a text page that contains straight text, and a text page containing a question. Since these examples are facsimiles of actual printouts, they do not look exactly like the actual screen.

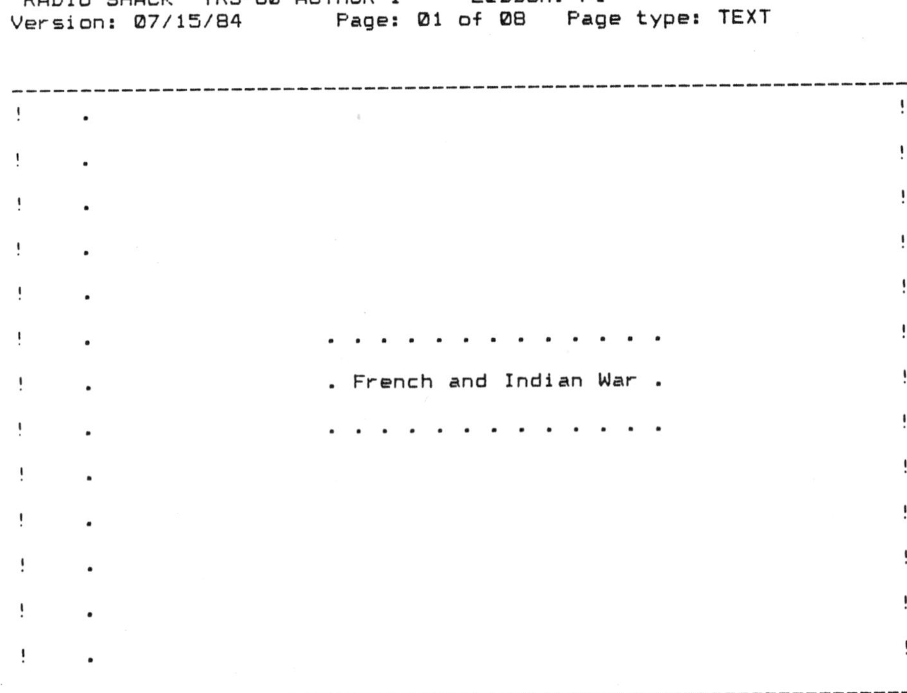

Fig. 5.11. Title page from **Author I.** Used with permission from Tandy Corporation/Radio Shack.

```
RADIO SHACK   TRS-80 AUTHOR I      Lesson: FI
Version: 07/15/84        Page: 02 of 08   Page type: TEXT


   -------------------------------------------------------------
   !    .                                                      !

   !    .                                                      !

   !    .     The French and Indian War was fought between the !

   !    .British and the citizens of their colonies, on one side, !

   !    .and the French and their Indian allies, on the other side. !

   !    .The war was fought to see who would control the land west !

   !    .of the Appalachian Mountains.  The French wanted the land !

   !    .for the rich furs that could be gotten there.  The Indians !

   !    .wanted the land to live on and to hunt on.  It had always !

   !    .been theirs.  The English colonists wanted more land for !

   !    .farming and the Crown just wanted more land. !

   !    .                                                      !

   !    .                                                      !

   -------------------------------------------------------------
```

Fig. 5.12. Text page with straight text from **Author I**. Used with permission from Tandy Corporation/Radio Shack.


```
RADIO SHACK   TRS-80 AUTHOR I      Lesson: FI
Version: 07/15/84        Page: 05 of 08   Page type: TEXT


   -------------------------------------------------------------
   !    .                                                      !

   !    .                                                      !

   !    .                                                      !

   !    .                                                      !

   !    .                                                      !

   !    .                                                      !

   !    .                                                      !

   !    .     The name of the colonist sent by Governor Dinwiddie !

   !    .to protest the French claims was:                     !

   !    .A) Jefferson, B) Amherst, C) Washington, D) Hamilton  !

   !    .                                                      !

   !    .                                                      !

   -------------------------------------------------------------
```

Fig. 5.13. Text page containing multiple-choice format. Used with permission from Tandy Corporation/Radio Shack.

A text page that asks a question can be generated in three forms: one that requires a short typewritten answer; one that offers a multiple-choice option in which the student presses the key that corresponds to his or her choice; and one that offers a multiple-choice option that requires the student to slide the flashing cursor under the correct answer and then press the Enter key. While these are all objective questions, they do provide a reasonable amount of flexibility. Figure 5.13 illustrates the first multiple-choice format. Figure 5.14 illustrates the same question requiring a short typewritten answer. Figure 5.15 illustrates the same question designed for the sliding cursor response. Although the second format is more challenging, there is little difference in the design of the question. However, the variation of format can help to relieve student boredom and fatigue.

If a question is asked on a text page the user must next generate a question page. The function of a question page is *not* to ask a question, but to tell the computer how to respond to the student's answer.

On the question page the user

1. states the correct answer

2. requires the teacher to mark with an x if using the single-keystroke response

3. specifies how many tries the student may have

4. assigns a weight to the question, which will be used in computing the final score

5. provides a positive message for a correct answer

6. may provide a hint to be given after an incorrect first answer. (The hint may be automatic after a specified number of tries or varied on the basis of the first response through the use of "triggers.")

7. may provide a message to be used in response to an incorrect answer

8. may assign a code to the question that can be used either to group questions for a subtest score or to branch the student to another part of the program (either for tutorial help or to skip a portion of the program).

The question page provides a great deal of flexibility and allows the creative teacher to make programs to fit a wide variety of needs. When the user is designing a question page, the system displays the bottom of the text page on which the question was asked, for the convenience of the user. An example of a question page containing a question, the question response portion of the page, and a "tries/hints" page is shown in figure 5.16.

A control page is used only if the program creator uses the coding option, which allows the teacher to create subtests or branch students making a specified score to a different portion of the program than other students. The control page allows the coding of questions into groups—to include, for example, a pretest, developmental test, and posttest. The score report will analyze the scores for these tests separately and report subscores, as well as a total score. This special page tells the computer whether to branch the student or in what way to calculate the score. This is the feature which makes individualization of content possible, both for students who need remedial work and those competent enough to skip some portions of the program.

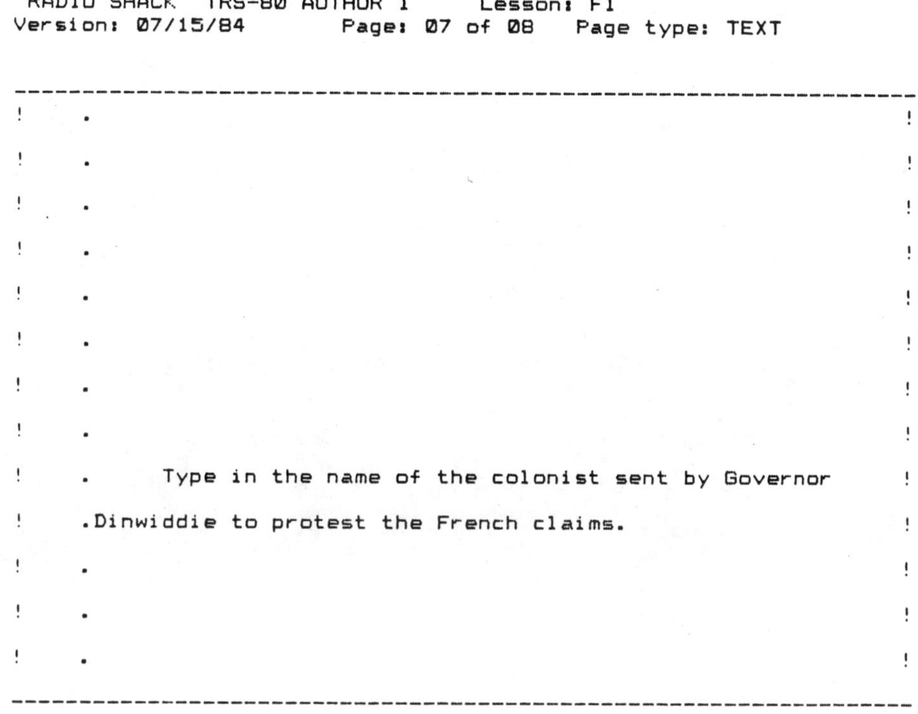

Fig. 5.14. Text page requiring short answers. Used with permission from Tandy Corporation/Radio Shack.

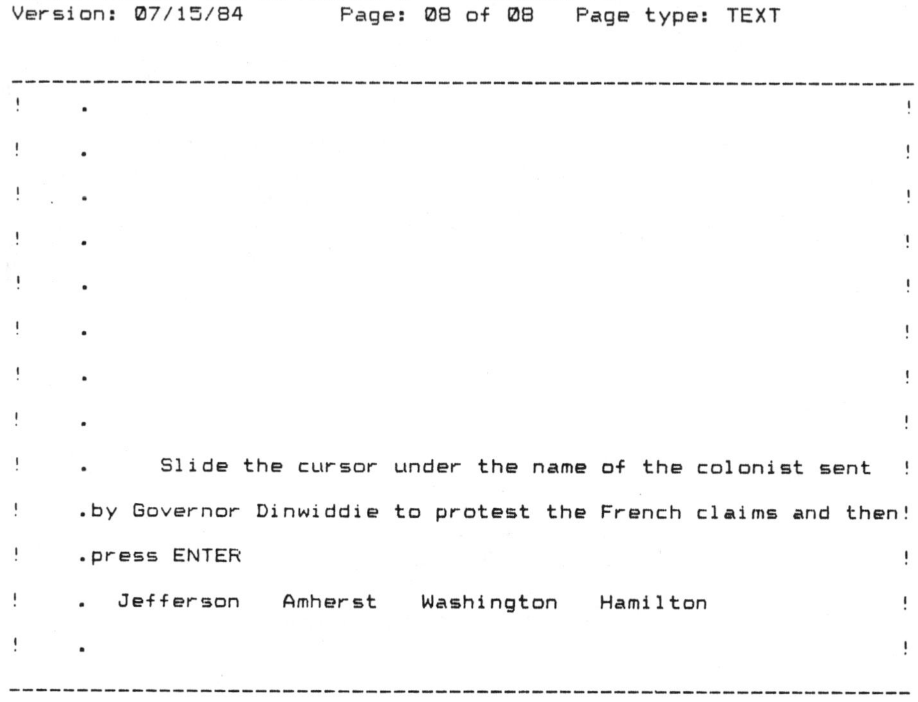

Fig. 5.15. Text page requiring a sliding cursor response. Used with permission from Tandy Corporation/Radio Shack.

```
         RADIO SHACK  TRS-80 AUTHOR I     Lesson: FI
         Version: 07/15/84       Page: 06 of 08   Page type: QUESTION


         ------------------------------------------------------------
         !            The name of the colonist sent by Governor Dinwiddie  !

         !      to protest the French claims was:                          !

         !      A) Jefferson, B) Amherst, C) Washington, D) Hamilton       !

         !                                                                 !

         !                                                                 !

         !ANSWER:                                                          !

         !C                                                              . !

         !         Mark here for single keystroke response: x.            !
         !MAX. TRIES: 03. WEIGHT: 20. GROUP:       . ANSWER LABEL:      . !
         !POSITIVE MESSAGE: Yes, this is when he first became known.    . !

         !                                                              . !

         !NEGATIVE MESSAGE: Sorry, it was George Washington.            . !

         !                                                              . !


         ------------------------------------------------------------
         ------------------------------------------------------------
         !                        TRIES HINT                            !

         !Appear after how many tries:                                  !

         !HINT:                                                       . !

         !                      TRIGGERED HINTS                         !

         !Triggers: A                                                 . !

         !HINT: He was not a military man.  Try "Father" of our country. . !

         !Triggers: B                                                 . !

         !HINT: This is a made up name.  Try the "Father" of our country.. !

         !Triggers: D                                                 . !

         !HINT: He was too young.  Think of the "Father" of our country. . !

         !Triggers:                                                   . !

         !HINT:                                                       . !
```

Fig. 5.16. "Tries/Hints" page from **Author I**. Used with permission from Tandy Corporation/Radio Shack.

The final type of page is the glossary page. It allows the teacher to present words or terms as long as nineteen characters and to give definitions of as much as 100 characters. Once terms are entered into the program, the student may use the glossary function by pressing the / key on the computer. He or she then types in the needed term. If the teacher has entered this term into the program, the student is given the definition. This can be very helpful for less able students. An example of a glossary page is given in figure 5.17.

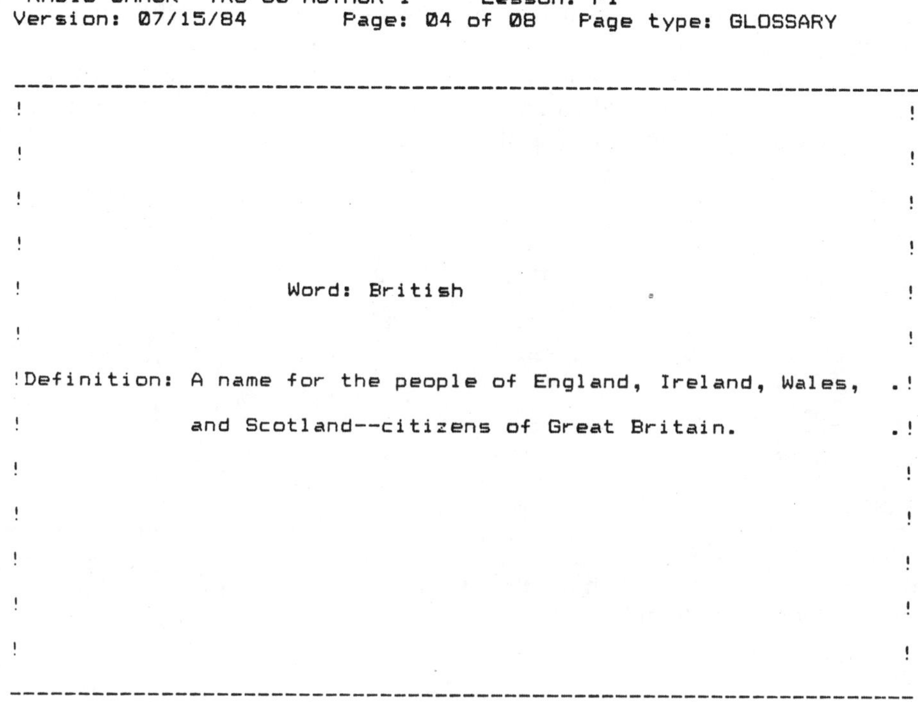

```
RADIO SHACK   TRS-80 AUTHOR I      Lesson: FI
Version: 07/15/84        Page: 04 of 08   Page type: GLOSSARY

  ------------------------------------------------------------
  !                                                          !
  !                                                          !
  !                                                          !
  !                                                          !
  !                    Word: British                         !
  !                                                          !
  !Definition: A name for the people of England, Ireland, Wales, .!
  !              and Scotland--citizens of Great Britain.       .!
  !                                                          !
  !                                                          !
  !                                                          !
  !                                                          !
  !                                                          !
  ------------------------------------------------------------
```

Fig. 5.17. Glossary page from **Author I**. Used with permission from Tandy Corporation/Radio Shack.

With these four types of pages, the teacher can create an individualized, self-paced, computer-assisted lesson. The program can teach, ask questions, evaluate answers, and give corrective feedback. And, since it is created by the teacher, it can be tailor-made for his or her curriculum. As mentioned before, these lessons can be created by teachers with little computer knowledge or experience. The main knowledge needed is how to design an effective lesson. The procedure for using the "Teach" module is inconvenient. Students must first type and enter the word *teach*. Then, after the module is loaded, the name of the program must be entered. Finally, the student enters his or her name and password. This not only takes time but also provides an opportunity for errors that can cause delay or require teacher assistance, at least until students become familiar with the system. Such a procedure, however, appears to be common to authoring systems.

The "Student" module of the **Author I** system allows the teacher to add and delete students from the file. No student will be allowed to take the lesson unless his or her name is entered in the "Student" module. Each qualified student is assigned a password that must be used to gain access to the program. If kept a secret by students, the password is a protection. For example, without a password system, if Tom Smith is mad at Bill Jones, he could take the lesson under Bill's name and purposely score poorly.

The "Student" module also allows the teacher a choice as to how many times to allow a student to take the lesson and as to how successive scores are recorded. The teacher might choose to allow each student to take the lesson only once, and could bar students access to the program after that. If the teacher wanted to allow students multiple attempts, he or she has two choices as to how the scores are recorded: an average could be computed for all the times the student took the lesson, or only the most recent score could be reported.

The computer can not only report a total score and subscores, it can also report the amount of time a student used to take the lesson. This can be useful information, allowing the teacher to assess the competence, for example, of two students with scores of 80, one of whom completed the program in ten minutes, the other in twenty-five. All scores are available on the screen or on paper. Figures 5.18 through 5.20 demonstrate the output of the "Student" module. On the first page the total score for each student is printed and a class average is given. There is also room for ten subtest scores. On the second page a distribution of scores is given. The third page contains the amount of time each student used to complete the lesson and an average time is given. It is possible to report five subtest timings as well.

```
LESSON: FI                                    TODAY'S DATE:   02/22/85

        NAME                     TOTAL   1   2   3   4   5   6   7   8   9   10
                                 SCORE

    1   TOM        SMITH           80
    2   BILL       JONES          100
    3   SUSAN      RICHARDS        80
    4   RITA       GARCIA         100
    5   BOB        BROWN           80

        AVERAGE SCORE              88
```

Fig. 5.18. Output page from "student" module showing student score and average for class. Used with permission from Tandy Corporation/Radio Shack.

```
LESSON: FI                                    TODAY'S DATE:   02/22/85

SCORE GROUPS:                    TOTAL   1   2   3   4   5   6   7   8   9   10
                                 SCORE

    0%-10%                         0    0   0   0   0   0   0   0   0   0   0
    11%-20%                        0    0   0   0   0   0   0   0   0   0   0
    21%-30%                        0    0   0   0   0   0   0   0   0   0   0
    31%-40%                        0    0   0   0   0   0   0   0   0   0   0
    41%-50%                        0    0   0   0   0   0   0   0   0   0   0
    51%-60%                        0    0   0   0   0   0   0   0   0   0   0
    61%-70%                        0    0   0   0   0   0   0   0   0   0   0
    71%-80%                        3    0   0   0   0   0   0   0   0   0   0
    81%-90%                        0    0   0   0   0   0   0   0   0   0   0
    91%-100%                       2    0   0   0   0   0   0   0   0   0   0
```

Fig. 5.19. Output page from "student" module showing score distribution. Used with permission from Tandy Corporation/Radio Shack.

```
LESSON: FI                                    TODAY'S DATE:   02/22/85

        NAME                     TOTAL      1        2        3        4        5
                                 TIME

    1   TOM        SMITH         01:05
    2   BILL       JONES         01:33
    3   SUSAN      RICHARDS       00:29
    4   RITA       GARCIA         00:22
    5   BOB        BROWN          07:57

        AVERAGE TIME             02:17
```

Fig. 5.20. Output page showing student time and average time for group. Used with permission from Tandy Corporation/Radio Shack.

The fourth module is the "Print/Verify" module. This module is used for two purposes. First, it can print a paper copy of the lesson, which the teacher can use to respond to students' questions while they are taking the lesson. It is also easier for some teachers to proofread a printout rather than trying to proofread off the screen. The second function of this module is to verify the lesson. This simply means that it will check the coding of answers and the branching to be sure the creator hasn't made any errors.

The **Author I** system may seem complicated in a written description, but it is easy to operate. It can be learned in two to three hours unless, perhaps, the learner is computer phobic. Once the system is learned, lessons can be created with relative ease.

Using an authoring system to create lessons does not, of course, guarantee high-quality lessons. Hodges (1985) states that with authoring programs "there is a great potential for creating dull, boring lessons ... simple drill and practice programs or uninteresting tutorials." Computer-assisted lessons created by the teacher will be only as good as the creativity and curriculum designing skills of the teacher allow them to be.

Authoring Resources

In this section eleven different authoring systems will be described. Questionnaires were sent to fifteen software manufacturers who produce authoring systems, and those presented in this section are the ones who responded. Each of the systems described will operate on at least one of the major brands of computers. Given this range, each reader should find one compatible with his or her equipment. The systems are listed in alphabetical order, and no attempt has been made by the authors to determine which system is "best"—an impossible task in any event, since different features and capacities will appeal to different readers. Any of the manufacturers will send additional information upon request.

System name:	**Author I**
Ordering address:	Tandy Corporation Fort Worth, TX 76102
Compatible computer(s):	TRS-80 Models I, III, and 4
Training manual or supporting materials:	A 146-page manual and a sample program, which is contained on one of the disks, comprise the self-instructional materials.
Approximate training time:	Three to four hours of training are necessary. The time needed to create lessons will vary with the complexity of the lesson.
Level of audience:	Elementary through adult
Can text and questions both be presented?	Yes, and several varieties of questions can be asked—first, two types of multiple choice questions in which the student selects an answer with a single keystroke or by sliding the cursor under the correct answer, and second, short-answer questions to which the response is typewritten.
Is branching possible?	Yes, although this is one of the more difficult parts of the program to learn.

Is there a student management program?	Yes. Student names and passwords must be entered. As students take the lessons, scores are automatically recorded. Three options are available for successive scores. A variety of printouts is also possible.
Can graphics be included?	Yes. Both special symbols and the ability to draw simple pictures are available.
Is a separate presentation disk required?	Yes
What is the price and what is included?	$149.95 includes disks that contain the sample program and separate programs for authoring, student records, presentation of lessons, printing a copy of the lesson, and retrieving student scores. There is also the manual, previously mentioned.

System name:	**CATGEN/CAT**
Ordering address:	Dynacomp, Inc. P.O. Box 18129 Rochester, NY 14618
Compatible computer(s):	TRS-80 Models III and 4 with 48K and one disk drive. Printer optional.
Training manual or supporting materials:	Thirty-page manual
Approximate training time:	One hour
Level of audience:	Any grade level
Can text and questions both be presented?	Yes. Multiple-choice questions may be asked.
Is branching possible?	No
Is there a student management program?	Yes. The students' scores are automatically recorded.
Can graphics be included?	No
Is a separate presentation disk required?	Yes
What is the price and what is included?	$39.95 includes disks and the manual.

System name:	**CLAS (Computerized Lesson Authoring System)**
Ordering address:	Touch Technologies 9990 Mesa Rim Road Suite 220 San Diego, CA 92121
Compatible computer(s):	IBM PC, Apple II family, Commodore 64, and Acorn
Training manual or supporting materials:	A ninety-five page manual in a three-ring binder
Approximate training time:	Two hours
Level of audience:	Elementary through college
Can text and questions both be presented?	Yes. Multiple-choice, true/false, and fill-in-the-blanks questions are possible, and they can be integrated into the text, all on one screen.
Is branching possible?	Not in this version. The company plans a new version that will allow branching.
Is there a student management program?	A score is given on the screen, but the score is not recorded on the disk.
Can graphics be included?	Only in the IBM version. Simple graphic characters in the character set may be utilized.
Is a separate presentation disk required?	Yes. The student disk must be preloaded.
What is the price and what is included?	$89.95 includes the authoring disk, tutorial program, student disk, and user's guide. The disks are copy protected, but the company will negotiate a licensing arrangement to allow unlimited copies in a school. CLAS-CBT is an advanced version available for IBM PCs at $229.00.

System name:	**EnBASIC Authoring System**
Ordering address:	COMPress P.O. Box 102 Wentworth, NH 03282
Compatible computer(s):	Apple II family
Training manual or supporting materials:	Ninety-four-page user's manual and pocket reference guide

Approximate training time:	Varies based on the type of lesson one wishes to be able to create.
Level of audience:	Elementary through college
Can text and questions both be presented?	Yes. In addition to being able to present questions, the text may include sixteen different sizes of print, subscripts, superscripts, and diacritical markings.
Is branching possible?	No
Is there a student management program?	No
Can graphics be included?	Yes. Colored boxes, diacritical markings, Cyrillic and Greek letters, and special "markup symbols" (which are used to evaluate the students' responses) can be used.
Is a separate presentation disk required?	No
What is the price and what is included?	$175 includes a master diskette, one backup copy, a demonstration diskette, the user's manual, and the pocket reference guide.

System name:	**MicroTutor II: EZ Author Plus System**
Ordering address:	Scandura Training Systems 12149 Greentree Lane Narberth, PA 19072
Compatible computer(s):	Apple II family. A two-disk drive computer is necessary for authoring, but only one is necessary for using the lesson that is created.
Training manual or supporting materials:	Provided are a twenty-six page manual, one start-up direction sheet, and a sample lesson to demonstrate the different question formats.
Approximate training time:	Two to three hours. Lessons can then be created in forty-five minutes to one hour if the material has been thought out ahead of time.
Level of audience:	Elementary through college
Can text and questions both be presented?	Yes. True/false, multiple-choice, and short-answer questions are possible. There is an automatic review of missed questions.
Is branching possible?	Incorrect items are repeated, but there is no true branching.

Is there a student management program?	Yes. All student records are automatically recorded. The system can hold the records of ten groups of fifteen students each. Either individual or group records can be printed.
Can graphics be included?	Inverse words and flashing words or letters can be used for reinforcement.
Is a separate presentation disk required?	Lessons are recorded on a separate diskette so that the student only has to use one diskette.
What is the price and what is included?	$175 includes the manual, EZ Author Plus disk, and EZ Tutor disk. Individual EZ Tutor disks, on which the lessons are recorded, are $15, or $120 for ten.

System name:	**TAS — Teacher Authoring System**
Ordering address:	Teach Yourself by Computer Software 2128 West Jefferson Road Pittsford, NY 14534
Compatible computer(s):	TRS-80 Models III and 4 with 48K
Training manual or supporting materials:	A user's manual and a sample lesson on one of the disks are provided.
Approximate training time:	Two to three hours
Level of audience:	Elementary through college
Can text and questions both be presented?	Yes, but only ten pages of text can be included with each lesson.
Is branching possible?	Yes
Is there a student management program?	Yes. A variety of information is recorded and available to the teacher: response time and answers for each question, information about total questions completed, number correct, and percentage correct.
Can graphics be included?	Yes. Any Model III characters, including special ones, may be used.
Is a separate presentation disk required?	Yes
What is the price and what is included?	$159.95 includes the authoring disk and a backup, the presentation disk, and the manual.

REFERENCES

Alexander, Mary, ed. 1984. "Document of the Month: Close Encounters with the Fourth Dimension." *Social Education* (March): 188-190.

Belenko, Viktor. 1984. "What Really Happened to KAL Flight 007?" *Reader's Digest* (January).

Beyer, Barry K. 1987. *Practical Strategies for the Teaching of Thinking*. Boston: Allyn and Bacon.

______. 1985. "Critical Thinking: What Is It?" *Social Education* (April): 270-276.

Brady, Holly, ed. 1988. "The Top Seven." *Classroom Computer Learning* (February): 29.

Carter, Richard. 1984. "CCL Picks: *Story Tree.*" *Classroom Computer Learning* (November/ December): 16-17.

Clement, Frank J. 1981. "Affective Considerations in Computer-Based Education." *Educational Technology* (April): 28-32.

Daetz, Denney. 1987. Review of *TimeLiner. Classroom Computer Learning* (September): 18-20.

Deakin, Rose. 1984. *Database Primer*. New York: New American Library.

Dodge, Bernie, and June Dodge. 1987. "Selecting Telecommunications Software for Educational Settings." *The Computing Teacher* (April): 10-12, 32.

Edelhart, Mike, and Owen Davies. 1983. *Omni Online Database Directory*. New York: Macmillan.

Friel, Susan. 1983. "Lemonade's the Name, Simulation's the Game." *Classroom Computer News* (February): 34-39.

Goldberg, Fred S. 1988. "Telecommunications and the Classroom: Where We've Been and Where We Should Be Going." *The Computing Teacher* (May): 26-30.

Handler, Marianne. 1989. "Microzine Jr." *The Computing Teacher* (February): 42-44.

Hannah, Larry H. 1987a. "Teaching Data Base Search Strategies." *The Computing Teacher* (June): 16-23.

______. 1987b. "The Data Base: Getting to Know You." *The Computing Teacher* (August/ September): 17-18, 41.

Hannah, Larry, and Charles Matus. 1984. "Teaching Ethics in the Computer Classroom." *Classroom Computer Learning* (April/May): 32-36.

Henney, Maribeth. 1988. "Reading and Writing Interactive Stories." *The Computing Teacher* (May): 45-47, 60.

Hodges, James O. 1985. "Developing Your Own Microcomputer Courseware with Authoring Tools." *Social Education* (January): 59-60, 62.

Hume, Ivor Noel. 1979. "First Look at a Lost Virginia Settlement." *National Geographic* (June): 735-767.

Hunter, Beverly. 1987. "Knowledge—Creative Learning with Data Bases." *Social Education* (January): 38-43.

______. 1985. "Problem Solving with Data Bases." *The Computing Teacher* (May): 20-27.

Lippitt, R., R. Fox, and L. Schaible. 1969. *Deciding and Doing.* Social Science Laboratory Units, Project Book 6. Chicago: Science Research Associates.

McCauley, Jim. 1987. "Decisions, Decisions Urbanization: The Growth of Cities." *The Computing Teacher* (May): 38-40.

Olds, Henry F. 1987. "Review: Decisions, Decisions Immigration: Maintaining the Open Door." *Classroom Computer Learning* (January): 19-21.

Parisi, Lynne. 1985. *Computer Databases: Applications for the Social Studies.* Boulder, Colo.: ERIC Clearinghouse for Social Studies/Social Science Education. ERIC, ED264167.

Parker, Janet. 1986. "Tools for Thought." *The Computing Teacher* (October): 21-23.

Salpeter, Judy. 1988. "CD-ROM Update: A Report from the International Conference on CD-ROM." *Classroom Computer Learning* (May/June): 78-81.

Scriven, Michael. 1976. *Reasoning.* New York: McGraw-Hill.

Scrogan, Len. 1987. "What's New in Online Information Services." *Classroom Computer Learning* (April): 48-50.

Stanford, Gene. 1977. *Developing Effective Classroom Groups.* New York: Hart.

Tanner, Dennis F., and Robert K. Bane. 1988. "CD-ROM: A New Technology with Promise for Education." *T.H.E. Journal* (August): 57-60.

Vlahakis, Robert. 1988. "The Computer-Infused Social Studies Classroom." *Classroom Computer Learning* (November/December): 58-61.

______. 1987. Review of *TimeLiner. The Computing Teacher* (October): 54-55.

Watson, Jim, and Neal Strudler. 1988-89. "Teaching Higher Order Thinking Skills with Databases." *The Computing Teacher* (December/January): 47-50, 55.

White, Charles. 1984. "Software: Side by Side, Six Economics Simulations." *Electronic Learning* (September): 60-61.

6

INTEGRATING SOFTWARE INTO THE CURRICULUM TO DEVELOP THINKING

The purpose of this chapter is to provide guidelines for designing instruction using the computer as a mediating device or tool. We will begin the chapter by discussing the elements of instructional design and then will move into the discussion of three teaching strategies: direct instruction, classification of information, and the interpretation of data. We will illustrate how an instructional environment is created through a set of teacher actions, a mediating device, and student actions. Such an environment allows the teaching of the following set of thinking skills, all of which are goals of social studies education:

recalling ideas and facts

explaining these ideas

identifying relationships

developing conclusions and generalizations

evaluating generalizations

The last section will consider the value of writing in social studies education.

THE ELEMENTS OF INSTRUCTIONAL DESIGN

The Purpose of the Lesson

Teaching is a process of transmitting knowledge, skills, and values to an individual or group of individuals through a selected set of experiences. The teacher's task is selecting or designing the best set of experiences to accomplish his or her goals in these areas. In chapter 2 several philosophies of social studies were discussed. Most social studies teaching involves the integration of several of these approaches. The emphasis a teacher chooses will depend on the philosophy of the school system, the background of the students, and the teacher's personal preference. If a purpose focused on knowledge or skill is selected, the emphasis will be on developing the children's ability to recall an idea or fact

explain or transpose an idea or fact

use information or ideas in new situations

identify relationships between component parts

draw conclusions or infer relationships

evaluate ideas or situations

If values are to be developed, the students must learn to

show willingness to attend to certain behaviors

show willingness to respond in a specified manner

tend to behave in a specified manner

integrate a behavior into their individual value systems

encourage others to behave in a similar manner

The Objective of the Lesson

Performance objectives get the teacher down to specifics. There are essentially four elements to be considered in deciding how to direct instruction: audience, behavior, condition, and degree. These elements tell us for whom the instruction is intended, what behavior is expected, which materials are to be used, and what have been specified as the performance criteria.

Performance objectives are helpful in two ways. First, they help clarify expectations of learning episodes—the teacher actions, student actions, and resultant learning that take place in a lesson sequence. Some "playing with the computer" should be allowed for the purpose of motivation and exploration, but it is only through directed use, with performance objectives clearly in mind, that instructional goals will be accomplished. If the teacher is using a spreadsheet program, what group of students should be involved? What specific behaviors should students exhibit? Are the students to *develop* or *use* row and column formulas? What degree of accuracy is expected? All of these questions are answered through the statement of performance objectives.

Second, performance objectives help teachers communicate intentions to students, their parents, and teachers' peers and superiors. A teacher having trouble justifying his or her use of computers might find a solution in the careful explication of his or her objectives.

Diagnosis

The teacher's next task is determining the knowledge, skills, and values of the students. The important point to remember is that computers and software are media devices and tools that require a specific set of skills. These skills must be taught. It is also important to remember that this device transmits a set of knowledge, skills, and values of its own, as discussed in chapter 2.

Instructional Interaction

With purposes and objectives clearly in mind, and having assessed the needs and abilities of their students, teachers must next select a set of activities or experiences that will allow students to reach the intended goals. Experiences are obtained through instruction—a set of teacher actions (TA), using some mediating device (M), allowing student actions (SA) that produce a resultant outcome. This idea is illustrated in the following diagram:

$$\text{Content} \longrightarrow \text{TA} + \text{M} + \text{SA} \longrightarrow \text{Resultant Outcome}$$

There are two important principles here. First, changing any one of these components influences the outcome of learning. The selection of a mediating device *does* make a difference. It affects both the teacher's actions—the things the teacher must do in the lesson sequence—and the students' actions—the things students must do to succeed in the learning situation. Similarly, changing the teacher's actions in any teaching episode will alter the outcome. It will affect the students' actions and the effectiveness of the mediating device. Second, the teacher's intervention will influence the result of the learning experience. It is highly desirable that teachers be strongly involved in the instructional sequences using computers. The balance of this chapter will present effective ways of intervening.

Evaluation

The interactive model of instruction presented above has implications in evaluation also; indeed, evaluation is much like a two-edged sword. The supporting rib of the sword is the lesson, learning sequence, or instructional device. One edge of the blade is the teacher's behavior; the other edge is the student's behavior. If students fail to reach the planned objectives, the problem may lie in any of the three elements: the lesson, teacher behavior, or student behavior. Stated another way, if the student does not perform according to expectations, perhaps the wrong computer-mediated lesson has been used, or the teacher could have failed to provide enough background or training for the software. Another possibility is that the student has not gone through the lesson sequence in an effective way. Of course, it is also possible that the problem exists because of a combination of these elements. An effective evaluation of an instructional episode is multifaceted.

SELECTED TEACHING STRATEGIES USING COMPUTER SOFTWARE

This section will discuss some teaching strategies—teacher actions that create a set of student actions in a social environment—that can be used with computer software. As noted above, effective actions improve a teacher's chances of getting expected student outcomes.

The Direct Instruction Strategy: Implementing Thinking

The most perplexing problem facing most teachers is that of teaching concepts and skills. Although much pressure has been applied to teach these elements, too little attention has been given to the strategy used to teach them. *Direct instruction* is a relatively new term that refers to academically focused, teacher-directed lessons using sequenced, structured activities and materials (Rosenshine 1979). In the initial stage of learning a new concept or skill, even a thinking skill, direct instruction is an effective strategy. This approach is designed, in the case of skills, to ensure acceptable performance, which is a necessary prerequisite to unsupervised practice or application.

Rosenshine's review of the related research indicated at least five important ideas. First, teachers who most successfully promoted gains in achievement played the role of a strong leader. Second, the frequency of factual, single-answer questions was positively related to gains in achievement. Third, academically focused, direct questions at the two lower levels of Bloom's (1956) cognitive taxonomy resulted in the increased acquisition of basic skills. Fourth, factual questions of the teacher question/student response/teacher feedback variety produced gains in achievement. Fifth, students made greater progress when they spent time on material and in activities that produced low error rates. These findings support the usefulness of direct instruction.

We must provide some clarification of our meaning of direct instruction. You'll notice that Rosenshine's position is teacher-directed instruction. Our position is more clearly stated as *active instruction*, a term credited to Thomas Good, an educational psychologist who has done extensive work in classroom instruction. As Jones and Jones (1986) point out, research consistently indicates the most effective teaching method varies according to such context variables as the student's age, ability, and personal characteristics, and the intended instructional goals. Our purpose is simply to point out that if one is to teach a student a low-level skill, that's one goal; to teach a child to transfer and use a decision-making strategy is another goal. It requires a careful examination of the student's age, ability, and characteristics. As we have clearly illustrated, our goal is active instruction. In fact, our direct instruction strategy makes way for active involvement of the learner. Thinking can be taught in no other way.

Returning to the concept of instructional interaction, the direct instruction strategy calls for student actions that require the recall of facts or ideas and their use. The strategy creates an interactive environment in which the student is given direct instruction, provided feedback on his behavior, and given direction toward correct responses.

The strategy also serves as an organizer for teacher actions. By following the steps of the direct instruction strategy the instructor can teach concepts and skills using the computer. We have found it useful to refer to this strategy as we plan our own instructional sequences.

The direct instruction strategy is similar in structure to that presented by Gagné (1974) in his discussion of the delivery of instruction. The complete strategy has six steps: motivating, providing a model, imparting information, allowing active student participation, giving knowledge of results, and presenting guidance (see figure 6.1).

Strategy Step	Teacher Action	Student Action
1. Motivating	Presents problem, need, or discrepant event	Attends
2. Providing model	Presents visual or verbal model	Copies or discusses elements
3. Presenting information	Explains elements of model, adding information	Attends, asks for information for clarification
4. Allowing active participation	Designs activities which require student response	Tests knowledge through participation
5. Giving knowledge of results	Attends to student responses	Compares behavior against model
6. Presenting guidance	Asks questions which focus student attention on model	Responds to questions on performance

Fig. 6.1. The Direct Instruction Strategy showing elements of instructional interaction.

We are going to describe a teaching episode illustrating the use of this strategy to teach an application of a spreadsheet program. This lesson is based on an article in which a simulation was used to integrate several of the social science skills (Friel 1983).

Illustrating Direct Instruction

The first step in the strategy is motivating the students. This can be accomplished in many ways; it is often done by either showing a need or presenting a problem. There are other ways, but basically teachers must attempt to answer the students' implied question, "Why should I listen to or learn this?"

Assuming that the students have played the simulation **Lemonade Stand** (distributed by K-12 Micromedia Software) and developed some charts on their data, they may begin asking a few "what if" questions. One might continue running the game, inserting their proposed changes to see the results, but another way to approach this problem is through the use of one of the spreadsheet programs. The problem of finding out what would happen if expenses increased is sufficient motivation to begin a teaching episode. The teacher begins the lesson by telling the students:

> The electronic spreadsheet automates and combines the pencil, calculator, and paper worksheet into a display. Spreadsheets can be used to store and display data, predict outcomes based on data and formulas, and perform calculations on rows or columns of numeric data. I have placed the information you collected from playing **Lemonade Stand** into my **VISICALC** program [shown in figure 6.2].

Providing a model is the next step in the strategy. The model needs to present the student with a visual or verbal illustration of the skill or concept that should be successfully exhibited at the end of the teacher-learning sequence. The model shows the students what they are supposed to learn. Models of mastery come in many forms. Figure 6.1 is one example; the illustration in figure 6.2 is another. Models of mastery should precede skill or concept presentations.

```
LEMONADE STAND
--------------------------------------------------------------------------------------
Day        1     2     3     4     5     6     7     8     9    10
--------------------------------------------------------------------------------------
SIGNS      1     2     3     4     5     6     7     8     9    10
SOLD      41    48    53    55    57    58    59    59    59    59
INCOME  4.10  4.80  5.30  5.50  5.70  5.80  5.90  5.90  5.90  5.90
EXPENSE 0.97  1.26  1.51  1.70  1.89  2.06  2.23  2.38  2.53  2.68
PROFIT  3.13  3.54  3.79  3.80  3.81  3.74  3.67  3.52  3.37  3.22
```

Fig. 6.2. Model of mastery for **Lemonade Stand** using **VISICALC** spreadsheet program.

The third step in the direct instruction strategy is imparting information to explain the model, information that puts meaning into seemingly vague generalities. The terms *columns, rows, cells, labels, values, formulas, predict,* and *calculate* are all concepts that must be illustrated and developed as the lesson continues. The sample lesson moves on as follows:

> An electronic spreadsheet is like an electronic table or chart. It is made up of *columns* and *rows*, as I have illustrated for you in figure 6.3. The columns run vertically from top to bottom on the computer screen and are referred to by letters. The rows run horizontally from left to right and are referenced by numbers. *Cells* are formed at the intersection of rows and columns. In our figure, cell A5 contains "signs," and cells A2 and A4 the ends of the horizontal lines that separate the "Day" row from the rest of the rows. Note that this means the first row of actual values is row 5, and the first column of values is column B.

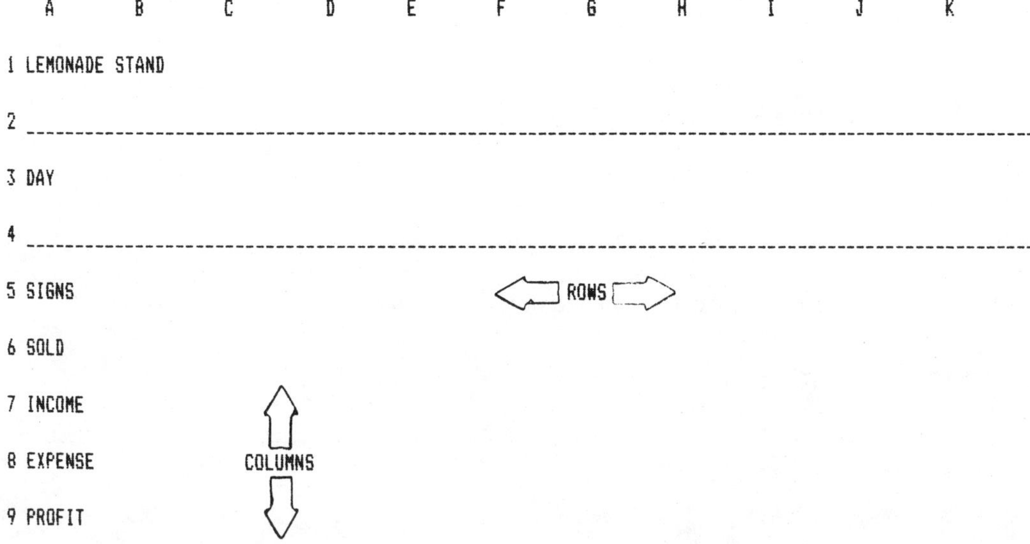

Fig. 6.3. Elements of a spreadsheet.

Three kinds of information can be entered into the cells of the spreadsheet, words called *labels*, numbers called *values*, and *formulas*. "Signs" is one of the labels we need to tell us what our first row of values in figure 6.4 is, the number of signs you used on each day. In the rows labeled "Signs" and "Sold" in figure 6.4 are the values I placed into my spreadsheet. You will notice that the column letters and row numbers are not printed on the paper copy I received on the printer.

```
LEMONADE STAND
------------------------------------------------------------------------
Day      1    2    3    4    5    6    7    8    9    10
------------------------------------------------------------------------
SIGNS    1    2    3    4    5    6    7    8    9    10
SOLD     41   48   53   55   57   58   59   59   59   59
INCOME
EXPENSE
PROFIT
```

Fig. 6.4. Illustration showing "labels" and "values."

It is time now to allow for active participation, the fourth step in effective learning. (Note-taking is *not* active participation.) Breaking the large group into buzz groups to generate ideas, having all students identify correct and incorrect examples, or even having them list the steps in the presented procedure allows for practice and the application of the knowledge or skills being taught. The students benefit from having the opportunity to approximate the desired behavior. The handout below might be useful:

Feedback Quiz
Spreadsheets

1.   On a spreadsheet rows run _______ or from _______ to _______.

2.   Columns run _______ or from _______ to _______.

3.   What number appears in cell D6 in figure 6.2? This number is called a _______.

4.   Write a label that appears on the spreadsheet printout. _______.

5.   Spreadsheets are like _______ or _______.

This leads directly to the fifth step, knowledge of results. All of us have watched good teachers move around the classroom correcting errors made by individual students. As the student attempts the required behavior he or she needs feedback. Often, and possibly most desirably, the teacher asks questions that help correct student errors. These teachers are offering knowledge of results or, as Bloom (1976) states it, presenting correctives. In addition, the instructor is gaining feedback from the student that allows the instructor to pace the instruction—to reteach needed elements or to move more quickly to new material.

The use of correctives provides the sixth step of the strategy, guidance. Guidance answers the student's covert question, "Why did I get that wrong?" It does more than allow knowledge of results in that it provides the reasoning behind the correct behavior, supplies the missing step, or reveals the missed perception. Now it's time to move back to the teaching episode:

>   *Formulas* are used to *calculate* values we want in our spreadsheet. When you ran your simulation game you received the information in figure 6.5 on the screen.

```
LEMONADE STAND
-----------------------------------------------------------------------------
Day        1      2      3      4      5      6      7      8      9     10
-----------------------------------------------------------------------------
SIGNS      1      2      3      4      5      6      7      8      9     10
SOLD      41     48     53     55     57     58     59     59     59     59
INCOME   4.1    4.8    5.3    5.5    5.7    5.8    5.9    5.9    5.9    5.9
EXPENSE
PROFIT
```

Fig. 6.5. Illustration showing calculation using formulas.

The computer program you used produced it. In my spreadsheet I had to use formulas to get these values. The value in cell B7 (4.1) was generated using the formula .1 * B6 — the amount charged for each glass, ten cents, multiplied by the number of glasses sold. This same formula was used to get the other income values on row 7. What formula could we use to obtain the values for the rows 8 and 9? Get into groups of three. Those of you on my right side make up a formula for row 8, the Expense row. Those of you on my left side, make up a formula for row 9, the Profit row. I'll get our computer ready and try out your formulas.

You'll notice that we have moved back to the first step again, presenting a model for the student to follow. Next the information the student needs to understand the model is presented. Then comes the time for active participation.

Small groups are excellent for allowing active participation. Being able to call upon the knowledge of others makes it easier to take on new behaviors. The groups should return with the following formulas: for row 8, (.02 * B6) + (.15 * B5) (the parentheses are required for **VISICALC**); for row 9, +B7−B8. (Here again the formula looks a bit strange, but it must be written this way to allow it to be entered as a value.) The careful reader will also notice a format change in the "Income" row of figure 6.6. This change can be accomplished in **VISICALC** to make the information more readable.

```
LEMONADE STAND
------------------------------------------------------------------------------
Day          1      2      3      4      5      6      7      8      9     10
------------------------------------------------------------------------------
SIGNS        1      2      3      4      5      6      7      8      9     10
SOLD        41     48     53     55     57     58     59     59     59     59
INCOME    4.10   4.80   5.30   5.50   5.70   5.80   5.90   5.90   5.90   5.90
EXPENSE   0.97   1.26   1.51   1.70   1.89   2.06   2.23   2.38   2.53   2.68
PROFIT    3.13   3.54   3.79   3.80   3.81   3.74   3.67   3.52   3.37   3.22
```

Fig. 6.6. Illustration showing format and calculation.

After the formulas are entered and replicated by the teacher, the demonstration lesson continues:

> Yesterday, you began asking some questions like "What if our cost changes?" We could have answered those questions by playing **Lemonade Stand**, but we can also answer them using a spreadsheet. Notice what happens to profits when I increase the cost of the lemonade in cell B8, figure 6.7.

```
LEMONADE STAND
------------------------------------------------------------------------------
Day          1      2      3      4      5      6      7      8      9     10
------------------------------------------------------------------------------
SIGNS        1      2      3      4      5      6      7      8      9     10
SOLD        41     48     53     55     57     58     59     59     59     59
INCOME    4.10   4.80   5.30   5.50   5.70   5.80   5.90   5.90   5.90   5.90
EXPENSE   1.38   1.74   2.04   2.25   2.46   2.64   2.82   2.97   3.12   3.27
PROFIT    2.72   3.06   3.26   3.25   3.24   3.16   3.08   2.93   2.78   2.63
```

Fig. 6.7. Illustration showing predicting and forecasting.

This process is called predicting or forecasting and is one of the most valuable uses of spreadsheets. They allow us to predict what will happen because formulas are used to produce the values in the cells. The method we use requires us to change our formulas to allow us to predict.

Predicting Population Growth

In the social studies curriculum electronic spreadsheets can be used for many purposes; the ability of the instrument to calculate both horizontally (in rows) and vertically (in columns) demonstrates to students the relationship between data and calculated solutions. Spreadsheets become powerful problem-solving tools that are capable of going far beyond simple one-step solutions. At the same time, students develop thinking skills that encourage higher-level cognitive processes. The following lesson (through p. 129, and used here with permission) was designed by Rick Tullis, formerly a secondary science teacher and now employed at Cameron University, Lawton, Oklahoma.

As we pointed out above, the teacher can use spreadsheets for forecasting and predicting. It is often desirable to discuss with students subjects that are conceptually comprehensible, but beyond the scope of students' calculating mastery. Spreadsheets can aid the students and provide a mechanism whereby they can practice with concepts of this type. Two reasons can be given for using spreadsheets for this purpose. First and most obvious, many students lack the technical calculating skills needed to arrive at appropriate solutions. Consequently, these students would become frustrated and easily discouraged when practicing with such concepts. In these cases, the motivational reasons for using computers in the curriculum would be quashed. Furthermore, there is always the dilemma of time, which frequently leads to the use of teaching examples that do not allow for student practice or participation. In the end, many powerful social studies concepts are either ignored or restricted, diluting an otherwise powerful message. Fortunately, spreadsheets provide an interesting solution.

Creating Instructional Spreadsheets. Instructional spreadsheets are defined as spreadsheets that teach concepts while providing a model that can be used for predictive practice. Spreadsheets that fit this definition can introduce or reinforce social studies concepts. Although reasons can be given for the inclusion of student-constructed models under the definition, it must be remembered that instructional spreadsheets model complex concepts that complement the curriculum. As such, these models by definition must include instructional directions and messages, ultimately fulfilling instructional objectives. Thus, they should be teacher designed and constructed.

The easiest way to begin using instructional spreadsheets is to look for simple data. Such information can be found in newspapers, magazines, and journals that talk about social issues and trends. A good example might be the impact of drought on corn production, or the spread of certain diseases. Topics such as these are excellent choices for spreadsheet prediction matrixes. For example, take a value (say the number of cars on American highways) and an amount that is connected to the first value (pollution each car emits), and use spreadsheets to calculate or make predictions based on these data. However, that task would be easily accomplished by students with pencil and paper. What if students wanted to know how much pollution would be produced each year for fifty years? Calculating this value by hand would be both repetitious and time-consuming.

Spreadsheets offer a solution. By knowing the percentage increase and percentage attrition of cars on the highway per year, it is possible to construct a spreadsheet that not only predicts the number of cars on the highway fifty years in the future, but that also connects the pollution data to these predicted values. Students, after entering initial data into the model, can create graphs from the results. And the graphs can then be used for further prediction. This is all possible without calculation by the student. In this fashion, students can then manipulate complicated data, changing the variables in the modeled outcomes. Experiences of these types encourage students to work with previously unmanageable concepts.

Population Growth Spread Sheet. One topic always interesting to students is the growth of populations. However, it is never easy to make predictions of population growth because of indeterminate variables like declining food resources, improvements in medical treatments, or disease. Nevertheless, the United Nations publishes periodic reports detailing the growth of national populations. Data of this type are very appropriate for spreadsheets.

These lessons were constructed using the spreadsheet feature of **Appleworks**. The Population Growth Spreadsheet (figure 6.8), which has three categories of data, is designed to allow the comparison of two countries, Libya and Norway. Note that the data entry instructions are included in the spreadsheet. The instructions included in our lesson not only specify the type of data needed, but also the location as illustrated in figure 6.8. A format of this design allows for less confusion (than students referring to documentation away from the monitor) and enhances the continuity of the lesson.

```
File:    Pop SS Example                                      Page 1

Population Growth Spread Sheet        STUDENT:

                Enter Country 1                   Enter Country 2
                 in Cell B5                        in Cell D5
                   Libya                             Norway

              Enter % Growth Rate 1           Enter % Growth Rate 2
                 in Cell B9                       in Cell D9
                           4.0                                  .4

   Enter Year    Enter Population 1              Enter Population 2
   in Cell A13       in Cell B13                     in Cell D13
          1985         3,600,000                        4,144,000
          1986         3,744,000                        4,160,576
          1987         3,893,760                        4,177,218
          1988         4,049,510                        4,193,927
          1989         4,211,491                        4,210,703
          1990         4,379,950                        4,227,546
          1991         4,555,148                        4,244,456
          1992         4,737,354                        4,261,434
          1993         4,926,849                        4,278,479
          1994         5,123,923                        4,295,593
          1995         5,328,879                        4,312,776
```

Fig. 6.8. Template for predicting population growth.

An interesting component of the spreadsheet is its ability to attach a date (year) to the population census, as shown in figure 6.9. The spreadsheet calculates and displays these values very easily. In cell A14 the following information is entered: + A13 + 1. The first plus sign (+) tells the computer a formula follows. The computer then adds the numerical value 1 to the value entered in cell A13. For example, if the value (year) 1985 was entered in cell A13, the computer would display 1986 in cell A14. Pressing the ⌘ and C keys simultaneously accesses the copy sequence. Using the appropriate key strokes, it is then possible to extend the calculations down the column. The spreadsheet we designed extended 100 years and the data was astounding.

The example we will use involves the use of the direct instruction strategy and the population spreadsheet. The two countries that will be compared were chosen for two reasons. First, each country has approximately the same 1985 population. Second, the countries have growth rates that are very different (Libya has ten times the growth rate of Norway). The only formula needed to construct the spreadsheet is entered in cells B14 and D14 (the formulas are the same relationally speaking). Cell B14 reads "+ B13 + ((B9/100)*B13)". That is, B13, the current population, is multiplied by the growth rate (which is calculated by dividing the numeric value in B9 by 100) to calculate the annual population increase. Then add the calculated value to cell B13. The result is displayed in B14. Now it is possible to extend the calculations as far as desired using the copy sequence. Choose "relational changes" for each B13 but not B9. The formula in cell B15 should read "+ B14 + ((B9/100)*B13)." Similar formulas are entered in column D using the same copy technique. Two columns result, each capable of calculating population growth independently.

```
File: POPULATION SS              REVIEW/ADD/CHANGE              Escape: Main Menu
==========A===============B==============C===============D================E====
  1|Population Growth Spreadsheet       Student:
  2|
  3|                   Enter Country 1              Enter Country 2
  4|                     in Cell B5                   in Cell D5
  5|
  6|
  7|                 Enter % Growth Rate 1         Enter % Growth Rate 2
  8|                     in Cell B9                   in Cell D9
  9|
 10|
 11| Enter Year    Enter Population 1           Enter Population 2
 12| in Cell A13      in Cell B13                 in Cell D13
 13|
 14|+A13+1         +B13+((B9/100)*B13)          +D13+((D9/100)*D13)
 15|+A14+1         +B14+((B9/100)*B14)          +D14+((D9/100)*D14)
 16|+A15+1         +B15+((B9/100)*B15)          +D15+((D9/100)*D15)
 17|+A16+1         +B16+((B9/100)*B16)          +D16+((D9/100)*D16)
 18|+A17+1         +B17+((B9/100)*B17)          +D17+((D9/100)*D17)
 -----------------------------------------------------------------------------
A1: (Label) Population Gr

Type entry or use @ commands                               @-? for Help
```

Fig. 6.9. Illustration showing formulas used for population growth.

Population Growth Spreadsheet Lesson. The first step of the direct instruction strategy necessitates motivating the student. One very powerful motivating aid (for this lesson) might be magazine articles depicting the plight of people in over-populated countries. However, demonstrating that a problem exists is usually not enough to ensure motivation. Instead, involve students in small discussion groups, encouraging them to speculate about overpopulated living conditions. These "buzz" groups generally create more questions than solutions, and disagreement is common. However, buzz groups accomplish the task of motivation and initiate the second step of the strategy.

The second step of the strategy requires the use of a model. The teacher should focus on the concept of population growth and perform a few simple calculations demonstrating the principles behind the concept. To motivate student use of the spreadsheet, the teacher should demonstrate the limitations of "hand calculating" with data from the model. To ensure student mastery of the model, the teacher should demonstrate the use of the spreadsheet.

In the third step of the direct instruction strategy, the teacher describes the model. The inclusion of technical terms and concepts is appropriate at this point. In this light, the teacher should describe the elements of a spreadsheet (rows, columns, cells) and illustrate the difference between formulas and values. Then, using the calculations of step two as a beginning, it is appropriate to demonstrate both how formulas are used and how they are entered into the spreadsheet.

Step four of the direct instruction strategy calls for active student participation with the model. Aside from providing the computer and spreadsheet template, the teacher should also supply the initial data needed for the demonstration. The population growth spreadsheet requires data of population census and growth rate. Since these values are generally calculated for a specified year, these data should also be available.

Remember, this is an instructional spreadsheet. As such, it should be used in a designed activity. Careful choice of countries that illustrate the issues of population growth subsequently enhances the efficacy of the activity. In this example, the populations of two countries (Norway and Libya) are compared. To simplify the comparison, the 1985 populations of the countries were roughly equivalent. After the student has entered the requested information, the fifth step of the strategy is entered, "knowledge or results."

Two phases exist within the "knowledge of results" step. First, students should extract specific information from the spreadsheet. For example, looking at the projected information, ask the students, "When will the two populations be approximately equal?" Also, "When will Libya's population be double that of Norway?" The first phase of this step requires students to exhibit a behavior or demonstrate mastery of the concept. The second phase involves teacher feedback and guidance. Thus, if the student responds, "Libya and Norway will have equal populations in 1989," the teacher provides encouragement and positive feedback. However, if the student says, "Libya and Norway will have equal populations in 1990," the teacher should provide guidance directing the student to a correct response by asking questions. In this way, the student is motivated to continue using the model.

Providing guidance is the sixth step of the model. This step really began in step five (knowledge of results). Going beyond simple right or wrong answers, guidance provides information critical to understanding the structure of an error. Thus, students gain knowledge of "why" a response is wrong, not just that it is or is not correct.

After guidance, the application of the spreadsheet model to another set of countries is appropriate. Again it is important to choose data that fulfills the intended instructional goal. For example, locate the current population and growth rate for both the United States and Mexico. Enter these values into the population growth spreadsheet and be amazed at the results. Now that the students have learned the value of such a tool, it may be time to connect what will happen if such growth continues. Are there examples in history? What have been the effects of such growth in the past? Can you find some examples? The use of the spreadsheet, and the power it provides, is a laboratory for beginning questions on possible causes and effects.

In summary, by following the direct instruction strategy—creating an interactive environment in which the student is given direct instruction, provided feedback on his behavior, and given direction toward correct responses—the instructor can teach concepts and skills using the computer. Many times students are given a program and told to learn it. *This is not good teaching*, nor is it an effective way to use computer software. The steps of the strategy provide a useful checklist for the teacher who wants to become a successful teacher of concepts and skills using computer software.

Using the Classification Strategy to Organize Information for Use in Databases: Implementing Thinking

Since one goal of social studies is to teach students to process information, interactive environments in which they *think* must be created. Perhaps the most carefully researched procedures for developing thinking skills are those devised by the late Hilda Taba, a recognized theorist and researcher in the area of school curriculum. Her research indicates that teacher behavior determines the level of thinking in the classroom. Figure 6.10 has been compiled from her findings (Taba 1967).

Creating an interactive environment means that the teacher's actions must place the student in charge of his own thinking. The critical elements in creating such an environment are (1) effective questions, (2) an open, encouraging atmosphere, and (3) patience.

Through the use of effective, open-ended questions the teacher becomes the manager of the instructional environment. As an associate at Texas Tech, Charles Geer, says, "The teacher becomes the guide on the side, instead of the sage on the stage." Using mediating devices, the teacher places the students in structured situations and guides them toward the use of organizing techniques.

Guiding students' thinking in an open environment has three advantages: (1) it gives the teacher insight into the conceptions of students; (2) the students are encouraged to examine their own thinking; and (3) students are taught a process of manipulating information.

Strategy Step	Teacher Actions	Student Actions
1. Listing information	Asks, "What do you know, read, see, or hear?" Encourages wide participation.	Identifies facts
2. Grouping facts	Asks, "What items seem to go together?"	Identifies groupings
3. Explaining groupings	Asks, "Why are you placing those things together?"	Explains groupings of items
4. Labeling groups	Asks, "What would you call this group?"	Places label on grouping
5. Regrouping	Asks, "Is there another way we can group this information?"	Searches for alternative categories

Fig. 6.10. The Classification Strategy showing elements of instructional interaction.

Examining one's own thinking and considering the ideas of others is productive activity that can be enhanced by the teacher's style of questioning. Rowe's (1979) research indicates that teachers can improve the level of children's thinking by using what she calls first and second wait-times. The first wait-time is the pause a teacher uses after a question is asked. This wait-time encourages children to respond to the question. The second wait-time is used after a student responds to the question. When teachers wait a few seconds before commenting on a student's response, other children often respond to the idea presented. If one combines an extending question (such as "Are there other things that might be included in this category?") with increased wait-time, students will soon start extending the conversation themselves, improving the level of thinking.

Using databases in the classroom can encourage the kind of thinking we are discussing. Pon (1984) introduced database management into her fourth-grade classroom, using Taba's (1967) classification strategy. Databases require a structure carefully planned in advance so that information can be retrieved by categories. The problem facing the data organizer is the formation of useful groupings.

Pon's first step was to have the students gather information on the Maidu Indian tribe in California from which categories could be developed. Her first question was likely "What information have you found on the Maidu tribe?" This is the listing step. The goal of the teacher is to get wide participation. Every student is encouraged to respond through the asking of open-ended questions and the teacher's verbal and nonverbal actions. Generally the bits of information are recorded on the board or on butcher paper. This keeps the information out in front of the group so they can all use the data.

The second step in the strategy is the grouping step. Again, an open-ended question is used to start this step: "What information seems to go together?" At times some "wild" responses may arise, but the wise teacher will refrain from making evaluative comments and accept all suggestions. Often, when a thinker *explains* a grouping a good idea is revealed. When explanations of the groupings are requested in step three, necessary corrections will likely be made by the students. If an erroneous category is not corrected, the teacher can reintroduce it for discussion later. Steps two and three are often combined because they flow together.

The fourth step involves labeling the groups. It, like step two, takes some patience. Students rarely come up with the labels teachers expect. After all, they have not had the same conceptual experiences as adults, so why should they have the same concepts? The information listed by Pon's group appears in figure 6.11.

Information Collected	Label or Attribute Given Later
Their houses were made of tules. They were round. They looked like bowls.	Home
They lived near or in the Butte Mountains. The city nearby is called Yuba City. It is in Sutter County. They lived near Feather River.	Location
They mostly ate acorns. They ate deer and small animals. They fished. Ate seeds.	Food
Men hunted and fished. Women gathered acorns and cooked.	Jobs
They danced and made musical instruments with reeds, especially at acorn harvest. They told stories. Had albino deer and acorn ceremonies.	Recreation, Special ceremonies
They used mortars and pestles to grind acorns with. They hunted with bows and arrows and fished with harpoons.	Tools
They wore hides and rabbit skins in winter. They used moccasins with high ankle covers for mountains.	Clothing

Fig. 6.11. Sample of a primary data chart on Maidu tribe. Source: Kathy Pon, "Databasing in the Elementary (and Secondary) Classroom." Reprinted with permission from *The Computing Teacher* (November 1984). Published by the International Council for Computers in Education.

The fifth step in the strategy is the regrouping step, which is especially useful in preparing information for database management. Here the students should be cautioned that the categories need to be distinct so that they will store their data in the same way each time, enabling them to retrieve the information they want. The labels Pon's (1984) students used changed as they began putting their data into a database, as shown in figure 6.12. Their changes may have allowed more distinct categories. Regrouping is an important step in the strategy generally because it allows students to gain some flexibility in their thinking and expands their concepts.

One of the problems facing the teacher using database programs is helping children organize seemingly unrelated data. The classification strategy discussed in this section provides the needed information-processing technique that helps children list, group, explain, label, and regroup information. The computerized database is an important tool for teaching thinking in the social studies. But what the teacher does to help children prepare information for the use of this device is even more important.

Using the Interpretation-of-Data Strategy with Databases: Implementing Thinking

Taba's (1967) interpretation-of-data strategy can be used to help students find relationships, identify cause and effect, compare and contrast data drawn from different sources, and draw conclusions. Whatever the task, the same basic procedure is used. This section will describe the procedure and how it can be used with databases. The steps in the strategy are illustrated in figure 6.13. Some of the steps look similar to those of the classification strategy, shown in figure 6.10, but the classification strategy is designed to allow students to formulate categories or concepts, whereas the interpretation-of-data strategy is intended to help them organize data so they can draw conclusions.

```
TRIBE          MAIDU
LOC            N V BUTTE MTNS YUBA CITY
CLI            COOL WINTERS & HOT SUMMERS
HOME           BARK OR BRUSH, BOWL SHAPE
               TEMPORARY
FOOD MAJ       ACORN DEER FISH
FOOD MIN       NUTS SEEDS BERRIES
JOB M          HUNTING TRAPPING FISHING
JOB FM         GATHERING FOOD PREP KIDS
CLO            SKINS IN WINTER MOCCASINS
SPEC TOOLS     DIGGING STICK MORTAR NETS
OUTSTD         ACORN & ALBINO DEER CERE.
 FEAT          USED SWEATHOUSES

TRIBE          MIWOK---MOUNTAINS
LOC            C V CHAW-SE PARK NEAR YOSEMIT
CLI            MILD-COOL WINTERS & HOT SUMMERS
HOME           TULE BRUSH SHELTERS---TEMPORARY
FOOD MAJ       ACORN FISH
FOOD MIN       ROOTS BULBS SM GAME
JOB M          HUNTING FISHING
JOB FM         GATHERING FOOD PREP
CLO            LIGHT TO NONE---BAREFOOT
SPEC TOOLS     MORTAR & PESTLE
OUTSTD         SWEAT NECESSARY FOR UNT SOME AGGRESSIVE
 FEAT

TRIBE          POMO---NORTHEASTERN
LOC            N V CLEARLAKE & N COASTAL MTN
CLI            COOL WINTERS & HOT SUMMERS
HOME           BARK TIPI-LIKE OR BRUSH---TEMPORARY
FOOD MAJ       FISH ELK DEER SEA OTTERS
FOOD MIN       NUTS SEEDS BERRIES
JOB M          HUNTING FISHING TRAPPING
JOB FM         COOKING GATHERING KIDS
CLO            SKINS IN WINTER, LITTLE---MOCCA.
SPEC TOOLS     BALSA BOATS NETS HARPOONS
OUTSTD         MADE BEAUTIFUL TWINED AND COILED
 FEAT           BASKETS CLAMS **
```

Fig. 6.12. Completed student computer database file. Source: Kathy Pon, "Databasing in the Elementary (and Secondary) Classroom." Reprinted with permission from *The Computing Teacher* (November 1984). Published by the International Council for Computers in Education.

Strategy Step	**Teacher Actions**	**Student Actions**
1. Gathering information	Asks, "What did you read, see, or hear?"	Identifies facts
2. Relating facts	Asks, "What relationships do you see?"	Identifies relationships
3. Explaining inferences	Asks, "How do you explain the relationship? Why do you think that is so?"	Explains relationship; justifies position
4. Drawing conclusions	Asks, "What can you conclude from what's been seen?"	Generalizes

Fig. 6.13. The Interpretation-of-Data Strategy showing elements of instructional interaction.

Step one, the information-gathering step, is the process of getting data for interpretation. The idea is to collect data from which students can relate important ideas, determine cause and effect, or find likenesses and differences. As described in the previous section, Pon (1984) used the classification strategy to lead her students to organize the information on the Maidu tribe shown in the top third of figure 6.12. The classification strategy provided the base, actually a model, for Pon's students' work. Using the categories created in that study, small groups of children could begin gathering new data on other tribes. The lower two-thirds of figure 6.12 illustrate the information Pon's class found on two other tribes. It is extremely important that the data be recorded in such a way that the ideas can be related and that the questions that open this part of the study be broad, yet focused. The teacher should test the questions used to guide research before a research session.

The second step in the interpretation-of-data strategy is relating the data. At this point there are several directions the process can take. The direction is determined by the purpose of the lesson. One can find relationships such as main ideas or sequence of events, compare likenesses and differences (comparison and contrast), or determine cause and effect.

Determining likenesses and differences is a bit of a problem for some youngsters. It generally requires looking at the data and formulating a list of similarities and differences. Pon does an excellent job of illustrating likenesses and differences by using the Venn diagram shown in figure 6.14. This comparison-and-contrast tool is excellent for helping youngsters draw conclusions or generalizations from information gathered from several sources.

The use of two-dimensional data retrieval charts is very important with older children and for larger amounts of data. Such a chart, for example, might have population age ranges down the left side and various years across the top. These charts compress data so it can be analyzed. Using such a chart a teacher could ask a question like: "In what years do you see larger groupings of people?" This same question can be answered more quickly by the database, but such techniques allow students insight into this computer tool.

It takes careful instruction and instructional intervention to use computer tools, as with any other instructional device. Returning to the model for instructional design discussed earlier, the purpose is to teach the skill of processing data. The performance objective might read: "Using a database on California Indian tribes, the fourth-graders will form four to five generalizations about their similarities and differences." Pon's (1984) assessment of her group indicated that they would need some help processing the data. To facilitate this processing, she changed her teacher actions by using a Venn diagram. This placed the students in a less active role than the use of the database would have, but it likely allowed a more meaningful experience for most of her students. Her action probably increased her students' resulting performance.

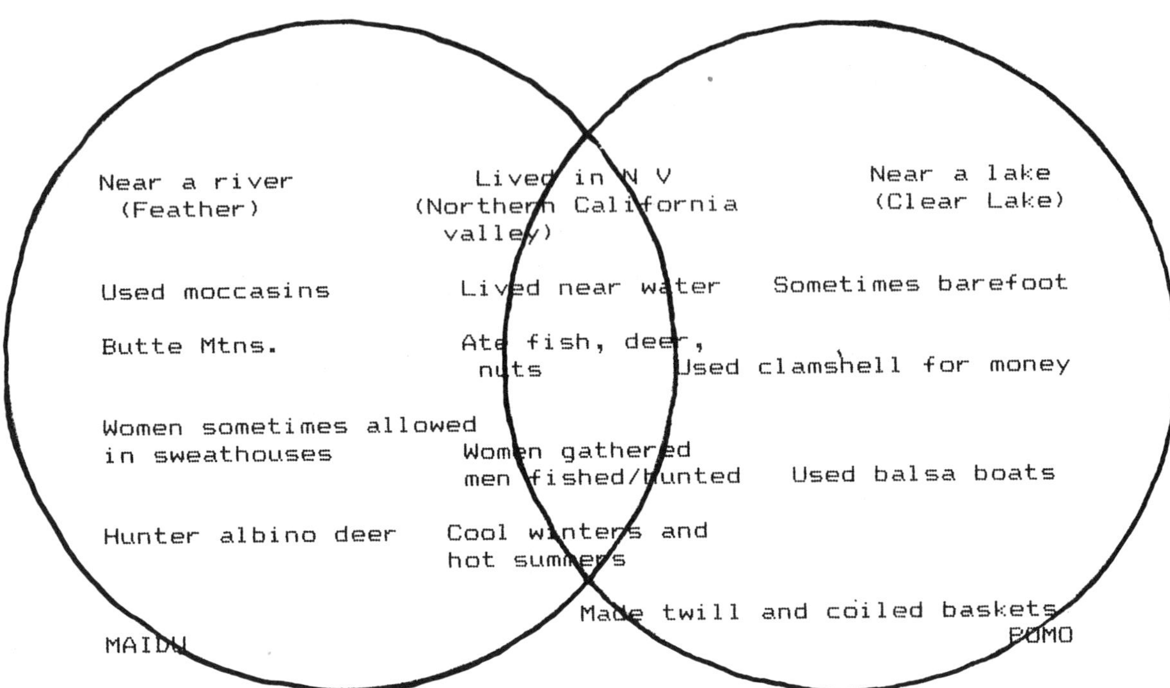

Fig. 6.14. Venn diagram for two tribe comparisons. Source: Kathy Pon, "Databasing in the Elementary (and Secondary) Classroom." Reprinted with permission from *The Computing Teacher* (November 1984). Published by the International Council for Computers in Education.

The dynamics of the cause-and-effect element of the strategy, which may not be used with all of the children, amaze most teachers. Children can really chain cause-and-effect ideas, and the process helps them think about "if/then" situations. A small group of Pon's students took generalizations made earlier and turned them into "if/then" statements, such as "If Indians ate acorns, then they used mortars and pestles." They then tested them for cause-and-effect relationships.

The third step in the interpretation-of-data strategy is explaining inferences; it is the justification step. The difficulty teachers experience in learning this strategy is in seeing this as a separate step. The focusing question is generally, "Why do you think that's so?" or "How do you account for that?" One often gets a shocked look from students asked to analyze their reasoning.

Inferences go beyond the data, although they are supported by the data. They are the educated guesses; explaining requires an intuitive leap. Teachers can extend the discussion and get more students involved by asking another question: "Does someone have a different idea about that?" Such an exchange moves the conversation around the group and deepens the level of thought.

Forming a generalization or conclusion is the fourth and final step in the strategy. It involves pulling relationships together and making tentative generalizations. Children need practice in the skill of generalizing. It is not an automatic by-product of maturation, although experience does play a large part in improving children's generalizing skills. Children can learn—and can be taught—to make good generalizations.

Three important ideas must be remembered. First, the purpose of a generalization is to allow predictions about the behavior of people and things over time and space. A generalization applies to identical or similar situations. Second, when teachers ask students to generalize, they are saying to them, "Now you have given me several ideas; could you put them together into a meaningful statement?" This requires a synthesis of information presented. Third, the teacher must summarize what has been said and help the students recall the central thoughts. After the central thoughts have been recalled, most students can provide generalizations.

Organizing databases is one step in helping students process information, but interpreting the data placed in the database requires another set of skills. Taba's interpretation-of-data strategy can help students find relationships, identify cause and effect, compare and contrast data drawn from different sources, and draw conclusions on data they have collected. Watson and Strudler (1988-89) extend our discussion by adding Taba's application of principles strategy to the use of databases.

ENCOURAGING WRITING USING WORD AND IDEA PROCESSING

What purpose does writing serve in social studies education? Marcus (1984) has identified two. The first purpose for encouraging students to write is to allow them to record what they know in term papers, reports, and essays. But a very different—and possibly more valuable—purpose for writing is enabling students to discover their ideas, sharpen their thoughts, and order their thinking.

We will consider these purposes as we enter this section, continuing our focus on the effective use of computer software. We will begin by discussing an instructional model for teaching writing and move to the discussion of specific computer programs for the communication of ideas.

There are four basic steps in all writing: prewriting, writing, rewriting and sharing—the PWRS model. PWRS is an abbreviation for powers. This writing process model will increase your students' writing power, exponentially.

Prewriting

The purpose of prewriting is to get one's thoughts into some format that can be used to generate ideas. Marcus (1984) indicates that 85 percent of a writer's time is spent on prewriting: musing, thinking, talking, brainstorming, taking notes, outlining, predrafting. Writers pick and choose, of course, among these strategies. Either of the teaching strategies previously discussed—classifying or interpreting data—can be used with children to aid them in prewriting experiences. After all, what good are ideas if children can't use them to discover other ideas?

There are now computer programs that can be used at the prewriting stage. Such programs present a coherent set of questions modeled on those a teacher might ask to elicit ideas. Such programs can be used with large or small groups by the teacher who wishes to employ the direct instruction strategy. They can also be used as tutorials to help children having difficulty with the skills of organizing ideas.

Think Tank, developed for the Apple II and IBM PC by Living Videotext, is one program that can be used from primary grades to high school. This program received a *Classroom Computer Learning* Annual Software award in January 1985. Its prime function is to allow the user to organize ideas. The student or group of students first create the major headings or ideas for a paper or report and then develop subheadings. Headings or subheadings can be turned into paragraphs whenever a student wishes.

Suttles (1984) reviews six other writing programs with a variety of purposes. The advantages of such programs are that they take children through a thinking process and allow them to manipulate ideas quickly. Three of the programs he rated highest are listed below.

Kidwriter
Spinnaker Software Corp.
One Kendall Sq.
Cambridge, MA 02139
Developed for the Apple II family and Commodore (both with 64K).

Story Maker: A Fact and Fiction Tool Kit
Scholastic, Inc.
2931 East McCarty St.
P.O. Box 7502
Jefferson City, MO 65102
Developed for the Apple II family (64K).

Quill
D. C. Heath & Co.
125 Spring St.
Lexington, MA 02173
Developed for the Apple II family (64K) by DCH Educational Software.

Writing anxiety is a major obstacle for some writers, impeding their ability to function even in the prewriting stage. Parham (1986) adds several types of programs that will aid in overcoming the blank page. He not only deals with idea processing but moves to programs that assist in freewriting, prompted writing, story starters, and word play. **Activity Files for the Bank Street Writer: Writing Activities and Language Skill Builders** (grades six through eight), developed for the Apple, Atari, Commodore, and IBM PC computers by Scholastic, is an excellent tool for helping children overcome some writing fears and learn a word processing program at the same time. One of the activities helpful in prewriting is "Darken," in which students turn down the brightness knob on their computer monitors so that they are unable to edit what they write. This allows ideas to flow more easily.

Another activity in the Bank Street **Activities Files** is called "Fantasy." It involves a technique called imaging, in which students write about what they see in their mind's eye. This is a very useful trick for helping students imagine other times and places. "Fan 1" and "Fan 2" are fantasy trips that present ideas upon which the writer builds. One trip is taken alone, the other with a friend. These prewriting episodes create motivation and provide a reason for writing.

Writing

A comparatively short amount of the writer's time is spent in the actual writing stage, putting the words on the paper or screen, filling up that awful, empty space. The major objective is getting one's ideas down. This is the most difficult part for most students who are subject to writing anxiety. Many children will falter at this point. Such anxiety-prone children eagerly participate in group discussions about a situation or event and then clam up, instantly, when they are asked to write. Some nearly go into a cold sweat.

The writing step should begin with group experiences and move toward individual writing. Some group work is encouraged in **Activity Files for the Bank Street Writer. The Writing Skills Bank** is a set of 40 preassembled lessons and 164 writing activities. The material is of the simple drill and practice type, a workbook on the computer. Instruction must precede the use of such packages so that children have models to follow. If students do not know how to construct a series of sentences stating a position, practice will not help. **The Writing Skills Bank** can be useful in helping children practice such skills as writing sentences and paragraphs, descriptions, and narrative passages as long as instructional models have been provided. These materials are based on a writing philosophy contrary to the position of Graves (1982), who takes a more holistic view of writing.

Rewriting

Students—and teachers—need to understand that "writing" is not the end of the process. They are allowed to reorganize, edit, revise, and polish their work. The word processor is an important tool in this stage.

Teaching and modeling the ability to rewrite is a key to helping students acquire good writing skills. Fourteen percent of a writer's time is spent rewriting, yet students seem to feel that once words go on a page, they are locked there forever. Changing this attitude requires constructive, productive experiences.

One set of experiences in the **Writing Activities Files** is "Friendly Peer Editing." This activity allows one student to make comments on another student's writing, completing fifteen sentences such as "The way you did the assignment . . . "; "One thing you might work on is . . ."; "If someone had said to me some of the things I've said to you, I'd . . .": True, the teacher would have to create and foster an environment for proper attitudes, but such activities would be preferred over mere teacher grading. Developing proper attitudes is part of social studies.

Green's (1984) interview with Donald Graves, a writing expert and author of *Writing: Teacher and Children at Work,* contains "Tips for Writing Conferences," a technique that helps students clarify and evaluate their own work (Green 1984, 23). Conferences allow children to grow in writing ability. Conferencing provides the knowledge-of-results and guidance steps in the direct instruction strategy.

Some editing procedures are taught in the **Writing Skills Bank**, another volume in the **Activity Files for the Bank Street Writer** (grades 4 through 6). Children seem to exert more effort while working on the computer, especially in those situations that call for editing and revising.

Kathy Pon (1988) offers several suggestions for revising. One is to use a check sheet, which she uses before students enter the revising stage. She offers a number of interesting techniques concerning the process approach we are discussing.

An interesting controversy is introduced by the availability of spelling checkers, programs that contain a word list with which words presented in a document can be compared. If the program finds an incorrectly spelled word, it indicates it by a flashing cursor, allowing the author to correct the word. The cursor then moves to the next word in question. Garvey (1984) explores the research on spelling and concludes that spelling checkers aid the poor spellers. Kessner (1984) lists eight spelling checkers. Three are listed below:

Bank Street Speller
Broderbund Software
17 Paul Dr.
San Rafael, CA 94903
For use with the **Bank Street Writer** and the Apple family (with 48K), available for $69.95.

Scripsit Dictionary; Super Scripsit Dictionary
Radio Shack Computer Centers throughout the United States
For use with **Scripsit** and TRS-80 Models III and 4 (with 48K), available for $149.00.

WordPro 3 + /64
Professional Software, Inc.
51 Fremont St.
Needham, MA 02194
For use with **WordPro 3 + /64, Paper Clip** for the Commodore 64 (64K), available for $79.00.

Eiser (1988) presents an extensive review of this tool explaining how they work, delimits different types, and presents a variety available for different types of computers.

In addition to the spelling checkers, there are a growing number of general error checkers like those listed by Wresch (1988): **Writers Helper**, published by Conduit, **Sensible Grammar**, by Sensible Software, **RightWriter**, by RightSof.

O'Brien (1984) presents three possible reasons for the popularity of word processors. First, with word processing everyone creates neat, well-formed copy with a professional look. Second, the tasks of reorganizing, editing, revising, and polishing texts, especially lengthy ones, suddenly become enjoyable. And third, since rewriting takes less time, the author can spend more time and energy considering the form and format of the presentation. One would expect these advantages to attract top students. But teachers like O'Brien report the tool to be especially appealing to slower students.

There are several word processing programs on the market that are used widely by ages eight to eighty. Solomon (1984) reviews five such programs and ranks the following three most highly:

Milliken Word Processor
Milliken
100 Research Blvd.
P.O. Box 21579
St. Louis, MO 63132
Developed for the 48K Apple II. 1984 version. Available for $69.95.

Bank Street Writer
Scholastic, Inc.
2931 East McCarty St.
P.O. Box 7502
Jefferson City, MO 65102
Developed for the 64K (new version) 48K (original) Apple II and IBM compatibles. 1982 (revised 1984). Available for $95.00.

The Writer's Assistant
Interlearn, Inc.
Box 342
Cardiff by the Sea, CA 92007
Developed for the 64K Apple II. 1983. Available for $89.95.

A recent review by Dana (1985) describes **Magic Slate**, a word processing program designed for the Apple II family by Sunburst Communications. This program is intended to change as the student grows—an interesting idea, considering the fact that changing word processing programs involves changing well-learned procedures and habits. Even the operation of the same familiar programs often requires the use of the handbook.

Sharing

Another important consideration is sharing what has been written with others. Graves (1982) feels that this is one of the keys to helping children develop good writing skills. Sharing can take place without the use of the computer, but word processing makes it much easier because the product is more professional looking.

Pon (1988) makes several suggestions for publishing children's work in terms of what a teacher must take into account and activities in which classes can take part. She also provides a list of publishers who will actually publish the work of students. A number of options are open in the area of desktop publishing which we will discuss in chapter 7.

Summary

Writing is learned through a set of developmental experiences based on some model. This model can be furnished by the teacher, mediating device, or peers, but it must be present. The student learns to write through actively attempting to approximate the established model. Some feedback must be provided through interaction with the teacher, and ideally with supportive peers as well. This is the reason for sharing.

The act of writing requires some experiential base, either vicarious or real, from which ideas develop. This base for writing can be created by the teacher or classroom group or facilitated through computer programs. Word processing seems to be a useful tool for getting ideas on paper because it facilitates the editing process.

REFERENCES

Bloom, Benjamin S. 1976. *Human Characteristics and School Learning*. New York: McGraw-Hill Book Company.

Bloom, Benjamin S., ed. 1956. *Taxonomy of Educational Objectives: Handbook I: Cognitive Domain*. New York: David McKay.

Dana, Ann. 1985. "Magic Slate" in "Educational Software Report," edited by Tom Spain. *Electronic Learning* (January): 53.

Eiser, Leslie. 1988. "I Luv to Write." *Classroom Computer Learning* (November/December): 50-57.

Friel, Susan. 1983. "Lemonade's the Name, Simulation's the Game." *Classroom Computer News* (February): 34-39.

Gagné, Robert M. 1974. *Essentials of Learning and Instruction*. Hinsdale, Ill.: Dryden Press.

Garvey, Ian. 1984. "Spelling Checkers: Can They Actually Teach Spelling?" *Classroom Computer Learning* (November/December): 62-65.

Graves, Donald. 1982. *Writing: Teacher and Children at Work*. Exeter, N.H.: Heinemann Educational Books.

Green, John O. 1984. "Computers, Kids and Writing: An Interview with Donald Graves." *Classroom Computer Learning* (March): 21-28.

Jones, Vernon F., and Louise S. Jones. 1986. *Comprehensive Classroom Management: Creating Positive Learning Environments*. Boston: Allyn and Bacon.

Kessner, Arthur. 1984. "Spelling Checkers for Word Processing." *Classroom Computer Learning* (November/December): 64.

Marcus, Steven. 1984. "Computers in the Curriculum: Language Arts." *Electronic Learning* (October): 54-58.

O'Brien, Peggy. 1984. "Using Microcomputers in the Writing Class." *The Computing Teacher* (May): 20-21.

Parham, Charles. 1986. "Conquering the Dreaded Blank Page." *Classroom Computer Learning* (September): 39-44.

Pon, Kathy. 1988. "Process Writing in the One-Computer Classroom." *The Computing Teacher* (March): 32-37.

______. 1984. "Databasing in the Elementary (and Secondary) Classroom." *The Computing Teacher* (November): 28-30.

Rosenshine, Barak V. 1979. "Content, Time, and Direct Teaching." In *Research on Teaching: Concepts, Findings, and Implications*, edited by Penelope L. Peterson and Herbert J. Walberg. Berkeley, Calif.: McCutchan Publishing Corporation.

Rowe, Mary Budd. 1979. *Teaching Science as Continuous Inquiry: A Basic*, 2nd ed. New York: McGraw-Hill.

Solomon, Gwen. 1984. "Software: Side by Side, Five Word Processing Programs." *Electronic Learning* (October): 60-61.

Suttles, Al. 1984. "Software: Side by Side, Six Writing Programs." *Electronic Learning* (October): 62, 64.

Taba, Hilda. 1967. *Teacher's Handbook for Elementary Social Studies*, introductory edition. Reading, Mass.: Addison-Wesley.

Watson, Jim, and Neal Strudler. 1988/89. "Teaching Higher Order Thinking Skills with Databases." *The Computing Teacher* (December/January): 47-50.

Wresch, William. 1988. "Six Directions for Computer Analysis." *The Computing Teacher* (April): 13-16.

7
TEACHER USES OF THE COMPUTER

The purpose of this chapter is to explore the ways teachers can use the computer as a tool to help them in their daily tasks. We will discuss computer managed instruction (CMI), which involves the use of the computer in keeping records, preparing lessons and assignments, and designing tests.

THE COMPUTER AS A MANAGEMENT TOOL

When computers first arrived in classrooms, teachers had a need for a variety of special-purpose tools. We needed, or at least most of us thought we needed, a program for a gradebook; a database program we could use to enter the addresses of our children and their parents, and other information on students; and a word processing tool with which we could prepare lessons, write notes home to parents, and prepare the numerous reports for which we are responsible. These programs exist today in what are called integrated programs, mentioned briefly in chapter 2.

Using Integrated Software Packages to Maintain Student Records

Two popular programs are **AppleWorks**, which we introduced in chapter 5, and **Microsoft Works**, which we will discuss here:

Title: **Microsoft Works**

Grade Level: Intermediate and above

Source: Microsoft Corporation
16011 N.E. 36th Way
Redmond, WA 98073-9719

System Requirements: Apple Macintosh with 400K or 800K drives, 512K RAM
minimum and IBM compatibles, 512K RAM minimum

Skills Required:
Familiarity with the keyboard

Introduction to the program through instruction or one to two hours per application with *Microsoft Works Lessons*, a part of the manual that comes with the package.

This integrated package consists of a spreadsheet, database, and word processor, as well as a limited graphing program drawing tool and telecommunications tool. The use of the graphing tool will be discussed in the following section; telecommunications was reviewed in chapter 5. The purpose of integrated software is to provide individual tools that work together. In other words, you can use information from a spreadsheet in the word processor, database, and telecommunications tool. When you are writing reports, you can use information from the database, spreadsheet, graphing, and telecommunications tools in your report. The features of the program were reviewed by Anderson (1987).

Uses for Spreadsheets

Until a couple of years ago, the authors had not used an integrated tool. One simply didn't exist for the 48K Radio Shack. When one of us upgraded to a Macintosh, there seemed little reason to use an integrated program except with taxes and budgetary types of projects. A friend had used one and recommended it very highly. In fact, that was the only Macintosh product he used, and he wrote rather profusely. Then one of us was assigned a class of ninety-six undergraduates. Grading that many papers, searching for that many students on a grade role, and assigning that many grades correctly, meant that a change in work habits had to follow. With the need created, the solution was **Microsoft Works**. After having used **Works** for a semester, the old system of using and entering information in a standard gradebook seems antiquated, time-consuming, and generally a waste of effort. In a research study reviewed in Ehman and Glenn (1987), teachers found that using a gradebook program was more useful than paper and pencil gradekeeping. They felt that students worked harder because of the weekly posting of computer-generated grades, and parents overwhelmingly liked the computer-generated grade reports. The researchers concluded that computer-generated reports could not have been produced as economically by hand-recording systems.

With an integrated program a complete spreadsheet can be designed that is more legible and easier to prepare; moreover, all of the work for the semester in terms of totaling and averaging is done at the same time. Reports of student performance can be easily produced. Next semester, all I have to do is put new names into my prepared template—a blank form—and possibly add or delete a few lines, which can be accomplished easily without creating additional formulas. My new gradebook is then ready to use.

A product similar to figure 7.1 can be designed in twenty to thirty minutes. That's the one advantage of a spreadsheet over a grading program; once your template is prepared, as illustrated in figure 7.3, only minor revisions need to be made. The second advantage is that you have learned an application that can be used for several projects, as suggested below. It does take time to learn a new program, but it is invested time that can pay interest down the line. Like money, time is something most of us can't waste.

Guidelines for creating a gradebook template follow.

1. The first thing to do is enter the students' names into the spreadsheet. Since most of the forms we use require the last name first, generally this is the way the names are entered. If a report is to be made, then the spreadsheet information can be utilized in the report. **Microsoft Works** allows the adjustment of the cell size to fit the name.

2. Now it is time to enter the types of activities you plan to grade, as illustrated in figure 7.1. Again, cell size can be made smaller; this is important later when you print your gradebook.

Student Name	Quiz 1	Quiz 2	Quiz Total	Test 1	Test 2	Test Total	Report 1	Report 2	Tot. Score	Grade
Abbot, Sally	21	24	45	92	88	180	100	95	420	
Anderson, Sydney	24	23	47	88	90	178	90	95	410	
Bower, Norma	16	16	32	74	88	162	85	90	369	
Clay, Alice	18	18	36	96	93	189	75	80	380	
Dozier, Pat	22	25	47	84	88	172	75	85	379	
Edwards, Martin	25	24	49	90	96	186	95	90	420	
Green, Gene	20	22	42	84	88	172	75	80	369	
Montez, Carlos	20	20	40	86	90	176	85	90	391	
Nogalles, Patti	22	16	38	83	88	171	90	85	384	
Rosser, Madeline	23	25	48	87	96	183	75	95	401	
Sanchez, Rosa	16	23	39	96	74	170	90	90	389	
Sills, Janice	24	22	46	88	89	177	85	100	408	
Stern, Will	25	21	46	96	90	186	100	90	422	
Willard, Paul	18	19	37	79	86	165	85	90	377	
Wolf, Allan	23	18	41	82	80	162	90	85	378	
Average	21.13	21.07	42.20	87.00	88.27	175.27	86.33	89.33	393.13	
Std Dev						8.31			18.21	

Fig. 7.1. Gradebook constructed using **Microsoft Works** spreadsheet.

3. At this point you must enter your cell formulas. This is really a simple process in **Microsoft Works**. The sample formulas are provided in the manual. One simply selects by pointing the cursor arrow at the cell in which one wants the formula and clicks the mouse button. Touch the = key and type **"Sum (B3:C3),"** as shown in the sample window in figure 7.2. When scores are placed in the spreadsheet a total will be shown in that cell. A similar procedure is followed for placing averages and standard deviations in the spreadsheet, as shown in figure 7.3. (Note: The double lines indicated by the arrows in figure 7.2 illustrate the split screen feature of the program, which allows one to have the list of names in front of them on the screen and still record scores in columns that would normally be off the screen.)

4. A complete gradebook template, showing all the remaining formulas needed, is illustrated in figure 7.3 in a reduced format created by **Microsoft Works**. The formulas for the remaining cells in a column can be inserted just by pulling down the Edit Menu and selecting "Fill Down." Similarly, the average formula was duplicated in the rows by selecting "Fill Across" from the same menu.

Computer Screen Print

	A	G	H	I	J
1					
2	Student Name	Test Total	Report 1	Report 2	Tot. Score
3	Abbot, Sally	=Sum(E3:F3)			=D3+G3+H3+I3
4	Anderson, Sydney				
11	Nogalles, Patti				
12	Rosser, Madeline				
13	Sanchez, Rosa				
14	Sills, Janice				
15	Stern, Will				
16	Willard, Paul				
17	Wolf, Allan				
18					
19	Average	=Average(G3:G17)	=Average(H3:H17)	=Average(I3:I17)	=Average(J3:J17)
20	Std Dev				
21					
22					
23					
24					

Fig. 7.2. Illustration showing sum and average functions and split screen feature (**Microsoft Works**).

Gradebook Template

Student Name	Quiz 1	Quiz 2	Quiz Total	Test 1	Test 2	Test Total	Report 1	Report 2	Tot. Score	Grade
Abbot, Sally			=Sum(B3:C3)			=Sum(E3:F3)			=D3+G3+H3+I3	
Anderson, Sydney			=Sum(B4:C4)			=Sum(E4:F4)			=D4+G4+H4+I4	
Bower, Norma			=Sum(B5:C5)			=Sum(E5:F5)			=D5+G5+H5+I5	
Clay, Alice			=Sum(B6:C6)			=Sum(E6:F6)			=D6+G6+H6+I6	
Dozier, Pat			=Sum(B7:C7)			=Sum(E7:F7)			=D7+G7+H7+I7	
Edwards, Martin			=Sum(B8:C8)			=Sum(E8:F8)			=D8+G8+H8+I8	
Green, Gene			=Sum(B9:C9)			=Sum(E9:F9)			=D9+G9+H9+I9	
Montez, Carlos			=Sum(B10:C10)			=Sum(E10:F10)			=D10+G10+H10+I10	
Nogalles, Patti			=Sum(B11:C11)			=Sum(E11:F11)			=D11+G11+H11+I11	
Rosser, Madeline			=Sum(B12:C12)			=Sum(E12:F12)			=D12+G12+H12+I12	
Sanchez, Rosa			=Sum(B13:C13)			=Sum(E13:F13)			=D13+G13+H13+I13	
Sills, Janice			=Sum(B14:C14)			=Sum(E14:F14)			=D14+G14+H14+I14	
Stern, Will			=Sum(B15:C15)			=Sum(E15:F15)			=D15+G15+H15+I15	
Willard, Paul			=Sum(B16:C16)			=Sum(E16:F16)			=D16+G16+H16+I16	
Wolf, Allan			=Sum(B17:C17)			=Sum(E17:F17)			=D17+G17+H17+I17	
Average	=Average(B3:B17)	=Average(C3:C17)	=Average(D3:D17)	=Average(E3:E17)	=Average(F3:F17)	=Average(G3:G17)	=Average(H3:H17)	=Average(I3:I17)	=Average(J3:J17)	
Std Dev			=StDev(D3:D17,Average(D3:D17))			=StDev(G3:G17,Average(G3:G17))			=StDev(J3:J17,Average(J3:J17))	

Fig. 7.3. "Completed" **Microsoft Works** grading template, 50 percent reduced.

There are a number of grading programs on the market. Eiser (1987b) reviews and comments on a number of commercial grading programs for classroom teachers. She provides an in-depth analysis. The two big disadvantages of using commercial programs is that, first, you must learn to operate a new program, and second, you must find a grading program that meets your expectations or adapt your way of grading to meet the requirements of the program.

As Nogales and McAllister (1987) point out in their discussion of the use of **AppleWorks**, spreadsheets can also be used in the development of seating charts, which in most classrooms are changed often. This simple technique is handy for a quick preparation for a substitute teacher. Spreadsheets are also useful in the yearly preparation of a materials request list. Their usefulness here is increased by one's ability to compare items in determining whether budget allowances have been observed.

Uses for Databases

Integrated software packages also contain databases. We have used databases extensively throughout this book. Again, Nogales and McAllister show their use in the preparation of test items, which we will discuss again later. Databases are also useful in preparing and maintaining student record cards, developing mailing lists, preparing mailing labels, and performing a number of other tasks. One example of a special application is using a database to develop a bibliography; in fact, this book's bibliography was prepared using **Microsoft Works'** database and word processor.

Uses for Word Processors

It is difficult to express the real value of a word processor to a person who hasn't used computers. One of the authors' recent experience is relevant. Some graduate students in a course were evaluating the instructional design features of textbook materials they were using. The process required them to prepare a set of goals, apply these goals to objectives, determine whether the material fit the purposes and the designed objectives, and, finally, assess a set of tests to determine whether the objectives tested were actually in the instructional materials. Two-thirds of the group were not computer users. Since there were computers accessible to the group, the computer users decided to help the nonusers become users because there was considerable complaining concerning the amount of typing and retyping such an assignment would require. Within the first week of use, the nonusers were avid users of word processing.

Much of the written work we do as teachers can be accomplished more easily using a word processor. **Microsoft Works** is a better word processor than is usually available in integrated packages. Page numbers appear in a scroll bar, margins and indentations are easy to set, and editing is a snap. In addition, a spelling checker is included in the program, which increases its usefulness. *This spelling checker can be used only on the word processor.* The ability to import pictures into the word processor and to type in and around the illustration is a powerful advantage of this tool. It allows the production of attractive teacher-prepared materials, a few examples of which follow.

Using the Computer to Create Course Materials

One use of integrated software is the creation of structural organizers—tools that provide students a framework that facilitates recalling, learning, and gaining insight from instruction. Helpful in the teaching and learning of knowledge, skills, or values, structural organizers come in many forms—structural overviews, data retrieval charts, diagrams, semantic maps, and timelines, for example. We shall discuss structural overviews, diagrams, data retrieval charts, and semantic maps here; we discussed timelines in chapter 5.

Structural Overviews

An example of a structural overview that is useful at an adult instructional level is the Alternative Curriculum Model, illustrated in figure 7.4. Developed by one of the authors a few years ago, this model summarizes the book *The Process of Education*, and is used to explain the ideas Bruner (1960) presented. Jerome Bruner, a learning psychologist who conceptualized the curriculum reforms of the 1960s, proposed that national teams should develop curriculum for the schools. This model takes as its content base the structure of knowledge (nature, conceptions, and methods of a discipline) defined by the scholars. Representatives from the foundational disciplines, rather than educators, would select the elements of knowledge to be taught in the schools. Theoretically the use of this model would prevent the selection of outdated concepts and methods used in the preparation of curricula.

Alternative Curriculum Model

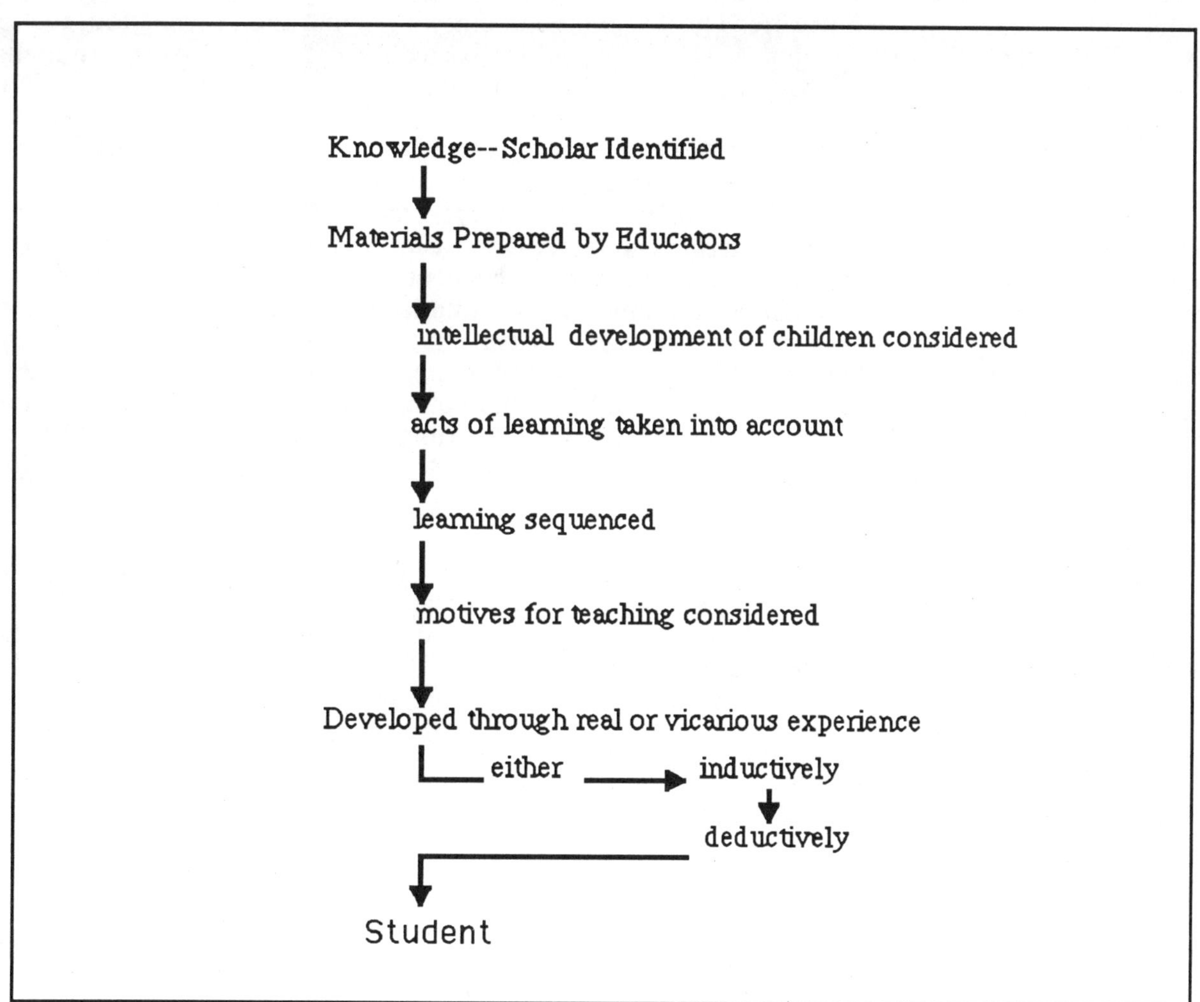

Fig. 7.4. An advanced organizer illustrating the concepts presented in a book.

The substantive structure would then be translated by professional educators into teaching materials that would take into account the intellectual development of children as described by Jean Piaget, the famous Swiss psychologist. The translation of the content must also take into account the acts of learning — what the child must do with the information. The third element, according to figure 7.4, that must be considered is that of the learning sequence. The student must experience the major concepts of the subject at increasing levels of difficulty as the student progresses through the curriculum; this is the now-famous *spiral curriculum* concept. Bruner also felt that the best learning was delivered to the student through real experience, but since this was not always possible, educators should use experiences that were as near to real as practical. He also indicated that either inductive or deductive teaching techniques could be used in the delivery of instruction.

As an aside, Bruner's ideas influence many of the concepts discussed in this book and in social studies education today. The idea of getting instructional experiences as near to real as possible is one reason simulation and the use of databases is emphasized so heavily. Although Bruner mentioned both inductive and deductive teaching techniques, he was misinterpreted by many educators at the time to have placed heavy emphasis upon inductive techniques. In addition, the concept of the teacher as a manager of instruction also comes directly out of *The Process of Education*. The instructional organizer shown in figure 7.4 was created in **SuperPaint**, published by Silicon Beach Software. This program combines a graphic and drawing tool that is available for the Macintosh computer. The organizer was pasted into **Microsoft Works** using the *scrapbook* tool, a part of all Macintosh programs. This tool allows one to copy, store, and transport graphics and text.

Structural overviews, such as that shown in figure 7.4, are valuable because (1) they outline the important ideas to be presented (they provide a model in direct instruction terminology), (2) they leave the student with a model on which facts, concepts, and generalizations can be hung, and (3) they provide a simple structure that can be recalled easily. This is a simple model, yet the material from which the overview was created, and the concepts and generalizations it contains, represents nearly 100 pages of an important milestone in American education. It is very useful to us as adults. The point is: If we are going to teach students to think, then we must present them not only with information, but also with ways of organizing that information so it can be recalled and used. Another useful technique has been called visual notemaking. It meets the needs of the pictorially oriented child; we must remember that we are primarily a visually oriented society.

Diagrams

The "stickman" diagram, figure 7.5, was used by Stein (1987) in a biographic study of George Washington. But as one can see, the tool could be used in any biographic study. The student merely attaches notes, which might come from a book, film, or lecture, to one of the eleven areas on the stickperson in such a way that

A — stands for ideas (brain)

B — is visions and hopes (the eyes)

C — represents the important words spoken (mouth)

D — describes actions taken (hands)

E — are the important feelings (heart)

F — are important trips made (feet)

G — shows weaknesses

H — illustrates strengths perceived

I — stands for the birth of the person (important dates placed at ground level)

J — describes the death of the person (other important events can be placed along the timeline)

K — tells about the person's background (roots).

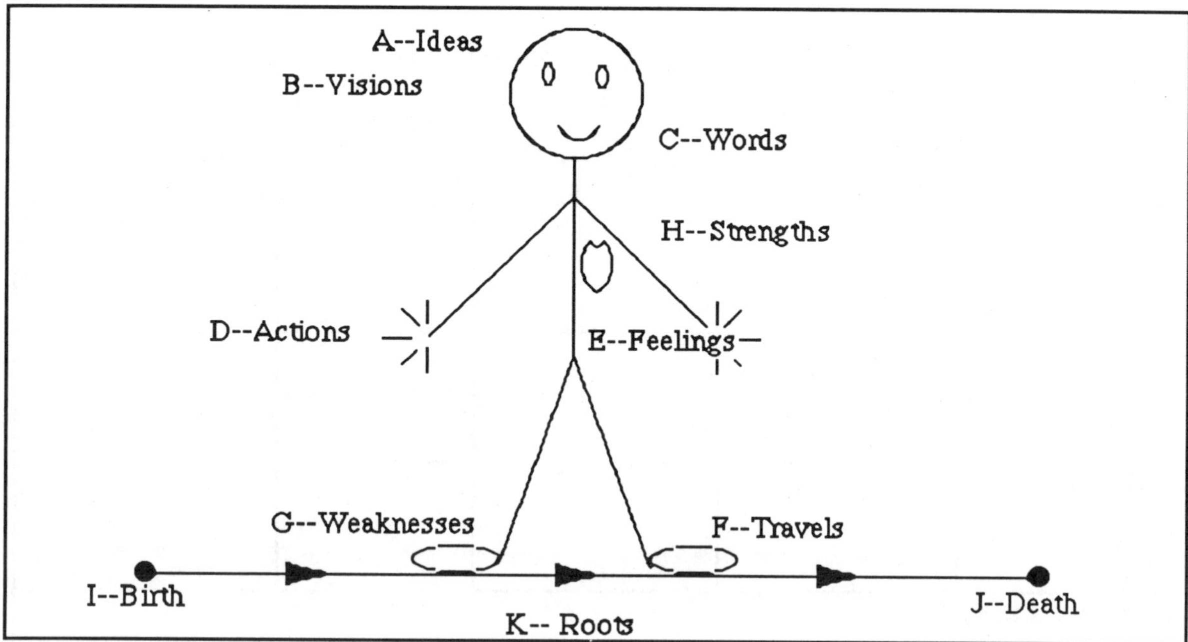

Fig. 7.5. "Stickman" used for organizing biographic information. Adapted from Harry Stein, "Visualized Notemaking: Left-Right Brain Theory Applied in the Classroom." *The Social Studies*, July/August 1987: 163-68. Reprinted with permission of the Helen Dwight Reid Educational Foundation. Published by Heldref Publications, 4000 Albemarle St., N.W., Washington, D.C. 20016. Copyright © 1987.

The value of such a tool is that it aids the child in systematically organizing information he has gathered. The student can then move to collecting information on another figure in American history or comparing his character's life with that selected by another child. Figure 7.5 was drawn using **MacPaint**, which is published by Apple Computer Company. The graphic was then imported into **Microsoft Works**.

Data Retrieval Charts

Another useful tool for helping children organize information is the data retrieval chart. One of the ways we can help students in late primary and intermediate schools to develop skills in reporting is through the use of reporting templates. Templates are simply blank forms. Hennings (1986) developed what she called "A Data Retrieval Chart for Reporting." Her data retrieval chart is a valuable writing tool. But she makes an error, commonly made by professionals in attempting to develop children's thinking—she asks students to generalize before they have explained their inferences. As you will recall from chapter 6 when we discussed the interpretation of data strategy, the steps in helping children make a comparison of likenesses and differences are to have the students recall what they have read, find relationships in the information and make inferences, explain their inferences, and draw conclusions. In figure 7.6 we have revised Hennings's form to follow this strategy.

This reporting template can be used in a variety of settings, on a variety of topics, to direct children's thinking. But to direct children's thinking is not to teach them to think. We must have students explain what they are doing, examine orally difficulties they have encountered doing it, and discuss ways they have overcome these difficulties. In addition, to really teach thinking we must ask students to name the steps they are using, ask what they have learned, ask how the process they have used can be transferred to other learning tasks, and encourage them to make transfers and applications to other thinking tasks.

CHART FOR REPORTERS

Directions: Fill in the chart by reading in a reference book located in the Reading Corner. Work with 2-3 friends on this assignment.

Native America Group	Kind of Home in which They Live	Kind of Clothing They Wear	Foods They Raise and Eat	Climate of Region
1. Hopi				
2. Iroquois				
3. Sioux				

Write four paragraphs.

Paragraph 1:
Describe the Hopi.

Paragraph 2:
Describe the Iroquois.

Paragraph 3:
Describe the Sioux.

Paragraph 4:
Explain the relationship between climate, food, homes, and clothing of a people.

Decide: How does the climate of the region where the group lives affect the kinds of homes, clothing, and food they use?

Fig. 7.6. An information chart can direct children's research. Source: Hennings, Dorothy Grant. *Communications in Action: Teaching the Language Arts*, 3d ed. Copyright © 1986 by Houghton Mifflin Company. Used with permission.

The real value of the data retrieval chart template is that it helps students to gather and organize information from which they can make generalizations. The template was developed here using the draw feature of the word processor in **Microsoft Works**. This feature makes the creation of forms or templates very easy. Again it illustrates the power of this integrated tool.

Semantic Maps

As Heimlich and Pittelman (1986) point out, recently both teachers and researchers have given a lot of attention to semantic mapping in reading content material and in the prewriting stages of factual composition. Semantic maps have been around for a number of years under the labels of semantic webbing (webbing), semantic networking, or plot maps (mapping). Semantic maps are diagrams that help students relate words or concepts. They are especially useful as an organizing tool for prereading and prewriting activities. If one wants to have the students build the web, then one would use the classification strategy as discussed in chapter 6. If one wanted to help students build the web, then one would use the direct instruction strategy. A teacher can draw the initial web structure using **MacPaint** and go in either direction. Figure 7.7 was imported into the word processing program. Heilborn (1985) has created an extremely useful book for individuals wanting to use **MacPaint**. For the average teacher using Macintosh, this is an important resource.

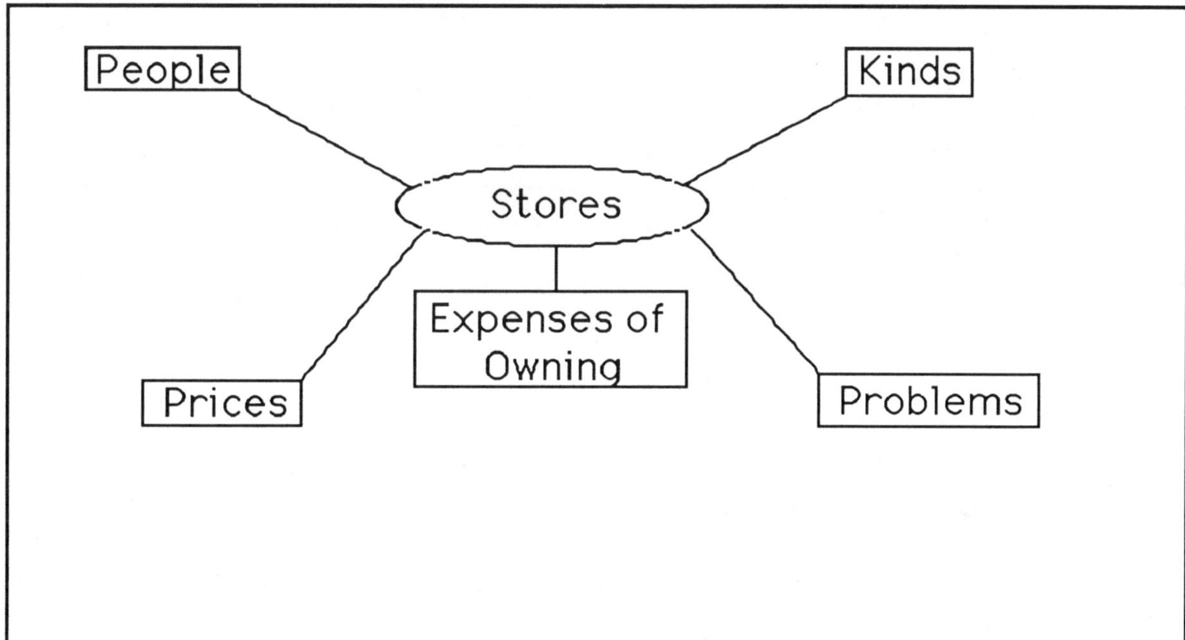

Fig. 7.7. Semantic map form for organizing ideas. Adapted with permission from Joan E. Heimlich and Susan D. Pittelman, *Semantic Mapping: Classroom Applications*. Newark, Del.: International Reading Association, 1986.

Graphs and Graphing

A group of skills that social studies teachers need to develop more systematically is the collection and presentation of quantitative data. We have discussed this in chapter 5 in connection with survey programs and our use of the Favorites database. But we have said little about the development and use of graphs as an important visual reporting tool. The skills involved in the preparation of graphs are

1. gathering data—involves collecting information, which then becomes a chart

2. classifying data—the making of charts

3. organizing data—the making of charts and preparation of scales to properly present the data

4. reporting data—the making of charts and graphs to communicate ideas

5. drawing conclusions—students interpreting their own graphs or those of others

6. evaluating conclusions—students assessing their conclusions and evaluating those of others.

These ideas can be illustrated best by an example in which we will use the data collected by a class that utilized the "Favorites" lessons from chapter 5. That was our data-collecting experience. The next task was to organize our data, so from that information we developed the chart shown in figure 7.8.

Graph Data Chart

Our Favorite Fast Food Restaurant	Number of Students
Burger King	8
McDonald's	3
Pizza Hut	3
Taco Bell	5

Fig. 7.8. Graphing chart constructed from "Favorites" data.

We then placed that data into the Microsoft spreadsheet program and selected the Draw Pie Chart feature from the Chart menu. This allowed us to create the circle graph shown in figure 7.9. This program is rather limited, since it can chart only a few sets of values, but for illustration purposes and initial instruction, it is adequate.

Figure 7.10 could be used with several of the programs reviewed by Mathis (1986), who lists software for elementary school students such as

MECC Graph, published by MECC

MECC Graph Primer, published by MECC

Easy Graph, published by Grolier

Exploring Graphs and Tables, published by Field Publications.

Collis (1988) offers several activities that can be used with database and graphing programs for both elementary and secondary classrooms.

Favorite Fast Food Restaurant

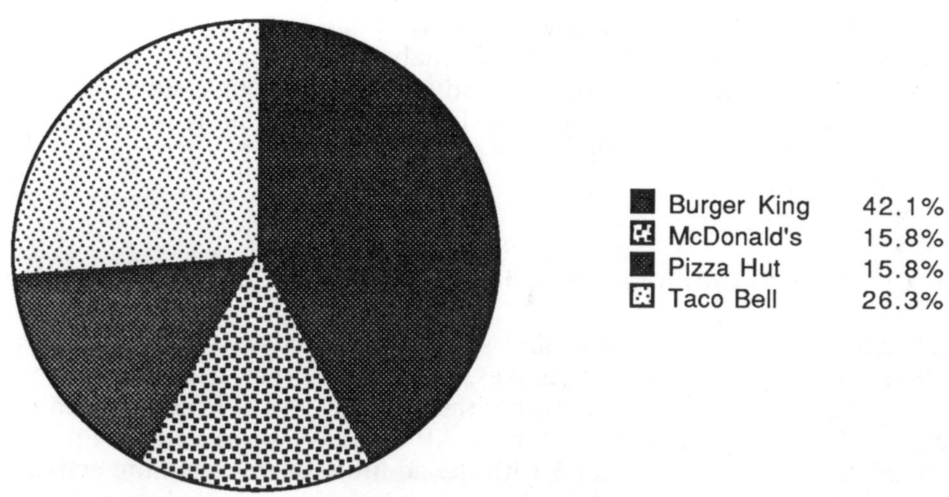

Fig. 7.9. Pie chart created with **Microsoft Works.**

OUR FAVORITE FAST FOOD RESTAURANT

From the data collected in the "Favorites" class survey, design a graph that shows the groups' favorite fast food restaurants.

Graph Data Chart

Our Favorite Fast Food Restaurant	Number of Students

Fig. 7.10. Graph data chart for "Favorites" class survey.

Mason (1986) paints a much grimmer picture at the secondary level, although **Graphic Analysis III**, published by Vernier Software, designed for this level has recently received an enhancement award from *Classroom Computer Learning*. In the same issue **Sampling: Probability and Prediction** and **Function Machine Level 1 and Level 2**, three separate programs, published by D. C. Heath, designed for statistical analysis and graphing at the elementary and junior high levels, also received the award (Brady 1988). Although statistical analysis and graphing have not received much attention in social studies in the past, the future looks much more promising because the technology is present; and the mathematics programs are teaching it. Social studies can come to life.

Using the Computer to Create Learning Activity Packages

Learning activity packages (LAPs) are sets of materials designed to accomplish a performance objective or set of related objectives. They differ from activity sheets because they follow teaching strategies and are complete within themselves. In fact, LAPs can contain a variety of activity sheets. The nearest example of an LAP we have produced in this book is the "Favorites" materials discussed in chapter 5 with the addition of the graphing activity shown in figure 7.10. In order for these materials to be a complete learning packet, a list of intended objectives, a pretest, and a posttest would have to be added.

It should be obvious that learning activity packets could easily be produced using the tools we have examined above. All the teacher would need to add is a clip-art tool such as **The Print Shop**, published by Broderbund Software, **MacArt Department**, published by Simon and Schuster, or a little time with **MacPaint** and you're off and running toward attractive packages. Certainly it takes time, but the kids will enjoy it! In addition, this tool can be used to direct children's thinking, because the learning packet can contain a teaching strategy that involves a thinking strategy, or at least a thinking skill.

The word processing portion of an integrated package can be a powerful tool when used to develop course materials. Used purposefully, the course methods can teach thinking.

Using the Computer to Create Tests

Perhaps one of the most difficult tasks a teacher performs is the preparation of tests. One answer may be a test-question database. In testing there are two choices. First, one has the choice of using the textbook questions, but because they don't always cover the material presented, those tests are either unfair or incomplete. A second choice is to develop a good teacher-prepared test. But, since they are hard to develop, such tests often suffer from overuse; and occasionally one will fall into the hands of students, making the test an invalid indicator of student performance. There are two solutions on the market today. The first is in the database programs we've discussed and the second solution is in test generators. Both can make test preparation easier.

Using Database Programs

Databases allow teachers to prepare their own test-item database using integrated software, as discussed by Nogales and McAllister (1987), or they can use publisher-prepared databases. As Nogales and McAllister point out, there are advantages to simply using the database software that comes in an integrated package such as **AppleWorks** and **Microsoft Works**. Their suggestions are for **AppleWorks**, but after some practice with **Microsoft Works** a teacher could make the translation. Using these programs, teachers can implement their own style of test making. Nogales and McAllister illustrate how to

1. develop a classification system that allows one to select subdivisions (areas) of the content

2. define categories that allow the generation of multiple-choice questions

3. code questions so that one can select specific questions

4. create alternate forms of the same test.

Teachers can now use test databases produced by the publishers of their textbooks. One example is the recently published *Scott, Foresman Social Studies Series* for grades 4-7. This text series is published with a software package that contains the Scott, Foresman **Test Generator/ Question Writer**. This program comes with an easy-to-follow (and it really is) instruction manual which introduces such features as

1. a bank of questions for each chapter that test content and skills in the areas of graphs, maps, timelines, and chronology

2. a method of item selection to allow teachers to test what they teach and to add their own questions to the test bank

3. a procedure of selection that allows the teacher to designate items for someone else to print — a way to put the instructional aide to work

4. the power to randomize test items and to create alternate forms

5. blackline masters for maps, charts, and graphs used on the tests

6. a quick scoring process for schools equipped with test scanners.

Using Test Generators

In addition to test generators published by textbook publishers, a number of commercial test generators are now on the market. These products were reviewed by Eiser (1988b). This author states that effective test generators should

1. contain all of the elements of a good word processor, such as word wrap around, what-you-see-is-what-you-get (WYSIWYG) viewing, full-screen editing, and insert and delete functions

2. have enough space to put in all of the questions, plus graphics

3. allow multiple-choice questions and answers to be displayed on the same screen

4. permit the use of matching-type items

5. contain the free-format feature, which allows the teacher to give instructions and to provide spacing to allow easy reading.

The reviewer indicated that the most powerful programs were **LXR Test** for the Macintosh, which is published by Logic eXetension Resources, and **Final Exam** from Earthware Computer Service, developed for the Apple family. Eiser selected these because of their ability to support the mixing of graphics and text and their support of database functions. The last product was unavailable for preview at the time Eiser's article was printed, but should now be on the market. Check it out using her suggestions.

The impact of the computer in the area of CMI has been slow in coming. This can partially be explained by the apparent lag in technology. For many years the computer industry has focused on the need for business management tools. As a result, some of these tools are being translated for use in the classroom. We do have some special needs, and the good news is that computers are very useful in filling needs associated with keeping records, preparing assignments, and designing tests. And there is even better news on the horizon. Desktop publishing may place teachers in situations where they can produce the materials children need, and the computer might also fill some motivational goals that have previously gone unfilled, or only partially filled.

DESKTOP PUBLISHING

What Is It?

What is it? That's the first question anyone wants to know about a relatively new concept. Desktop publishing, according to Stanley (1986), involves the use of computer software to create page design (e.g., to change typefaces and sizes, draw boxes around portions of text, and place text and graphics in documents). There was a time when a school newspaper, bulletin, or other classroom publication had to be typed, cut into strips, and pasted on another page. The editor had to find some clip art that could be reproduced, and finally, at best, the publication had to be photocopied for distribution. Two developments have transformed the personal computer into a personal publishing system: page assembly software tools and the laser printer. Software packages such as **Ready-Set-Go**, published by Letraset USA for the Macintosh computer and **Pagemaker**, published by Aldus Corporation both for the Macintosh and the IBM PC, can make the time-consuming task of pasteup obsolete in the production of printed matter. McCarthy (1988), Rose (1988), and Eiser (1988a) offer primers on getting started with such programs. Eiser makes specific recommendations as to which program to use with which hardware in addition to presenting a stepwise procedure. In addition, such software as **Newsroom**, published by Springboard Software and **Dazzle Draw**, published by Broderbund, as reported by McCarthy, can be used with the Apple family computers making the process available to any classroom. The Children's Writing and Publishing Center, published by The Learning Company, is a recent addition to the marketplace. These programs use the simple dot matrix printers.

Benefits

The greatest benefits of desktop publishing programs are (1) they allow the publication of children's writing in either newspaper or book format, (2), they permit the creation of better-looking teacher-prepared materials, and (3) they produce professional-looking products for communication with parents. Stanley (1986) explains why teachers of writing skills place a high value on publication. To Donald Graves, author and researcher on the process of writing, the question "Why publish?" is equivalent to the question "Why write?" Graves indicates that publishing gives writers a focus, a framework, and the incentive to write. It also gives them a record of past accomplishment and a benchmark to measure their growth. As we have pointed out earlier, sharing our ideas with others is what writing is all about. McCarthy (1988) reports that in a Detroit study, slow learners used desktop publishing to create storybooks. These fourth- and fifth-graders had reading comprehension scores 50 percent higher than the control groups at the end of the study. The researchers also found increases in self-esteem.

Cecilia Hunter produces a school newspaper, the *Santa Gertrudis School Bulletin*, which serves the basic purposes we cited above. It is the public relations tool between the school and her community. There is nothing that shows more of what a school accomplishes than the work of its students. What thrills children more than seeing their writing in print? In figure 7.12 Hunter provides useful pointers for developing such a tool. This illustration also shows some of the features of **Newsroom**. Lake (1986) describes this program as "pretty powerful because it contains a word processor, a graphics tool, and a telecommunications feature."

STAFF SELECTION NEEDED

The first step in the production of a newspaper is the selection of a staff. I have asked teachers to recommend to me  students in all grades who are task committed, and independent workers. Creativity is a nice, but not necessary, quality.

I then assign five students to be editors, one for each page, and an editor in chief, responsible for the layout of each page. I like to have a representative from each classroom who is the contact person for the staff.

NEWS DIVIDED BY SUBJECTS

The newspaper is divided into subject areas so that we have a news page, two feature pages, a class news page and a sports page. One student is responsible for each page. The editor is responsible for the layout of all pages. If a story is missing, he may leave a blank spot, with the by line of the student who did not submit the story. Or, he may get the story.

The sponsor must carefully proofread all materials and ask for rewriting if needed. 

STAFF SELECTS NEWS

At the beginning of each month the sponsor meets with the staff as a whole and plans the newspaper that will appear at the end of the month. Students are given assignment sheets and worksheets. The assignment sheets tell what stories they will be gathering and who should be talked to about that story. Students quickly learn some minor idiosyncrasies of each teacher, and share them with each other for more harmonious relations. 

NEWS MUST BE SOUGHT

After assignments are made students must then actively, and sometimes aggressively seek the news. Again, worksheets are given students with pointers on what to ask. Students must determine the "Who", "What", "What", "When", "Where", "Why" and sometimes "How" for each story.

Students are reminded that news that will happen is superior to news that has happened, unless it is an honor or award.

Students are also made aware of when teachers can be interviewed. 

writing stories difficult

Actually writing the stories is probably the most difficult part of the production of a school newspaper. Using Newsroom means a story must be long, or short enough to fit the predetermined size. I generally find there are enough graphics libraries to do a very adequate job, but matching story and picture takes careful consideration. Students must be careful to get complete and accurate 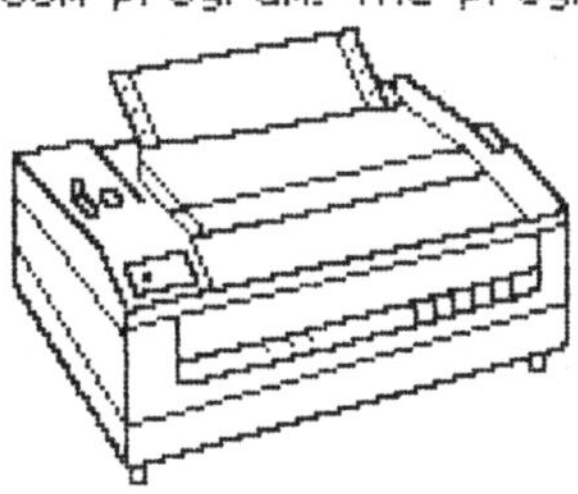 information and answer the Who, What, When, Where and Why questions in so far as it is possible. Generally, my students must return for more information.

Printing and distributing The paper ends process

The sponsor reviews each hand written story and suggests necessary changes, additions, or corrections. Then the story is typed by the reporter using the Newsroom program. The program is somewhat difficult to manage, due to the number of disks involved, but, most 5th grade students can master it. Then the editor determines the layout, and the papers are distributed.

Fig. 7.11. Process for preparing a school newspaper using **Newsroom**.

We have provided several examples of teacher-prepared materials, so we will not spend much time on them here, except to underline the importance of desktop publishing in the preparation of such materials. We're very aware of the fact that our textbooks are changing, because of pressures from professional organizations and state legislatures. The products we are now receiving have integrated, as we have illustrated, some of the new technology. But *textbooks don't meet the needs of many children* who are reading below grade level and who are poorly motivated and generally turned-off to learning, especially in social studies. Teacher-prepared materials are one way we can meet these needs.

If we can produce visually attractive materials and activities, better motivation is another possible result. Many teachers don't have the time to prepare such materials and some don't have the talent; but for those of us who do, the tools are waiting.

SPECIALIZED PRINTING PROGRAMS

As we discuss motivation, there are other tools that should be considered, for example, the award-making tools. As educators we have been in many school buildings across this country. The buildings to which we enjoy returning are the ones that contain children with smiles on their faces. Invariably, these are the buildings in which some attention is paid to the variety of achievements of the children and the faculty. Two programs exist on the market at present that allow the development of awards to recognize special efforts: **Certificate Maker**, published by Springboard Software, and **Award Maker Plus**, published by Baudville. Each program allows one to select from over 200 certificates, which then need only to be filled in with the special details. A variety of borders and fonts is available, and a list of names can be entered on the certificates. Official-looking seals come with the packages and a variety of special parchment can be purchased, which really makes the awards attractive and worthy of framing. We used **Award Maker Plus** to produce the certificate in figure 7.12. We encourage teachers to explore the great variety of other kinds of motivating printing programs one might consider for the software library. Eiser (1987a) reviews a variety of such programs that can create banners, comic strips, and cards.

CMI is off the ground and running. The integrated software packages offer the teacher many productivity tools in the areas of keeping and maintaining records, creating lessons and assignments, and preparing tests. Many teachers need nothing more than possibly a graphics tool. But for those of us who have a few extra resources, or can get the PTA, an appreciative parent, or some form of Santa to furnish the funds needed, there are gradebook programs, test generators, statistical and graphing tools, desktop publishing programs, certificate-making programs, and other print software that can make the job easier for us and learning more pleasant for our students.

Fig. 7.12. Example of a certificate produced using **Award Maker Plus** by Baudville, Inc. Used with permission.

REFERENCES

Anderson, Eric S. 1987. Review of *Microsoft Works*. *The Computing Teacher* (March): 39-41.

Brady, Holly, ed. 1988. "The 1988 Classroom Computer Learning Software Awards." *Classroom Computer Learning* (February): 28-38.

Bruner, Jerome S. 1960. *The Process of Education*. New York: Random House.

Collis, Betty. 1988. *Computers, Curriculum, and Whole Class Instruction*. Belmont, Calif.: Wadsworth.

Ehman, Lee H., and Allen D. Glenn. 1987. *Computer-Based Education in the Social Studies*. Bloomington, Ind.: Social Studies Development Center.

Eiser, Leslie. 1988a. "Choosing the Right Desktop Publisher." *Classroom Computer Learning* (November/December): 38-43.

――――. 1988b. "Test Generators: Teacher's Tool or Teacher's Headache." *Classroom Computer Learning* (May/June): 44-48.

――――. 1987a. "Print It! 101 Things to Print with Your Computer." *Classroom Computer Learning* (May): 32-39.

――――. 1987b. "HELP! I'm Drowning in Paperwork!" *Classroom Computer Learning* (February): 26-35.

Heilborn, John. 1985. *Macintosh Notebook: MacPaint*. Englewood Cliffs, N.J.: Prentice Hall.

Heimlich, Joan E., and Susan D. Pittelman. 1986. *Semantic Mapping: Classroom Applications*. Newark, Del.: International Reading Association.

Hennings, Dorothy Grant. 1986. *Communications in Action: Teaching the Language Arts*, 3rd ed. Boston: Houghton Mifflin.

Lake, Daniel T. 1986. "Telecommunications from the Classroom." *The Computing Teacher* (April): 43.

Mason, Margie. 1986. Review of "Software Side by Side: Graphing Programs." *Electronic Learning* (April): 46-47.

Mathis, Judy. 1986. "Statistical Sampling of Fish Populations." *The Computing Teacher* (June): 20-21.

McCarthy, Robert. 1988. "Stop the Presses: An Update on Desktop Publishing." *Electronic Learning* (March): 24-30.

Nogales, Patti D., and Carol H. McAllister. 1987. *AppleWorks for Teachers*. Irvine, Calif.: Franklin, Beedle & Associates.

Rose, Shelley Yorke. 1988. "A Desktop Publishing Primer." *The Computing Teacher* (June): 13-15.

Stanley, Milt. 1986. "Desktop Publishing." *The Computing Teacher* (November): 46-49.

Stein, Harry. 1987. "Visualized Notemaking: Left-Right Brain Theory Applied in the Classroom." *The Social Studies* (July/August): 163-168.

SOURCES AND RESOURCES FOR USING COMPUTERS IN SOCIAL STUDIES EDUCATION

The purpose of this chapter is to provide the reader with sources from which to obtain information on the use of computers in social studies education. First, we include an annotated bibliography of books and articles we have found to be useful in this relatively new interest area. Second, we provide a listing of periodicals that fill a variety of needs. Finally, we provide descriptions of more than 300 pieces of social studies software.

ANNOTATED BIBLIOGRAPHY

Books

Budin, Howard, Diane Kendall, and James Lengel. **Using Computers in the Social Studies**. New York: Teachers College Press, 1986. 118 pp.

This is a basic handbook on the use of computers in social studies. It contains information on ways the computer can be connected electronically with other devices. It also deals with the social issues of the computer in society, and ways to teach these issues.

Ehman, Lee H., and Allen D. Glenn. **Computer-Based Education in the Social Studies**. Bloomington, Ind.: Social Studies Development Center, 1987. 68 pp.

This interesting book reviews the research on the use of computers in the classroom. Good research is available, but there are many more questions than answers.

Hunter, Beverly. **My Students Use Computers**. Reston, Va.: Reston Publishing Company, 1984. 376 pp.

Although this book is not written directly to social studies educators, it contains many social studies activities and instructional ideas applicable to the use of social studies software.

Hunter, Beverly, and Erica K. Lodish. **On-line Searching in the Curriculum: A Teaching Guide for Library/Media Specialists and Teachers**. Santa Barbara, Calif.: ABC-Clio, Inc., 1989. 219 pp.

This is a book that can help a variety of computer users. It can help you prepare and conduct lessons for students and plan for use of on-line databases in your school, and it can be used as a model for the preparation of lessons which fit your own curriculum.

Knapp, Linda Roehrig. **The Word Processor and the Writing Teacher**. Englewood Cliffs, N.J.: Prentice Hall, 1986. 281 pp.

Teachers interested in improving writing in the classroom will find this a good resource book for all levels. It presents activities for all school age children and ideas for student publications.

Roberts, Jack L. **Scholastic Computing: An Introduction to Computers**. New York: Scholastic, 1984. 288 pp.

This book is written for computer literacy courses for grades six through nine. It contains clear, simple explanations of many confusing computer concepts as well as computer applications. It is often useful for teachers to get simple material to explain confusing concepts.

Roberts, Nancy, David F. Anderson, Ralph M. Deal, Michael S. Garet, and William A. Shaffer. **An Introduction to Computer Simulation**. Reading, Mass.: Addison-Wesley, 1983. 562 pp.

This book can be used to teach systems theory and computer simulation to high school and college undergraduate students. The book is clearly written and provides a place to begin for an adventuresome teacher facing a classroom of bright students. The development of the **Simulation Construction Kit** makes this an even more valuable resource.

Rubin, Charles. **Microsoft Works: On the Apple Macintosh**. Redmond, Wash.: Microsoft Press, 1986.

Most computer users agree that software manuals are difficult to use. We have discovered that books on the software application are usually helpful since they generally contain examples and projects.

Turner, Bobby, and Bobby Mimlitch. **Help Works**. Lubbock, Tex.: HELP WORKS Software Corporation, 1987.

This publication is a complete guide to **AppleWorks**. The material comes in a convenient notebook form which makes it easy to use at the computer.

Weaver, Dave. **Database Software for the Social Studies**. Portland, Oreg.: Northwest Regional Educational Laboratory, 1986.

This is a valuable guide for the development of student-prepared and ready-made databases in social studies.

Articles

Brown, Joan Marie. "Spreadsheets in the Classroom Part II." *The Computing Teacher* (February 1987): 9-12.

These are lessons three and four from the two-article series for helping students design spreadsheets (see also Brown 1986-1987).

______. "Spreadsheets in the Classroom." *The Computing Teacher* (December/January 1986-1987): 8-12.

These are the initial lessons on how to use spreadsheets. The prepared lessons that are often published in *The Computing Teacher* are extremely useful. Spreadsheets have not been utilized to the extent possible in any curriculum area at present. The use of statistical analysis and projection is on the horizon for social studies educators. The spreadsheet is a powerful tool.

Glenn, Allen D., and Steven J. Rakow. "Computer Simulations: Effective Teaching Strategies." *The Computing Teacher* (February 1985): 58-59.

Computer simulations may be divided into two basic types: continuous-time, which requires continuous interaction, and stop-time, which allows the user to stop at the end of a round and begin again. Meeting intended instructional goals requires an understanding of the type of simulation encountered. This article discusses these concepts.

Hannah, Larry. "The Data Base: Getting to Know You." *The Computing Teacher* (August/September 1987): 17-18.

This and the following article are similar to the two Brown articles. We made extensive use of these useful lessons.

———. "Teaching Data Base Search Strategies." *The Computing Teacher* (June 1987): 16-17.

This article could be considered a prepared database, except that one has to type it into the **AppleWorks** database. Its direct instruction technique is valuable.

Hodges, James O. "Developing Your Own Microcomputer Courseware with Authoring Systems." *Social Education* (January 1985): 59-62.

This is a well-written article with a good bibliography for those interested in the use of authoring systems. Hodges is past chairperson of the Special Interest Group/Computers and Social Education (SIG/CASE), which can be joined by writing Dr. James Hodges, Virginia Commonwealth University, 901 W. Franklin St., Richmond, VA 23284. SIG/CASE is an interest group of the National Council for the Social Studies.

Hunter, Beverly. "Problem Solving with Data Bases." *The Computing Teacher* (May 1985): 20-27.

This is an important article for teachers who want to use databases in their classrooms. The article discusses what a database is and why teachers and students use databases, and it presents steps to help teachers develop them in the classroom.

National Council for the Social Studies. "In Search of a Scope and Sequence." *Social Education* (April 1984): 249-262.

This is the latest statement from the National Council on the knowledge, skills, and values contained in the social studies curriculum.

Pon, Kathy. "Process Writing in the One-Computer Classroom." *The Computing Teacher* (March 1988): 32-37.

This is an important article for anyone interested in implementing the process approach to writing we have discussed in this book.

Rawitsch, Don. "The Computerized Database: Not a Simple Solution." *The Computing Teacher* (December/January 1987-1988): 34-37.

The inquiry movement of the 1960s may have been twenty years too soon. We now have the tool to accomplish the task. But as we have pointed out, teaching thinking is not accomplished by placing the student in front of a computer. Rawitsch's study is an important one.

Roberts, Nancy. "Who's Last in Line for Computers: The Social Studies Teacher." *Classroom Computer News* (November/December 1982): 17-18.

This article inspired the previous edition of this book. Many of its ideas have been implemented, but we have a ways to go.

Vlahakis, Robert. "The Computer-Infused Social Studies Classroom." *Classroom Computer Learning* (November/December 1988): 58-60.

This article stands in bright contrast in social studies and the use of the computer: from the extreme of the gloomy position painted by Roberts in "Who's Last in Line for Computers? The Social Studies Teacher" to the point that the social studies has the greatest number of recommended titles reviewed by the Educational Products Information Exchange (EPIE). The author explains how he has implemented some of the ideas and programs we have discussed.

Wheeler, Fay. "The New Ready-Made Databases: What They Offer Your Classroom." *Classroom Computer Learning* (March 1987): 28-32.

The use of prepared databases is an important element in preparing students for the information age. This article discusses the advantages of these databases and presents guidelines for purchasing them.

Willis, Jerry, and Dee Anna Willis, "But What Does the Research Say?" *Classroom Computer Learning* (March 1989): 28-35.

This article by one of the leading writers in computer education reviews the status of computer assisted instruction. In addition the author includes "some research sources" for those interested in deeper study and those interested in maintaining their expertise.

INFORMATION SOURCES FOR EDUCATIONAL COMPUTING

The rate of change in microcomputing is so rapid that it is difficult to stay up to date. This is especially true in the use of computers in social studies education, so it becomes necessary to depend upon recent periodical material. Therefore, this section is a particularly important one. It describes many of the educational computing periodicals, gives a brief description of the purpose of each publication, and provides an address through which the publisher can be contacted.

Educational Computing Periodicals

AEDS Journal and **AEDS Monitor**
Association of Educational Data Systems
1201 16th St. N.W.
Washington, DC 20036
The *AEDS Journal* is published four times a year and contains a variety of articles for different audiences. It publishes many research and conceptual articles. One finds fewer articles on using microcomputers in public school settings and more on the process of writing and developing educational software. The *AEDS Monitor* contains a variety of general articles that would be interesting to people involved in educational computing.

Classroom Computer Learning
5615 West Cermak Rd.
Cicero, IL 60065
CCL has produced authoritative articles on educational computing over the broad range of the public school curriculum. It has been especially alert to developments in social studies software. Some of the articles are similar to those found in *The Computer Teacher* but *CCL* also publishes a dates and events calendar of computer shows and conferences. It provides annual reports for outstanding software and also reviews new hardware and software. A very good publication for the practitioner.

Computers in the Schools
The Haworth Press
28 East 22nd St.
New York, NY 10010
This is a publication that focuses on the impact and applications of computers in education.

The Computing Teacher
International Council for Computers in Education
University of Oregon
1787 Agate St.
Eugene, OR 97403
  TCT was created by David Morsund, its editor, and a respected leader in the field for many years. One of the oldest journals on computing and teaching, it carries a range of articles on the uses of computers in the public schools and in university and college settings. *TCT* publishes reviews of significant software and quite a few descriptions of projects as well as courses.

Educational Technology
140 Sylvan Ave.
Englewood Cliffs, NJ 07632
  This is an established journal with a strong reputation. Although its purpose is to expand knowledge in educational technology in general, it contains many articles on educational computing. It is relatively expensive but is available in most university libraries.

Electronic Learning
Scholastic
902 Sylvan Ave.
Box 2001
Englewood Cliffs, NJ 07632
  Part of the Scholastic stable of educational publications, *Electronic Learning* is published eight times a year. It publishes articles similar to those found in *Classroom Computer Learning.* Every month it features a curriculum area and it can be depended upon for its reviews of software.

Journal of Computer-Based Instruction
Association for the Development of Computer-Based Instructional Systems
Computer Center
Western Washington University
Bellingham, WA 98225
  Like the *AEDS Journal,* the *Journal of Computer-Based Instruction* has a strong focus on research and conceptual articles.

Media & Methods
1511 Walnut St.
Philadelphia, PA 19102
  This journal is a publication of the American Society of Educators. It includes software reviews and articles about computers in education.

Social Education
National Council for the Social Studies
3501 Newark St., N.W.
Washington, DC 20016
  This journal, available to members of the NCSS, is designed for individuals who teach or support the teaching of social studies in the elementary, middle, or high schools. It features a section called "Computer Corner," which concentrates on social studies software. There are often feature articles on educational computing. The Special Interest Group/Computers and Social Education, SIG/CASE, an interest group of the National Council for Social Studies, also features an occasional newsletter.

The Social Studies
4000 Albemarle St., N.W.
Washington, DC 20016
   This journal publishes articles of interest to educators of all levels. The subject matter covered includes material dealing with the social studies, social sciences, history, and interdisciplinary studies.

T.H.E. Journal
Information Synergy
P.O. Box 992
Acton, MA 01720
   "T.H.E." stands for "Technological Horizons in Education." This journal publishes articles on many types of educational technology, including computers, video disks, and audiovisual equipment. *T.H.E. Journal* publishes descriptions of various computer projects in public schools, colleges, and universities. It also takes an international focus on computer applications. This publication is interesting for three reasons: first, it contains advertisements for computers, computer accessories, and software; second, it has a new products section; third, it is sent *free* to such individuals as principals, superintendents, and college program directors.

Teaching and Computers
Scholastic
730 Broadway
New York, NY 10003
   Geared to elementary teachers, this publication provides information and practical suggestions for integrating computers into the classroom. It includes nontechnical information about how computers work, teacher-developed lessons, and informative books and resources.

Techtrends (formerly *Instructional Innovator*)
Association for Educational Communications and Technology
1126 16th St., N.W.
Washington, DC 20036
   AECT publishes three journals for its members: *Techtrends, Journal of Instructional Development*, and *Educational Communications and Technology Journal*. Computers are not the only focus of *Techtrends*, nor is classroom learning. AECT's membership includes trainers in industry as well as educators in public schools and university faculty. All types of instructional media and technology are covered. Many university libraries carry all three journals.

General Computing Magazines

   The publications described in this subsection are not concerned specifically with educational applications of computers, although many of them regularly devote space to the subject. Several have even put together special issues with education as the focus. Most of the magazines listed here are available in well-stocked computer stores.

Byte
700 Main St.
Peterborough, NH 03458
   One of the first small-computer magazines, *Byte* is written for the sophisticated computer user. There are articles on programming languages, the construction of computer equipment, educational computing, artificial intelligence, and new computing techniques. Most beginners will find *Byte* too difficult. Computer users who have a strong electronics background, however, will find many interesting articles in this publication.

Compute!
Compute! Publications
324 West Wendover, Suite 200
Greensboro, NC 27408
Written for Apple, VIC, Commodore 64, and Atari users, this publication contains a mix of articles on hardware and software for beginners as well as advanced users. A strong point of *Compute!* is its articles on the nitty-gritty details of how each computer operates. It also publishes many programs you can type into your computer and use.

InfoWorld
1060 Marsh Rd.
Suite C-200
Menlo Park, CA 94025
Produced in a newspaper format, *InfoWorld* concentrates on two types of information — news and product reviews. In addition to a weekly education department, the magazine reports on computer graphics, databases, and new technology.

Popular Computing
Byte Publications, McGraw-Hill
700 Main St.
Peterborough, NH 03458
This magazine is put out by the publishers of *Byte*. Written for readers with little or no computer background, it contains a mixture of articles, product reviews, and applications suited to the needs and interests of the relatively inexperienced computer user.

Product-Oriented Publications*

Some magazines are produced for specific types of computers. Such publications carry product announcements, corrections of bugs, and descriptions of software developed specifically for one machine.

Commander
P.O. Box 98827
Tacoma, WA 98498
This monthly journal for Commodore users reports on the future of computers, compares computer equipment, analyzes educational software, and describes innovative ways to use computers.

Macintosh Hands On
52 Domino Dr.
Concord, MA 01742
This monthly magazine prints programs for the Mac. It reviews new software and hardware, provides news about the Mac world, and presents articles on how to get the best out of the software on the market.

MacUser
Ziff Davis Publications
1 Park Avenue
New York, NY 10016
This magazine is written for the general market and publishes articles on developments in Mac hardware and software. The magazine is filled with reviews of new software, news about the Mac world, and tips on ways to get better use of the Mac. If there's a new development, you'll see it here.

---

*Reprinted by special persmission of Classroom Computer Learning from "Directory of Educational Computing Resources 1984-85," © 1984 by Pitman Learning, Inc., 19 Davis Drive, Belmont, CA 94002.

Microcomputer Magazine
Commodore Computers
1200 Wilson Dr.
West Chester, PA 19380
     This bimonthly is for more advanced users of VIC 20 and Commodore 64. Sections on business and educational applications are included in every issue.

Nibble
52 Domino Dr.
Concord, MA 01742
     This magazine concentrates only on the Apple. It carries articles for beginners but also has many construction articles and program listings for the intermediate and advanced user.

PC World
555 De Haro St.
San Francisco, CA 94107
     This monthly magazine for IBM PCs and compatibles reports on the state of the art in local networks, telecommunications, databases, and second-generation software. Subscription includes two special issues: a hardware review and a software review.

SOFTWARE PROGRAMS FOR SOCIAL STUDIES

     "There isn't any software for social studies"—this complaint is often heard. Perhaps it is true in a relative sense—for example, when the amount of software in social studies is compared to that for mathematics. There does, however, appear to be more social studies software than is generally assumed. In this section more than 300 software programs for social studies are presented.
     The information in this section was gathered from a variety of sources, primarily publishers' catalogs and advertisements. One of the authors took this material, interpreted it, and made some assumptions regarding the type of program, grade level appropriateness, and subject matter area; he then entered it into a database. Some of these programs may be available from additional sources and perhaps can be used with other machines. In some cases, no doubt, the prices will have changed. Yet no other published source contains this many programs. For readers with questions about pricing or the equipment for which the programs are available, the addresses of the producers or distributors are listed in the section immediately following the list of programs and its indexes.
     Each entry lists the program's title and source, courses for which it is appropriate, approximate grade level for which it will be useful, price, type of program, systems on which it will operate, and a brief description of the program. Following the listings there are indexes to help the reader locate programs for a specific grade range or subject. To make it easier for teachers seeking programs for a specific level, we have added the codes **EL, JH, HS,** and **CO.**

Descriptions of Programs

Ad Game

Source(s): MicroEd
Course(s) for Which Appropriate: Social studies
Approximate Grade Levels: 5, 6, 7, 8, 9 **EL, JH**
Cost: $30
Type of Program: Tutorial
System(s) on Which It Will Run: Commodore 64
Description: The objective of this program is to teach the student how to read a vertical bar
     graph and interpret the data.

Adventure Island

Source(s): Queue, Intellectual Software
Course(s) for Which Appropriate: Elementary social studies, geography
Approximate Grade Levels: 3, 4, 5, 6, 7, 8 **EL, JH**
Cost: $60
Type of Program: Simulation
System(s) on Which It Will Run: Apple II family
Description: Working in small groups, students simulate being stranded on an island. In order to survive until they are rescued, students will need to use group decision-making skills, read maps and compasses, and demonstrate an understanding of coordinates. Ten maps and four booklets are included.

Africa

Source(s): Educational Activities
Course(s) for Which Appropriate: Geography
Approximate Grade Levels: 7, 8, 9, 10, 11, 12 **JH, HS**
Cost: $69
Type of Program: Tutorial, drill and practice
System(s) on Which It Will Run: Apple II family; TRS-80 Models III and 4
Description: The first disk is a tutorial program that covers several misconceptions most people have about Africa. Through graphics and information, these misconceptions are corrected. The second disk includes a drill and practice program on the geography of Africa.

African Geography

Source(s): Sunshine Computer Software
Course(s) for Which Appropriate: Geography
Approximate Grade Levels: 7, 8, 9, 10, 11, 12 **JH, HS**
Cost: $29
Type of Program: Drill and practice
System(s) on Which It Will Run: IBM PC
Description: A map of Africa is presented on the screen. The student uses the cursor control keys to select a country. The student is then asked to name the country, its capital, and the largest city. Correct answers produce the country's anthem. Help is available if needed.

Agent USA

Source(s): Scholastic
Course(s) for Which Appropriate: Geography
Approximate Grade Levels: 4, 5, 6, 7 **JH**
Cost: $40
Type of Program: Simulation
System(s) on Which It Will Run: Apple II family; IBM PC; Atari; Commodore 64
Description: The secret agent is traveling across the country trying to disarm a bomb. Students must help him by reading train schedules, maps, and train routes and making choices about the best route for the agent to use.

Air Pollution

Source(s): EME Corporation
Course(s) for Which Appropriate: Economics
Approximate Grade Levels: 9, 10, 11, 12 **HS**
Cost: $47-$52
Type of Program: Simulation
System(s) on Which It Will Run: Apple II family, TRS-80, IBM PC, Tandy 1000
Description: A simulation of carbon monoxide pollution in an urban environment. Students manipulate variables affecting carbon monoxide levels, use "worst case" analysis and determine safety margins. Program includes student lab booklets and a study guide.

Alexander the Great

Source(s): MicroEd
Course(s) for Which Appropriate: Elementary social studies, world history
Approximate Grade Levels: 5, 6, 7, 8 **EL, JH**
Cost: $30
Type of Program: Tutorial
System(s) on Which It Will Run: Commodore 64
Description: Acquaints students with the life of Alexander the Great, the young king who spread
Greek culture throughout the ancient world.

All about America

Source(s): Unicorn Software, Learning Arts
Course(s) for Which Appropriate: Geography, U.S. history, social studies
Approximate Grade Levels: 2, 3, 4, 5 **EL**
Cost: $70
Type of Program: Tutorial, game
System(s) on Which It Will Run: Apple II family
Description: Sixteen topics are covered for young children using large, easy-to-read text and eye-
catching graphics. The two-disk program also contains reading comprehension and vocab-
ulary questions which are presented in a game format. There is also a map disk and quiz.

Amendments to the Constitution

Source(s): Classroom Consortia Media
Course(s) for Which Appropriate: U.S. history, government
Approximate Grade Levels: 8, 9, 10, 11, 12 **JH, HS**
Cost: $70 IBM, $35 Apple
Type of Program: Tutorial
System(s) on Which It Will Run: Apple II family; IBM PC
Description: Presents explanations of major points in the constitutional amendments. Review
consists of crossword puzzles and multiple-choice questions. Two case studies of trials are
included and the student must be the "judge."

America Coast to Coast

Source(s): Mindscape
Course(s) for Which Appropriate: Geography, elementary social studies
Approximate Grade Levels: 4, 5, 6, 7, 8 **EL, JH**
Cost: $50
Type of Program: Drill and practice
System(s) on Which It Will Run: Apple II family
Description: Students learn the relative sizes of states, their locations, capitals, shapes, motto,
and industries.

America Moves West

Source(s): Orange Cherry Media
Course(s) for Which Appropriate: Elementary social studies, U.S. history
Approximate Grade Levels: 4, 5, 6, 7, 8 **EL, JH**
Cost: $78
Type of Program: Tutorial
System(s) on Which It Will Run: Apple II family; Commodore 64; TRS-80 Models III and 4
Description: This program looks at the importance of the Louisiana Purchase, the history of
Spanish lands, the gold rush, pioneer trails, and the everyday life of settlers. Each of these
programs is a separate unit on the disk.

American Explorers

Source(s): Aquarius
Course(s) for Which Appropriate: U.S. history
Approximate Grade Levels: 7, 8, 9, 10, 11 **JH, HS**
Cost: $35 (backup included)
Type of Program: Tutorial, simulation
System(s) on Which It Will Run: Apple II family; IBM PC; TRS-80 Models III and 4
Description: This program is part of the series America, An Early History, which gives the student insight into social, religious, economic, and political aspects of early America. Historical figures are used to "speak" to the student.

American Foreign Policy

Source(s): Focus Media
Course(s) for Which Appropriate: U.S. history
Approximate Grade Levels: 9, 10, 11, 12 **HS**
Cost: $119
Type of Program: Tutorial
System(s) on Which It Will Run: Apple II family
Description: Two double-sided disks contain four programs: The Emerging Nation Period; From Isolationism to Imperialism; From World War to Cold War; and Super Powers in the Nuclear Age. Can be used as introduction or reinforcement.

American Government

Source(s): Queue
Course(s) for Which Appropriate: Government
Approximate Grade Levels: 7, 8, 9, 10, 11, 12 **JH, HS**
Cost: $45 each part
Type of Program: Tutorial
System(s) on Which It Will Run: Apple II family; Macintosh; IBM PC
Description: This five-part program utilizes a highly interactive tutorial to teach about a wide range of topics in American government, including concepts of democracy, the Constitution, branches of government, political parties, the presidency, and elections. A management system is included.

American Government I-V

Source(s): Intellectual Software
Course(s) for Which Appropriate: Government
Approximate Grade Levels: 9, 10, 11, 12 **HS**
Cost: $35 each, $150 set
Type of Program: Tutorial
System(s) on Which It Will Run: Apple II family; IBM PC
Description: Five programs cover key concepts about democracy, the Constitution, elections, political parties, the presidency, the Congress, and the courts. The Apple programs are available with a student management system for an additional $10 per program.

American History

Source(s): Learning Arts
Course(s) for Which Appropriate: U.S. history
Approximate Grade Levels: 4, 5, 6 **EL**
Cost: $169
Type of Program: Tutorial
System(s) on Which It Will Run: Apple II family
Description: This is a six-disk, interactive program that uses a fictional or historical character to guide the student through activities related to the time period. If incorrect choices are made, the program branches to provide the information at a lower reading level. The program concentrates on the period 1607-1810.

American History: 1865-1912

Source(s): Queue
Course(s) for Which Appropriate: U.S. history
Approximate Grade Levels: 7, 8, 9, 10, 11, 12 **JH, HS**
Cost: $35
Type of Program: Tutorial
System(s) on Which It Will Run: Apple II family; Commodore 64; IBM PC
Description: Tutorial program gives explanations for every choice. "Help" screens and practice are given on important concepts. A testing mode is built in. Teacher and student materials are included with a two-sided disk.

American History Achievement I: To 1860

Source(s): Microcomputer Workshops Courseware
Course(s) for Which Appropriate: U.S. history
Approximate Grade Levels: 10, 11, 12 **HS**
Cost: $50
Type of Program: Drill and practice with explanations
System(s) on Which It Will Run: Apple II family
Description: Covers the development of American history from the pre-Columbian period to 1860. Explanations are provided for answers, feedback is provided, and questions are presented in the CEEB Achievement Test format. An approximate CEEB score is given with full error analysis.

American History Achievement II: 1860-1890

Source(s): Microcomputer Workshops Courseware
Course(s) for Which Appropriate: U.S. history
Approximate Grade Levels: 10, 11, 12 **HS**
Cost: $50
Type of Program: Drill and practice with explanations
System(s) on Which It Will Run: Apple II family
Description: Problems are designed to cover the period from the Civil War to "the beginnings of the technological revolution."

American History Adventure

Source(s): Queue
Course(s) for Which Appropriate: U.S. history
Approximate Grade Levels: 7, 8, 9, 10, 11, 12 **JH, HS**
Cost: $60
Type of Program: Game, problem solving
System(s) on Which It Will Run: Apple II family; IBM PC
Description: Students meet and must identify historical characters. In addition, they must be able to locate them in time and place.

American History Adventures

Source(s): Learning Arts
Course(s) for Which Appropriate: U.S. history
Approximate Grade Levels: 4, 5, 6, 7, 8 **EL, JH**
Cost: $150
Type of Program: Tutorial
System(s) on Which It Will Run: Apple II family
Description: Students explore historical events, identify the event taking place, and state evidence to support their conclusions. Includes programs on: Revolution and Constitution, Discovery and Exploration, Westward Expansion, and Civil War and Reconstruction. Each available separately for $40 with backup.

American History Games

Source(s): Queue
Course(s) for Which Appropriate: U.S. history
Approximate Grade Levels: 7, 8, 9, 10, 11, 12 **JH, HS**
Cost: $50
Type of Program: Game
System(s) on Which It Will Run: Apple II family; Commodore 64
Description: Presents a variety of games to review facts in history. Each game has two or more formats. For an additional $10 a utility disk can be purchased that allows the teacher to add new lists of facts.

American History Keyword Series

Source(s): Focus Media
Course(s) for Which Appropriate: U.S. history
Approximate Grade Levels: 7, 8, 9, 10, 11, 12 **JH, HS**
Cost: $45 each
Type of Program: Game, drill and practice
System(s) on Which It Will Run: Apple II family
Description: Students must determine an important vocabulary word from clues such as definitions, examples, synonyms, or references. Four programs are available: Civil War Keyword, Westward Ho! Keyword, World War II Keyword, and Changing America Keyword. Backups included.

American Indians

Source(s): Right On Programs
Course(s) for Which Appropriate: Social studies, U.S. history
Approximate Grade Levels: 4, 5, 6 **EL**
Cost: $25
Type of Program: Tutorial
System(s) on Which It Will Run: Apple II family; Commodore 64
Description: Indian tribes from all sections of the country are discussed. Each culture is described. Reproducible worksheets and a teacher's manual are included.

American Inventions

Source(s): Right On Programs
Course(s) for Which Appropriate: Social studies
Approximate Grade Levels: 5, 6, 7 **EL, JH**
Cost: $25
Type of Program: Tutorial
System(s) on Which It Will Run: Apple II family; Commodore 64
Description: Six major inventions and their impact are described in this program: vulcanizing rubber, the telephone, the electric light bulb, the airplane, xerography, and space ships. Reproducible worksheets and a teacher's manual are included.

American People

Source(s): Focus Media
Course(s) for Which Appropriate: U.S. history
Approximate Grade Levels: 5, 6, 7, 8, 9, 10, 11, 12 **EL, JH, HS**
Cost: $22.50
Type of Program: Game—quiz on facts
System(s) on Which It Will Run: Apple II family; Commodore 64; TRS Color Computer
Description: Students compete for "money" using six categories of questions: Women, Sports, Explorers, Inventors, The Arts, and At War. Questions vary in difficulty. Winners receive a "check" for the amount of money they win.

American Presidency

Source(s): MicroEd
Course(s) for Which Appropriate: Elementary social studies, U.S. history
Approximate Grade Levels: 4, 5, 6, 7, 8 **EL, JH**
Cost: $50
Type of Program: Tutorial
System(s) on Which It Will Run: Commodore 64
Description: Provides information about the duties and history of the presidency.

America's Presidents

Source(s): Intellectual Software
Course(s) for Which Appropriate: U.S. history
Approximate Grade Levels: 9, 10, 11, 12 **HS**
Cost: $35-$100 each
Type of Program: Tutorial
System(s) on Which It Will Run: Apple II family
Description: Five programs cover the presidents during various eras. Programs and prices are: Founding a Nation, Washington-Harrison, $50; Age of Conflict, Tyler-Grant, $100; Age of Growth Hayes-Taft, $35; World Wars, Prosperity, and Depression, Wilson-Truman, $35; and The Modern Era, Eisenhower-Reagan, $50.

Ancient Civilizations

Source(s): MicroEd
Course(s) for Which Appropriate: Elementary social studies
Approximate Grade Levels: 4, 5, 6 **EL**
Cost: $30
Type of Program: Tutorial
System(s) on Which It Will Run: Commodore 64
Description: Teaches students the geographical locations of ancient civilizations.

Ancient Civilizations

Source(s): Right On Programs
Course(s) for Which Appropriate: World history
Approximate Grade Levels: 6, 7, 8 **EL, JH**
Cost: $25
Type of Program: Tutorial, game
System(s) on Which It Will Run: Commodore 64; Apple II family
Description: Early Greek and Roman civilizations are presented, with emphasis on famous individuals and places. A game, teacher's guide, and reproducible worksheets are included.

Ancient Civilizations and the Middle Ages

Source(s): Focus Media, Opportunities for Learning
Course(s) for Which Appropriate: World history
Approximate Grade Levels: 6, 7, 8, 9, 10, 11, 12 **EL, JH, HS**
Cost: $129
Type of Program: Tutorial
System(s) on Which It Will Run: Apple II family
Description: Contains four programs: Ancient Middle East, Ancient Greece, Ancient Rome, and Middle Ages. Each is a tutorial with text and graphics. Review questions and a game are included for review. Students encounter major events from the dawn of history to the Age of Exploration.

Ancient Civilizations Keyword

Source(s): Focus Media
Course(s) for Which Appropriate: World history
Approximate Grade Levels: 7, 8, 9, 10, 11, 12 **JH, HS**
Cost: $55
Type of Program: Drill and practice
System(s) on Which It Will Run: Apple II family
Description: Students piece together clues (synonyms, examples, and definitions) to identify vocabulary related to the ancient civilizations in Egypt, Asia, India, the Middle East, and the Americas.

Ancient Rome

Source(s): Teach Yourself by Computer
Course(s) for Which Appropriate: World history
Approximate Grade Levels: 6, 7, 8, 9, 10, 11 **EL, JH, HS**
Cost: $40
Type of Program: Tutorial
System(s) on Which It Will Run: Apple II family
Description: Explores daily life in early Rome including recreation, clothing, legends, games, and education. Review questions, tests, and a manual are included.

"And If Reelected..."

Source(s): Focus Media
Course(s) for Which Appropriate: Government
Approximate Grade Levels: 9, 10, 11, 12 **HS**
Cost: $65
Type of Program: Simulation
System(s) on Which It Will Run: Apple II family; IBM PC
Description: Highly interactive program involves the student as a candidate for presidential reelection. A variety of situations arise that require decisions. These decisions affect popularity and support of twenty-one special-interest groups. The student's reelection depends on the decisions made. 1988 *Classroom Computer Learning* software award.

A New Continent Is Discovered

Source(s): Aquarius
Course(s) for Which Appropriate: U.S. history
Approximate Grade Levels: 7, 8, 9, 10, 11 **JH, HS**
Cost: $35 (backup included)
Type of Program: Tutorial, simulation
System(s) on Which It Will Run: Apple II family; TRS-80 Models III and 4; IBM PC
Description: Part of the series America, An Early History, which gives the student insight into social, religions, economic and political aspects of early America. Historical figures are used to "speak" to the student.

Annam: A Developing Country

Source(s): Educational Activities
Course(s) for Which Appropriate: World history
Approximate Grade Levels: 6, 7, 8, 9, 10, 11 **EL, JH, HS**
Cost: $63
Type of Program: Simulation
System(s) on Which It Will Run: Apple II family; TRS-80 Models III and 4
Description: Students assume the role of dictator of Annam, a Southeast Asian country. A variety of situations are presented and the student must make decisions, each leading to consequences that have impact on the final outcome. (Several events change from one playing to another.)

Around and about the Civil War

Source(s): Orange Cherry Media
Course(s) for Which Appropriate: Social studies, U.S. history
Approximate Grade Levels: 4, 5, 6, 7, 8 **EL, JH**
Cost: $39
Type of Program: Drill and practice, game
System(s) on Which It Will Run: Apple II family; Commodore 64
Description: Students are introduced to major battles of the Civil War as they race against the
clock to recall information and respond to questions.

Around and about the Revolutionary War

Source(s): Orange Cherry Media
Course(s) for Which Appropriate: Social studies, U.S. history
Approximate Grade Levels: 4, 5, 6, 7, 8 **EL, JH**
Cost: $39
Type of Program: Tutorial
System(s) on Which It Will Run: Apple II family; Commodore 64
Description: Students climb aboard a "lighter-than-air" balloon and are presented with a bird's
eye view of major battlefields of the Revolutionary War.

ASK: A Survey Kit

Source(s): D. C. Heath
Course(s) for Which Appropriate: Government, sociology
Approximate Grade Levels: 9, 10, 11, 12 **HS**
Cost: $51
Type of Program: Tool
System(s) on Which It Will Run: Apple II family
Description: The program allows students to create a survey and statistically analyze the data.
Descriptive statistics, cross tabulations, and scatter diagrams can be created.

Balance of Power

Source(s): Mindscape, Edu-Tron
Course(s) for Which Appropriate: Government
Approximate Grade Levels: 9, 10, 11, 12 **HS**
Cost: $55
Type of Program: Simulation
System(s) on Which It Will Run: Apple II family; IBM PC; Macintosh
Description: Students use research and reasoning skills to direct global politics. Maps and a data-
base provide accurate information for decisions. This program can be used by groups or
individuals and has four levels of difficulty. 1988 *Classroom Computer Learning* software
award.

Bank Street School Filer

Source(s): Sunburst
Course(s) for Which Appropriate: U.S. history, world history, government, economics,
sociology, geography
Approximate Grade Levels: 5, 6, 7, 8, 9, 10, 11, 12 **EL, JH, HS**
Cost: $99
Type of Program: Tool
System(s) on Which It Will Run: Apple II family; Commodore 64
Description: An easy to use filing program to create and edit databases and design and print
reports. A tutorial and a 175-page teacher's manual are included. For $59 each there are
prepared databases available on North America, the U.S., and Colonial Times which can be
used with this program.

Beginning Geography

Source(s): Right On Programs
Course(s) for Which Appropriate: Elementary social studies
Approximate Grade Levels: 1, 2 **EL**
Cost: $25
Type of Program: Tutorial
System(s) on Which It Will Run: Commodore 64; Apple II family
Description: The concepts of the four directions and map symbols for river, mountain, and other
    physical features are presented. Reproducible worksheets and a teacher's guide are included.

Beyond the Rising Sun: Discovering Japan

Source(s): Educational Activities
Course(s) for Which Appropriate: World history, world cultures
Approximate Grade Levels: 7, 8, 9, 10, 11, 12 **JH, HS**
Cost: $63
Type of Program: Simulation
System(s) on Which It Will Run: Apple II family
Description: Students simulate being members of a Japanese family. They must make typical
    decisions related to that culture from deciding what sport to play to whether to attend a
    "cram" school. Decisions affect success, money, and family harmony scores. Backup,
    management, and documentation are included.

BIFs: Basics in Forecasting

Source(s): Conduit
Course(s) for Which Appropriate: Government, economics, sociology
Approximate Grade Levels: 10, 11, 12+ **HS, CO**
Cost: $75
Type of Program: Simulation
System(s) on Which It Will Run: IBM PC
Description: An introduction to the basics of population and economic forecasting, this package
    helps students make forecasts through a number of different models. Students learn about
    some strengths and weaknesses of forecasts and also gain a better understanding of computer
    modeling.

Business Organization

Source(s): Queue
Course(s) for Which Appropriate: Economics
Approximate Grade Levels: 9, 10, 11, 12 **HS**
Cost: $110
Type of Program: Tutorial
System(s) on Which It Will Run: Apple II family
Description: A two-disk tutorial program that explores the nature of different types of business
    organizations and demonstrates decision-making procedures within them. A case study of
    Pepperidge Farm, which was founded in a kitchen and became a large corporation, is used.

Business Simulations Package

Source(s): Queue
Course(s) for Which Appropriate: Economics
Approximate Grade Levels: 9, 10, 11, 12+ **HS, CO**
Cost: $325
Type of Program: Simulation
System(s) on Which It Will Run: Apple II family
Description: Package consists of nine simulations, available separately for $40-$50. Included are:
    Measuring Price Elasticity; Wage Theory; Price Discrimination; Prospecting Game; Iron
    and Steel Location; Siting an Aluminum Plant; Workers and Machines; Competition,
    Mergers, and Control of Monopoly; and Real Estate Agent.

Calendar

Source(s): MicroEd
Course(s) for Which Appropriate: Elementary social studies
Approximate Grade Levels: 1, 2, 3 **EL**
Cost: $30
Type of Program: Drill and practice
System(s) on Which It Will Run: Commodore 64
Description: Helps students identify days of the week, months, and differences in dates.

Campaign

Source(s): Queue
Course(s) for Which Appropriate: World history
Approximate Grade Levels: 9, 10, 11, 12 **HS**
Cost: $50
Type of Program: Simulation
System(s) on Which It Will Run: Apple II family
Description: Students pretend to be Edward III during the Normandy campaign of the Hundred Years' War. From his landing in France to the Battle of Crecy they must make decisions as to what to do next. The program includes booklets that provide background material.

Campaign Math

Source(s): Mindplay
Course(s) for Which Appropriate: U.S. history, government, elementary social studies
Approximate Grade Levels: 3, 4, 5, 6, 7, 8, 9 **EL, JH**
Cost: $50
Type of Program: Simulation
System(s) on Which It Will Run: Apple II family; IBM PC
Description: One or two players research issues, raise funds, and choose advertising media to win an election. Each student creates his own election issues and statistics.

Canada

Source(s): Intellectual Software, Queue
Course(s) for Which Appropriate: World history
Approximate Grade Levels: 9, 10, 11, 12 **HS**
Cost: $25/$30
Type of Program: Drill and practice
System(s) on Which It Will Run: Apple II family; IBM PC; Commodore 64
Description: Covers the economy, cities, provinces, and physical features of Canada. A wall map is included, and for the higher price, Apple users receive a disk that includes a student management system.

Caravan: The Adventures of Marco Polo

Source(s): Queue
Course(s) for Which Appropriate: World history, elementary social studies
Approximate Grade Levels: 5, 6, 7, 8, 9, 10, 11, 12 **EL, JH, HS**
Cost: $60
Type of Program: Simulation
System(s) on Which It Will Run: Apple II family
Description: It is the year 1260. Students are departing on a caravan from Venice to the Orient. An understanding of economics and geography, as well as decision-making skills, are developed as students buy and sell products along the way. A copy of *The Travels of Marco Polo* is included.

Choice or Chance?

Source(s): Rand McNally
Course(s) for Which Appropriate: Geography, U.S. history
Approximate Grade Levels: 7, 8, 9, 10, 11, 12 **JH, HS**
Cost: $111
Type of Program: Tutorial
System(s) on Which It Will Run: Apple II family
Description: Covers historical events in three eras: exploration, expansion, and industrialization. Develops a recognition and understanding of the relationship between geography and history in terms of causes and effects. Teacher's guide and workbook masters included.

Choices, Choices: On the Playground

Source(s): Tom Snyder Productions
Course(s) for Which Appropriate: Elementary social studies
Approximate Grade Levels: K, 1, 2, 3, 4, 5, 6 **EL**
Cost: $89.95
Type of Program: Simulation
System(s) on Which It Will Run: Apple family (64K) and IBM
Description: Simulation sets the environment for teaching decision-making skills around a new kid at school who doesn't seem to fit in.

Choices, Choices: Taking Responsibility

Source(s): Tom Snyder Productions
Course(s) for Which Appropriate: Elementary social studies
Approximate Grade Levels: K, 1, 2, 3, 4, 5, 6 **EL**
Cost: $89.95
Type of Program: Simulation
System(s) on Which It Will Run: Apple family (64K) and IBM
Description: Simulation sets the environment for teaching decision-making skills around witnessing a bad deed at school and the children must decide whether to tell the truth or choose not to tattle on a friend.

Christopher Columbus

Source(s): MicroEd
Course(s) for Which Appropriate: Elementary social studies
Approximate Grade Levels: 4, 5, 6, 7, 8 **EL, JH**
Cost: $50
Type of Program: Tutorial
System(s) on Which It Will Run: Commodore 64
Description: Provides information about the life of Christopher Columbus.

Coast-to-Coast America

Source(s): Beard Sales
Course(s) for Which Appropriate: Geography
Approximate Grade Levels: 3, 4, 5, 6, 7, 8 **EL, JH**
Cost: $40/$50
Type of Program: Game, drill and practice
System(s) on Which It Will Run: Apple II family; Commodore 64; IBM PC
Description: Five games designed to review the names of the states, their capitals, major industries, mottos, and other details. The lower price is for the Commodore 64 version.

Communication

Source(s): Right On Programs
Course(s) for Which Appropriate: World history
Approximate Grade Levels: 6, 7, 8 **EL, JH**
Cost: $25
Type of Program: Tutorial
System(s) on Which It Will Run: Apple II family; Commodore 64
Description: The history of communications from tom-toms to laser beams is included. Reproducible worksheets and a teacher's guide are included.

Community Helpers

Source(s): Right On Programs
Course(s) for Which Appropriate: Elementary social studies
Approximate Grade Levels: 2, 3 **EL**
Cost: $25
Type of Program: Tutorial
System(s) on Which It Will Run: Apple II family; Commodore 64
Description: Community helpers and their services are explained. A game is also included. Reproducible worksheets and a teacher's guide are included.

Community Helpers: Public and Private

Source(s): Orange Cherry Media
Course(s) for Which Appropriate: Elementary social studies
Approximate Grade Levels: 3, 4, 5, 6 **EL**
Cost: $78
Type of Program: Tutorial
System(s) on Which It Will Run: Apple II family; Commodore 64; TRS-80 Models III and 4
Description: Using an innovative approach, children learn about various aspects of their community such as public safety, sanitation, health, and mail delivery. Services in the private sector that are included are commerce, medical services, communications, and housing.

Community Search

Source(s): McGraw-Hill Software
Course(s) for Which Appropriate: World history, geography
Approximate Grade Levels: 5, 6, 7, 8, 9 **EL, JH**
Cost: $180
Type of Program: Simulation
System(s) on Which It Will Run: Apple II family; TRS-80 Models III and 4
Description: Students are members of a society searching for a new homeland after theirs has been ruined by drought. By reading information and then recording and interpreting data, they are able to make decisions to benefit their community and find a hospitable place to live.

Congress

Source(s): Scholastic
Course(s) for Which Appropriate: U.S. history, government
Approximate Grade Levels: 7, 8, 9, 10, 11, 12 **JH, HS**
Cost: $60
Type of Program: Database
System(s) on Which It Will Run: Apple II family and a copy of AppleWorks
Description: Consists of databases and lesson plans to involve students in learning how federal legislative decisions are made. Students examine the roles of committees, voting patterns, and the influence of key lobbyists. Students develop position papers and learn how to influence Congress on issues of concern.

Congressional Bill Simulator

Source(s): Focus Media
Course(s) for Which Appropriate: Government
Approximate Grade Levels: 8, 9, 10, 11, 12 **JH, HS**
Cost: $55
Type of Program: Simulation
System(s) on Which It Will Run: Apple II family
Description: Students write a bill, determine to which committees it should be assigned, and make
   a number of important decisions. After intense lobbying students watch to see if the bill is
   passed by committees and by both houses of Congress.

Constitutional Amendments

Source(s): Queue
Course(s) for Which Appropriate: Government, U.S. history
Approximate Grade Levels: 8, 9, 10, 11, 12 **JH, HS**
Cost: $50
Type of Program: Tutorial
System(s) on Which It Will Run: Apple II family; IBM PC
Description: Attempts to develop comprehension and mastery of the amendments to the Constitu-
   tion. Graphics, problem-solving situations, and interactive exercises are used to meet this goal.

Constitutional Law

Source(s): Intellectual Software
Course(s) for Which Appropriate: Government, U.S. history
Approximate Grade Levels: 10, 11, 12 **HS**
Cost: $45
Type of Program: Tutorial
System(s) on Which It Will Run: Apple II family
Description: Basic principles of constitutional law are covered in these interactive disks.

Constitution and the Government of the U.S.

Source(s): Educational Activities
Course(s) for Which Appropriate: Government, U.S. history
Approximate Grade Levels: 7, 8, 9, 10, 11, 12 **JH, HS**
Cost: $179
Type of Program: Tutorial
System(s) on Which It Will Run: Apple II family
Description: Case studies help students explore issues related to the Constitution and the Bill of
   Rights. A management system, eight text booklets, backup disks, and documentation are
   included.

Constitution of the United States

Source(s): Learning Arts
Course(s) for Which Appropriate: U.S. history, government
Approximate Grade Levels: 7, 8, 9, 10, 11, 12 **JH, HS**
Cost: $255
Type of Program: Tutorial
System(s) on Which It Will Run: Apple II family
Description: Students are presented the historical background in addition to each article and
   amendment. They read each part and then receive an explanation followed by comprehen-
   sion questions. Five disks are included.

Consumers and the Law

Source(s): Educational Activities
Course(s) for Which Appropriate: Economics, government
Approximate Grade Levels: 7, 8, 9, 10, 11, 12 **JH, HS**
Cost: $179
Type of Program: Tutorial
System(s) on Which It Will Run: Apple II family
Description: Rights and problems of consumers, sales contracts, legal protections, warranty protections, consumer decision making are covered in this program. Included are three disks with backups, a management system, documentation, and eight text booklets. Case studies test thinking skills.

Continents and Countries

Source(s): Mindscape
Course(s) for Which Appropriate: Geography
Approximate Grade Levels: 5, 6, 7, 8, 9, 10, 11, 12 **EL, JH, HS**
Cost: $50
Type of Program: Database
System(s) on Which It Will Run: Apple II family
Description: Four activities help students use a database to answer questions regarding size, population, location, income, language, government, and religions of various countries.

Contracts Law

Source(s): Queue
Course(s) for Which Appropriate: Government
Approximate Grade Levels: 9, 10, 11, 12+ **HS, CO**
Cost: $45/$65
Type of Program: Tutorial
System(s) on Which It Will Run: Apple II family
Description: A tutorial on contracts law for high school or college. The higher price includes a student management program that records data on individual student performance. This program consists of two disks.

Creating the U.S. Constitution

Source(s): Educational Activities
Course(s) for Which Appropriate: U.S. history, government
Approximate Grade Levels: 7, 8, 9, 10, 11, 12 **JH, HS**
Cost: $60
Type of Program: Simulation
System(s) on Which It Will Run: Apple II family
Description: The student becomes a participant at the Constitutional Convention and must choose between being middle or upper class and from a small, middle, or large state. Based on these choices, the student is assigned a character. Decisions are then required, based on the character.

Credit and Banking

Source(s): Queue
Course(s) for Which Appropriate: Economics
Approximate Grade Levels: 9, 10, 11, 12 **HS**
Cost: $110
Type of Program: Tutorial
System(s) on Which It Will Run: Apple II family
Description: Demonstrates how a large economy systematizes the use of money through the many forms of money and banking as the means of storing, transferring, and lending it. A case study also illustrates how compound interest can increase the value of a savings account.

Credit: The First Steps

Source(s): MCE
Course(s) for Which Appropriate: Economics
Approximate Grade Levels: 9, 10, 11, 12 **HS**
Cost: $60
Type of Program: Tutorial
System(s) on Which It Will Run: Apple II family
Description: Covers issues involved with using credit: advantages, responsibilities, and dangers. Students are also guided through the process of filling out a loan application. A backup disk and an instructional guide are included.

Criminal Law

Source(s): Intellectual Software, Queue
Course(s) for Which Appropriate: Government
Approximate Grade Levels: 10, 11, 12 **HS**
Cost: $45
Type of Program: Tutorial
System(s) on Which It Will Run: Apple II family
Description: Principles of criminal justice are taught in this interactive tutorial program.

Criminal Procedure

Source(s): Intellectual Software, Queue
Course(s) for Which Appropriate: Government
Approximate Grade Levels: 9, 10, 11, 12 **HS**
Cost: $35
Type of Program: Tutorial
System(s) on Which It Will Run: Apple II family
Description: An interactive program to teach students about basic rights of the accused, bail, legal aid, plea bargaining, trial procedures, and parole.

Crosscountry California

Source(s): Didatech Software
Course(s) for Which Appropriate: Geography, elementary social studies
Approximate Grade Levels: 5, 6, 7, 8, 9 **EL, JH**
Cost: $50
Type of Program: Simulation
System(s) on Which It Will Run: Apple II family
Description: The program simulates truck transportation of commodities to 150 cities in California. It teaches geography, map reading, problem solving, major resources, and distances. The program includes excellent graphics, a wall map, cross reference cards, route maps, and a backup disk.

Crosscountry Canada

Source(s): Didatech Software
Course(s) for Which Appropriate: Geography, elementary social studies
Approximate Grade Levels: 5, 6, 7, 8, 9 **EL, JH**
Cost: $55
Type of Program: Simulation
System(s) on Which It Will Run: Apple II family
Description: The program simulates truck transportation of commodities to eighty cities. It teaches map reading, geography, problem solving, major resources, and distances. It includes excellent graphics, a wall map, cross-reference cards, route-planning maps, and a backup disk.

Crosscountry Texas

Source(s): Didatech Software
Course(s) for Which Appropriate: Geography, elementary social studies
Approximate Grade Levels: 5, 6, 7, 8, 9 **EL, JH**
Cost: $50
Type of Program: Simulation
System(s) on Which It Will Run: Apple II family
Description: The program simulates truck transportation of commodities between 135 cities in Texas. It teaches geography, map reading, problem solving, major resources, and distances. It includes excellent graphics, a wall map, cross-reference cards, route-planning maps, and a backup disk.

Crosscountry USA

Source(s): Didatech Software
Course(s) for Which Appropriate: Geography, elementary social studies
Approximate Grade Levels: 5, 6, 7, 8, 9 **EL, JH**
Cost: $50
Type of Program: Simulation
System(s) on Which It Will Run: Apple II family
Description: The program simulates truck travel between 180 major cities. It teaches map reading, problem solving, geography, major resources, and distances. It includes excellent graphics, a large wall map, cross-reference cards, and route-planning maps. A backup disk is included.

Day to Find Out

Source(s): Orange Cherry Media
Course(s) for Which Appropriate: U.S. history
Approximate Grade Levels: 7, 8, 9 **JH**
Cost: $67
Type of Program: Simulation
System(s) on Which It Will Run: TRS-80 Models III and 4; Apple II family
Description: Four simulations allow the student to try being president of the United States, an air traffic controller, a nuclear plant manager, and a submarine commander. A teacher's guide is included.

Decades Game 1, 2, and 3

Source(s): Queue
Course(s) for Which Appropriate: U.S. history
Approximate Grade Levels: 7, 8, 9, 10, 11, 12 **JH, HS**
Cost: $60 each
Type of Program: Game
System(s) on Which It Will Run: Apple II family
Description: One to four players determine the dates of events in U.S. politics, economics, technology, science, art, and literature.

Decisions

Source(s): EMC Publishing
Course(s) for Which Appropriate: Economics, consumer economics
Approximate Grade Levels: 9, 10, 11, 12 **HS**
Cost: $35 each, $295 set
Type of Program: Game, tutorial, simulation
System(s) on Which It Will Run: Apple II family
Description: Ten diskettes help students learn to make responsible economic decisions. Textbooks, workbooks, and teacher's manual included. Topics include making decisions, supply and demand, you and your paycheck, how to use your resources, and consumer rights and responsibilities.

Decisions, Decisions: The Budget Process

Source(s): Tom Snyder Productions
Course(s) for Which Appropriate: U.S. history, economics
Approximate Grade Levels: 8, 9, 10, 11, 12 **JH, HS**
Cost: $90
Type of Program: Simulation
System(s) on Which It Will Run: Apple II family; IBM PC; Tandy 1000
Description: Students simulate being the House of Representatives and must vote on a contro-
versial spending bill. Throughout the process students learn about the workings of Congress
and the federal budgeting process. A backup disk and extensive resources are provided.

Decisions, Decisions: Colonization

Source(s): Tom Snyder Productions
Course(s) for Which Appropriate: U.S. history
Approximate Grade Levels: 5, 6, 7, 8, 9, 10, 11, 12 **EL, JH, HS**
Cost: $90
Type of Program: Simulation
System(s) on Which It Will Run: Apple II family; IBM PC; Tandy 1000
Description: The goal of this program is to generate informed discussions about colonization
issues. It is the future. Students simulate being the president confronted with decisions about
colonizing outer space. Historical cases are used as background. The Decisions, Decisions
series was a winner of a 1988 *Classroom Computer Learning* software award.

Decisions, Decisions: Foreign Policy

Source(s): Tom Snyder Productions
Course(s) for Which Appropriate: U.S. history, world history
Approximate Grade Levels: 8, 9, 10, 11, 12 **JH, HS**
Cost: $90
Type of Program: Simulation
System(s) on Which It Will Run: Apple II family; IBM PC; Tandy 1000
Description: Students simulate being the leaders of a superpower. An important ally seeks help in
controlling a popular rebellion. Should they become involved in the internal affairs of
another country? Historical references provide background. Backup disk and supplementary
materials provided.

Decisions, Decisions: Immigration

Source(s): Tom Snyder Productions
Course(s) for Which Appropriate: U.S. history, sociology, government
Approximate Grade Levels: 5, 6, 7, 8, 9, 10, 11, 12 **EL, JH, HS**
Cost: $90
Type of Program: Simulation
System(s) on Which It Will Run: Apple II family; IBM PC; Tandy 1000
Description: Students simulate being the president and decide whether to allow thousands of
unwanted refugees to enter the country. Historical examples provide background. Backup
disk, teacher's materials, worksheets, and student reference books are included.

Decisions, Decisions: On the Campaign Trail

Source(s): Tom Snyder Productions
Course(s) for Which Appropriate: U.S. history, government
Approximate Grade Levels: 7, 8, 9, 10, 11, 12 **JH, HS**
Cost: $120
Type of Program: Simulation
System(s) on Which It Will Run: Apple II family; IBM PC; Tandy 1000
Description: Students assume the role of a third-party candidate for president. Running behind in the polls, they begin a final cross-country campaign tour. Students address various issues as they finalize their campaign platform.

Decisions, Decisions: Revolutionary Wars

Source(s): Tom Snyder Productions
Course(s) for Which Appropriate: U.S. history
Approximate Grade Levels: 5, 6, 7, 8, 9, 10, 11, 12 **EL, JH, HS**
Cost: $90
Type of Program: Simulation
System(s) on Which It Will Run: Apple II family; IBM PC; Tandy 1000
Description: The program uses a powerful "You Are There" format to generate informed discussions about issues involved in revolutionary wars. Students play the governor of a province experiencing a revolutionary movement. How will they control the situation? Historical cases serve as background.

Decisions, Decisions: Television

Source(s): Tom Snyder Productions
Course(s) for Which Appropriate: Social studies
Approximate Grade Levels: 5, 6, 7, 8, 9, 10, 11, 12 **EL, JH, HS**
Cost: $90
Type of Program: Simulation
System(s) on Which It Will Run: Apple II family; IBM PC; Tandy 1000
Description: The goal of this program is to generate informed discussions among students of the role of TV in American life and about media ethics. Students simulate being TV executives. A special they are planning is objected to by the sponsor. Should they broadcast it or change it?

Decisions, Decisions: Urbanization

Source(s): Tom Snyder Productions
Course(s) for Which Appropriate: U.S. history, world history, sociology
Approximate Grade Levels: 5, 6, 7, 8, 9, 10, 11, 12 **EL, JH, HS**
Cost: $90
Type of Program: Simulation
System(s) on Which It Will Run: Apple II family; IBM PC; Tandy 1000
Description: Students assume the role of mayor of a small town in which a valuable resource is discovered. Should they allow the town to grow? Should limits be set? Historical examples presenting conflicting views are used as background. Includes backup, teacher's guide, and worksheets.

Democomp

Source(s): Focus Media
Course(s) for Which Appropriate: U.S. history
Approximate Grade Levels: 6, 7, 8, 9, 10, 11, 12 **EL, JH, HS**
Cost: $49 each (backup included)
Type of Program: Maps
System(s) on Which It Will Run: Apple II family (all programs); Commodore 64 (programs 1 and 3)
Description: Programs contain maps of each era: Explorers of North America, Ownership of North America, The Thirteen Colonies, Territorial Expansion 1776-1959, America Moves West, and European Immigration.

Democracy

Source(s): Right On Programs
Course(s) for Which Appropriate: Elementary social studies
Approximate Grade Levels: 5, 6, 7 **EL, JH**
Cost: $25
Type of Program: Tutorial
System(s) on Which It Will Run: Apple II family; Commodore 64
Description: Explains private and public governments with an emphasis on democracy. Contrasts communist and democratic forms of government and discusses the Constitution and the Bill of Rights. Reproducible worksheets and a teacher's manual are included.

Demo-graphics: Populations and Projections

Source(s): COMpress, Conduit
Course(s) for Which Appropriate: Government, geography, sociology
Approximate Grade Levels: 9, 10, 11, 12 **HS**
Cost: $95
Type of Program: Database, simulation
System(s) on Which It Will Run: Apple II family
Description: Contains a database and statistical formulae to provide data and make projections for 147 countries. It can be updated as new information or conditions change. Projections can be made on real or simulated data. Space exists for adding up to ten additional countries.

Diffusion Game

Source(s): Conduit
Course(s) for Which Appropriate: Economics, sociology, U.S. history
Approximate Grade Levels: 10, 11, 12 **HS**
Cost: $55
Type of Program: Simulation
System(s) on Which It Will Run: Apple II family
Description: Students take on the role of change agents in this program about the diffusion of innovations. The students are to convince rural people to accept an innovation.

Dinosaur Days

Source(s): Teach Yourself by Computer Software
Course(s) for Which Appropriate: Elementary social studies
Approximate Grade Levels: 2, 3, 4, 5 **EL**
Cost: $40
Type of Program: Tutorial
System(s) on Which It Will Run: Apple II family
Description: A two-disk program full of information about dinosaurs, their environment, classifications, extinction theories, and fossils. Tests, review options, alternative text, and worksheets are included.

Dinosaur Dig

Source(s): Mindscape
Course(s) for Which Appropriate: Elementary social studies
Approximate Grade Levels: 3, 4, 5, 6 **EL**
Cost: $50
Type of Program: Tutorial
System(s) on Which It Will Run: Apple II family; IBM PC
Description: Students learn about the dinosaur's size, strength, and causes for disappearance.

Direction and Distance

Source(s): MicroEd
Course(s) for Which Appropriate: Elementary social studies
Approximate Grade Levels: 1, 2, 3, 4 **EL**
Cost: $30
Type of Program: Tutorial
System(s) on Which It Will Run: Commodore 64
Description: Teaches students the cardinal and intermediate directions.

Discover the World

Source(s): Hartley
Course(s) for Which Appropriate: U.S. history
Approximate Grade Levels: 5, 6, 7, 8, 9, 10 **EL, JH, HS**
Cost: $80
Type of Program: Simulation
System(s) on Which It Will Run: Apple II family (64K); IBM PC (256K)
Description: Student sails from one of five ports to find a route to the Orient. A variety of feedback about winds and dangers is provided as the student chooses the direction and makes other decisions. Classroom Computer Learning Software Award of Excellence 1987.

Disraeli and the Eastern Question

Source(s): Queue
Course(s) for Which Appropriate: World history
Approximate Grade Levels: 9, 10, 11, 12 **HS**
Cost: $60
Type of Program: Simulation
System(s) on Which It Will Run: Apple II family
Description: Students explore British foreign policy toward the Ottoman Empire as they decide how Disraeli should or might have acted during each stage of the Balkan Crisis. Rewards are based on how close their choice was to that of Disraeli.

Dr. Know's Geography

Source(s): MicroEd
Course(s) for Which Appropriate: Elementary social studies, geography
Approximate Grade Levels: 5, 6, 7, 8 **EL, JH**
Cost: $50
Type of Program: Drill and practice
System(s) on Which It Will Run: Commodore 64
Description: Helps students identify capitals of countries for any given continent.

Early Humans

Source(s): Right On Programs
Course(s) for Which Appropriate: World history
Approximate Grade Levels: 6, 7, 8 **JH**
Cost: $25
Type of Program: Tutorial
System(s) on Which It Will Run: Apple II family; Commodore 64
Description: The food, clothes, tools, and travel of prehistoric people are covered, including a
    game. Reproducible worksheets and a teacher's guide are included.

Eastern Europe

Source(s): MicroEd
Course(s) for Which Appropriate: Geography, world history
Approximate Grade Levels: 5, 6, 7, 8, 9, 10, 11 **EL, JH, HS**
Cost: $30
Type of Program: Drill and practice
System(s) on Which It Will Run: Commodore 64
Description: Teaches students to identify the countries of Eastern Europe by their placement on
    the map.

Easy Search

Source(s): Focus Media
Course(s) for Which Appropriate: Geography
Approximate Grade Levels: 5, 6, 7, 8, 9, 10 **EL, JH, HS**
Cost: $49
Type of Program: Database
System(s) on Which It Will Run: Apple II family
Description: Easy-to-use database program incorporated into a simulation that involves bringing
    together countries with parallel or complementary needs. Helps students develop research
    skills, compare information, and analyze statistics. Additional student workbooks available.

Easy Search: American Studies

Source(s): Focus Media
Course(s) for Which Appropriate: U.S. history, geography
Approximate Grade Levels: 6, 7, 8, 9, 10, 11, 12 **EL, JH, HS**
Cost: $49
Type of Program: Database, simulation
System(s) on Which It Will Run: Apple II family
Description: Contains two programs: The 50 States and American Inventions. Each contains a
    large database and utilizes a role-play simulation as a vehicle to get students to analyze
    information in the database. For example, students operate a relocation service to seek
    particular environments.

Economics Keyword

Source(s): Focus Media
Course(s) for Which Appropriate: Economics
Approximate Grade Levels: 9, 10, 11, 12 **HS**
Cost: $55
Type of Program: Drill and practice
System(s) on Which It Will Run: Apple II family
Description: Students attempt to identify a vocabulary term from synonyms, examples, and
    definitions. A wide range of economic terms is included.

Economics: What, How & For Whom?

Source(s): Focus Media
Course(s) for Which Appropriate: Economics
Approximate Grade Levels: 10, 11, 12 **HS**
Cost: $169 (backup included)
Type of Program: Tutorial
System(s) on Which It Will Run: Apple II family; TRS-80 Models III and 4
Description: Five programs on five disks: What Is Economics?; Economics: Definitions and Laws; Economic Systems: Traditional, Command, and Market; Capitalism, Communism, and Socialism; and Teacher's Classroom Demonstrations. Ideas for in-class or homework activities to interface with these lessons are given.

Editorial Forum Series (five individual titles)

Source(s): MicroEd
Course(s) for Which Appropriate: U.S. history, problems of democracy
Approximate Grade Levels: 9, 10, 11, 12 + **HS, CO**
Cost: $30 each
Type of Program: Tutorial, problem solving
System(s) on Which It Will Run: Commodore 64; Apple IIe
Description: Each program combines a computer program and a newspaper tabloid that present a wide range of current views on the topic. Issues include: Homeless People, License to Kill, Toxic Chemical Wastes, Weapons in America, and Powderkeg Prisons.

Elements of Economics

Source(s): Queue
Course(s) for Which Appropriate: Economics
Approximate Grade Levels: 9, 10, 11, 12 **HS**
Cost: $110
Type of Program: Tutorial
System(s) on Which It Will Run: Apple II family
Description: This two-disk program covers the following concepts: rationale for developing an economic system, supply and demand, efficiency in production and consumption, trade, specialization, division of labor, trade, and equilibrium price. A case study relating to tickets for a rock concert is used.

Eurographics

Source(s): Sunshine Computer Software Company
Course(s) for Which Appropriate: Geography, world history
Approximate Grade Levels: 7, 8, 9, 10, 11, 12 **JH, HS**
Cost: $29
Type of Program: Drill and practice
System(s) on Which It Will Run: IBM PC; IBM compatibles
Description: A map of Europe is created on the color graphics display. The student uses the cursor control keys to select a country. The student is asked to name the country, its capital, and the largest city. Help is provided if needed.

European Nations and Locations

Source(s): Edu-Tron
Course(s) for Which Appropriate: Elementary social studies, world history
Approximate Grade Levels: 4, 5, 6, 7, 8 **EL, JH**
Cost: $45
Type of Program: Drill and practice, game
System(s) on Which It Will Run: Apple II family; Commodore 64; IBM PC
Description: Facts and trivia about European countries and their locations.

European States and Traits

Source(s): Britannica Software
Course(s) for Which Appropriate: World history, geography
Approximate Grade Levels: 9, 10, 11, 12 **HS**
Cost: $30/$40
Type of Program: Drill and practice
System(s) on Which It Will Run: Apple II family; IBM PC; Commodore 64
Description: Students move outlines of countries to their correct location on the map. Then they answer questions about landmarks, capitals, neighboring countries, historical events, and current events. The lower price is for the Commodore 64 version.

Evaluating Presidential Leadership

Source(s): Focus Media
Course(s) for Which Appropriate: U.S. history, government
Approximate Grade Levels: 9, 10, 11, 12 **HS**
Cost: $49 (backup included)
Type of Program: Data analysis
System(s) on Which It Will Run: Apple II family
Description: Students conduct research and input the data into the computer. The data is analyzed and the results presented on the screen; results can be printed out.

Evidence

Source(s): Queue
Course(s) for Which Appropriate: Government
Approximate Grade Levels: 9, 10, 11, 12+ **HS, CO**
Cost: $45/$65
Type of Program: Tutorial
System(s) on Which It Will Run: Apple II family
Description: A two-disk tutorial covering the concept of evidence for high school and college. The higher-priced program includes a student management system that records data regarding individual student performance.

Expedition to Saggara

Source(s): Intellectual Software, Queue
Course(s) for Which Appropriate: World history, sociology
Approximate Grade Levels: 6, 7, 8, 9, 10 **EL, JH, HS**
Cost: $60
Type of Program: Simulation
System(s) on Which It Will Run: Apple II family
Description: A simulation based on a real archaeological site in Egypt. Students must obtain grants and permission to excavate, manage finances, map out the site, record the details of the excavation, and speculate on the meanings of the "finds."

Exploration to the Jeffersonian Era

Source(s): Queue
Course(s) for Which Appropriate: U.S. history
Approximate Grade Levels: 7, 8, 9, 10, 11, 12 **JH, HS**
Cost: $35
Type of Program: Tutorial
System(s) on Which It Will Run: Apple II family; Commodore 64; IBM PC
Description: Gives explanations for every answer and provides help screens and practice for important concepts. A test mode gives explanations for incorrect answers as well. Student and teacher materials included.

Explorers and Settlers

Source(s): Computer Island
Course(s) for Which Appropriate: U.S. history
Approximate Grade Levels: 6, 7, 8 **EL, JH**
Cost: $20 (tape), $25 (disk)
Type of Program: Drill and practice
System(s) on Which It Will Run: TRS-80 Color Computer with at least 32K
Description: Multiple-choice quiz on explorers and settlers of the new world.

Factory

Source(s): Sunburst
Course(s) for Which Appropriate: Economics, social studies
Approximate Grade Levels: 4, 5, 6, 7, 8, 9 **EL, JH**
Cost: $65
Type of Program: Problem solving
System(s) on Which It Will Run: Apple II family; Acorn; TRS-80 Models III and 4 and Color
    Computer; IBM PC
Description: Students are challenged to create geometric "products" on a simulated assembly line
    that they design. This program develops visual discrimination, spatial perception, under-
    standing of sequence, and logic.

Facts and Opinions

Source(s): MicroEd
Course(s) for Which Appropriate: Elementary social studies
Approximate Grade Levels: 3, 4, 5, 6 **EL**
Cost: $30
Type of Program: Tutorial
System(s) on Which It Will Run: Commodore 64
Description: The program is designed to help students distinguish between fact and opinion.

Famous Blacks in U.S. History

Source(s): Frontier Software
Course(s) for Which Appropriate: U.S. history
Approximate Grade Levels: 4, 5, 6, 7, 8 **EL, JH**
Cost: $40
Type of Program: Tutorial
System(s) on Which It Will Run: Apple II family
Description: Presents information about many of the great Blacks who have made major contri-
    butions to the United States and its history.

Famous American Women

Source(s): Computer Island
Course(s) for Which Appropriate: U.S. history
Approximate Grade Levels: 6, 7, 8 **EL, JH**
Cost: $25
Type of Program: Drill and practice, game
System(s) on Which It Will Run: TRS-80 Color Computer with at least 32K
Description: A who-am-I game based on a multiple-choice quiz with fifty questions.

Famous Women in U.S. History

Source(s): Frontier Software
Course(s) for Which Appropriate: U.S. history
Approximate Grade Levels: 4, 5, 6, 7, 8 **EL, JH**
Cost: $40
Type of Program: Tutorial
System(s) on Which It Will Run: Apple II family
Description: Presents information about women who have made major contributions to the United States and its history.

Farm Life

Source(s): Right On Programs
Course(s) for Which Appropriate: Elementary social studies
Approximate Grade Levels: 1, 2 **EL**
Cost: $25
Type of Program: Tutorial
System(s) on Which It Will Run: Apple II family; Commodore 64
Description: Introduces students to basic concepts of farms, farm animals, and products raised on farms. A teacher's guide and reproducible worksheets are included.

Financial Cookbook and Consumer's Guide

Source(s): South-Western Publishing
Course(s) for Which Appropriate: Consumer economics
Approximate Grade Levels: 9, 10, 11, 12 **HS**
Cost: $43
Type of Program: Problem solving
System(s) on Which It Will Run: Apple II family; IBM PC; Tandy 1000; Compaq
Description: The disk contains menu-driven programs for thirty-two "recipes" for solving financial problems. A manual is provided and the Consumer's Guide gives step-by-step instruction with sample problems and sample screens. Student workbooks cost $5.25 each and can be used for group or individual instruction.

French Revolution

Source(s): Frontier Software
Course(s) for Which Appropriate: World history
Approximate Grade Levels: 6, 7, 8, 9, 10 **EL, JH, HS**
Cost: $40
Type of Program: Tutorial
System(s) on Which It Will Run: Apple II family
Description: Presents causes, events, battles, and people of the French Revolutionary period.

Game of Presidents

Source(s): Intellectual Software
Course(s) for Which Appropriate: U.S. history
Approximate Grade Levels: 7, 8, 9, 10, 11, 12 **JH, HS**
Cost: $35
Type of Program: Game
System(s) on Which It Will Run: Apple II family
Description: The tables are turned. Students teach the computer about U.S. presidents by telling the computer what questions to ask to determine the identity of a randomly selected president. Students create their own questions and the teacher may review their files to find any misconceptions.

Game Show

Source(s): Advanced Ideas
Course(s) for Which Appropriate: Elementary social studies
Approximate Grade Levels: 3, 4, 5, 6 **EL**
Cost: $40 + +
Type of Program: Drill and practice
System(s) on Which It Will Run: Apple II family; IBM PC; Commodore 64
Description: A TV quiz show, complete with flashing lights and a cheering audience, provides the format for drill over information and vocabulary. An authoring system lets the teacher modify the program. Question disks are available in social studies for each grade 3-6 at $20 each/$50 for the set.

Geographics

Source(s): Sunshine Computer Software
Course(s) for Which Appropriate: Geography
Approximate Grade Levels: 7, 8, 9, 10, 11, 12 **JH, HS**
Cost: $29
Type of Program: Drill and practice
System(s) on Which It Will Run: IBM PC
Description: A map of the United States is presented in color graphics. The student uses the cursor control key to select a state. The student is asked to name the state, the capital, and the largest city. If needed, assistance is provided by typing "help."

Geography Keyword

Source(s): Focus Media
Course(s) for Which Appropriate: Geography
Approximate Grade Levels: 7, 8, 9, 10, 11, 12 **JH, HS**
Cost: $55
Type of Program: Game, drill and practice
System(s) on Which It Will Run: Apple II family
Description: Students attempt to uncover the mystery word through clues such as synonyms, examples, definitions, and places. In this way they learn new facts and terms related to land forms, bodies of water, maps, cities, countries, and climates.

Geography Games

Source(s): Intellectual Software
Course(s) for Which Appropriate: Geography
Approximate Grade Levels: 5, 6, 7, 8, 9 **EL, JH**
Cost: $40/$50
Type of Program: Game
System(s) on Which It Will Run: Apple II family
Description: Seven competitive games for two players. Tests ability to identify states when given a feature and to learn to spell names of states, cities, and geographic features. The higher price includes a utility disk that allows the teacher to add new lists of features.

Geography Quiz Series

Source(s): Learning Arts
Course(s) for Which Appropriate: Geography
Approximate Grade Levels: 7, 8, 9, 10, 11, 12 **JH, HS**
Cost: $63
Type of Program: Drill and practice
System(s) on Which It Will Run: Apple II family
Description: Three programs on three disks: Basics, Regions I (U.S., Canada, national parks, Middle East), Regions II (New Zealand, Australia, Africa, Asia, Europe). Review questions are presented in a variety of formats.

Geography Search

Source(s): McGraw-Hill Software
Course(s) for Which Appropriate: Geography, U.S. history
Approximate Grade Levels: 5, 6, 7, 8, 9 **EL, JH**
Cost: $180
Type of Program: Simulation
System(s) on Which It Will Run: Apple II family; TRS-80 Models III and 4
Description: Students are involved in a simulation related to sailing to the New World. Using the workbooks provided, students study the facts and make decisions. The program helps them navigate using the sun, stars, and trade winds. A teacher's manual is also included.

Geo World

Source(s): Tom Snyder Productions
Course(s) for Which Appropriate: Geography
Approximate Grade Levels: 5, 6, 7, 8, 9, 10, 11, 12 **EL, JH, HS**
Cost: $80
Type of Program: Database
System(s) on Which It Will Run: Apple II family
Description: Provides a powerful database of fifteen mineral resources and their location around the world. Interpretation of maps, charts, and cross-sectional diagrams is developed.

Globe Master II

Source(s): Learning Arts
Course(s) for Which Appropriate: Geography
Approximate Grade Levels: 5, 6, 7, 8, 9, 10, 11, 12 **EL, JH, HS**
Cost: $40
Type of Program: Drill and practice
System(s) on Which It Will Run: Apple II family
Description: With high-resolution color maps of various continents, students are asked questions about states, capitals, countries, and landmarks.

The Golden Spike: Building America's First Transcontinental Railroad

Source(s): National Geographic Society
Course(s) for Which Appropriate: U.S. history and geography
Approximate Grade Levels: 5, 6, 7, 8, 9 **EL, JH**
Cost: $109.50
Type of Program: Multimedia simulation
System(s) on Which It Will Run: Apple family 128K
Description: This program has print material, a filmstrip, and simulation which teaches creative problem solving, creative thinking, and decision making in small-group setting.

Government and the Market

Source(s): Queue
Course(s) for Which Appropriate: Economics, government
Approximate Grade Levels: 9, 10, 11, 12 **HS**
Cost: $110
Type of Program: Tutorial
System(s) on Which It Will Run: Apple II family
Description: This two-disk program considers the five kinds of market failure and how the power of government to spend, tax, and regulate operates when this happens. The effects of spending, taxing, and regulation are considered, as well as beneficial monopolies.

Government Keyword Series

Source(s): Focus Media
Course(s) for Which Appropriate: Government, U.S. history
Approximate Grade Levels: 7, 8, 9, 10, 11, 12 **JH, HS**
Cost: $89
Type of Program: Game, drill and practice
System(s) on Which It Will Run: Apple II family
Description: This game involves the student in determining the hidden words through clues such as synonyms, examples, definitions, and historical references. With each clue students learn to associate new facts with the terms. Useful for review of terms and concepts.

The Grand Tour of Western Europe

Source(s): Orange Cherry Media
Course(s) for Which Appropriate: World history, geography
Approximate Grade Levels: 7, 8, 9, 10, 11 **JH, HS**
Cost: $78
Type of Program: Tutorial
System(s) on Which It Will Run: Apple II family; Commodore 64; TRS-80 Models III and 4; IBM PC
Description: By running this program, a student uses the computer as a personal guide to each country of Western Europe. The student learns the geography, history, and the culture of the countries.

Great American History Knowledge Race

Source(s): Focus Media
Course(s) for Which Appropriate: U.S. history
Approximate Grade Levels: 9, 10, 11, 12 **HS**
Cost: $85
Type of Program: Drill and practice, game
System(s) on Which It Will Run: Apple II family; IBM PC; Tandy 1000; Commodore 64
Description: Using a game board on the screen student rolls computer dice to move on the board. Questions must be answered correctly in order to capture a space. Two programs with four categories each cover the entire range of U.S. history.

Great Depression

Source(s): Frontier Software
Course(s) for Which Appropriate: U.S. history
Approximate Grade Levels: 6, 7, 8 **EL, JH**
Cost: $40
Type of Program: Tutorial
System(s) on Which It Will Run: Apple II family
Description: Presents information about causes and events related to the Depression, including the stock market crash and Roosevelt's major recovery programs.

Great Knowledge Race: U.S. History Series

Source(s): Focus Media
Course(s) for Which Appropriate: U.S. history
Approximate Grade Levels: 7, 8, 9, 10, 11, 12 **JH, HS**
Cost: $45 each
Type of Program: Drill and practice, game
System(s) on Which It Will Run: Apply II family
Description: There are four series, each sold separately: exploration through colonization, revolution and union, Washington's administration through nationalism, and the Monroe Doctrine through the age of reform. Students choose a topic and are given questions. Good for competition.

Great States Race

Source(s): Milliken
Course(s) for Which Appropriate: Geography, elementary social studies
Approximate Grade Levels: 4, 5, 6 **EL**
Cost: $35
Type of Program: Drill and practice, game
System(s) on Which It Will Run: Apple II family
Description: Players race across the U.S. in hot air balloons. In order to fly over a state the player must correctly answer a question about that state. Questions include cities, capitals, rivers, famous people, historical events, and points of interest.

Great World History Knowledge Race

Source(s): Focus Media
Course(s) for Which Appropriate: World history
Approximate Grade Levels: 7, 8, 9, 10, 11, 12 **JH, HS**
Cost: $85 (backup included)
Type of Program: Drill and practice, game
System(s) on Which It Will Run: Apple II family; IBM PC; Tandy 1000; Commodore 64
Description: Contains two programs with four categories each. The first covers ancient peoples through the medieval world and the second covers the Renaissance through the twentieth century. A computerized game board and dice are used and questions given for each category.

Greek Mythology

Source(s): Teach Yourself by Computer Software
Course(s) for Which Appropriate: World history
Approximate Grade Levels: 7, 8, 9, 10, 11, 12 **JH, HS**
Cost: $40
Type of Program: Tutorial
System(s) on Which It Will Run: Apple II family
Description: This tutorial presents the most commonly told legends about the gods of Mt. Olympus and looks at the influence of Greek mythology on art and literature. Graphics supplement the text. There are also graded tests, review questions, and alternate text. A manual is included.

Growth of the United States

Source(s): Right On Programs
Course(s) for Which Appropriate: U.S. history
Approximate Grade Levels: 4, 5, 6 **EL**
Cost: $25
Type of Program: Tutorial
System(s) on Which It Will Run: Apple II family; Commodore 64
Description: Explains reasons for and causes of the growth of the United States into an industrial nation. A game is included. Reproducible worksheets and a teacher's manual are included.

Hail to the Chief

Source(s): K-12 MicroMedia
Course(s) for Which Appropriate: Government, U.S. history
Approximate Grade Levels: 7, 8, 9, 10, 11, 12 **JH, HS**
Cost: $30
Type of Program: Simulation
System(s) on Which It Will Run: Apple II family; Atari; TRS-80 Models III and 4
Description: Two players simulate a presidential campaign. Decisions must be made regarding style, media exposure, and whether to emphasize foreign or domestic issues. There are four levels of play.

Hat in the Ring

Source(s): MicroEd
Course(s) for Which Appropriate: Elementary social studies
Approximate Grade Levels: 5, 6, 7 **EL, JH**
Cost: $30
Type of Program: Tutorial
System(s) on Which It Will Run: Commodore 64
Description: Helps students learn about some of the factors that influence a presidential campaign.

Heart of Africa

Source(s): Edu-Tron
Course(s) for Which Appropriate: Geography
Approximate Grade Levels: 6, 7, 8, 9, 10, 11, 12 **EL, JH, HS**
Cost: $33
Type of Program: Simulation
System(s) on Which It Will Run: Commodore 64
Description: Students attempt to find the tomb of an ancient pharaoh by competing with adversaries to navigate seventeen rivers, sail to ten cities and learn the ways of twenty-two tribes. Many geographically accurate land forms are encountered.

Hill Railway

Source(s): Queue
Course(s) for Which Appropriate: Geography
Approximate Grade Levels: 8, 9, 10, 11, 12 **JH, HS**
Cost: $40
Type of Program: Simulation
System(s) on Which It Will Run: Apple II family
Description: Students learn the interrelationship between a landscape and the representation of its relief on a contour map by planning the building of a railway using a contour map and grid reference lines to plan the gradients of the line.

History and Geography

Source(s): Learning Arts
Course(s) for Which Appropriate: Geography, U.S. history
Approximate Grade Levels: 4, 5, 6, 7, 8, 9 **EL, JH**
Cost: $50 (backup included)
Type of Program: Drill and practice
System(s) on Which It Will Run: Apple II family
Description: Five drill and practice programs: Regions of the U.S.A., States and Capitals, Presidents, Country, and Revolutionary War Quiz.

The History Game

Source(s): Computer Island
Course(s) for Which Appropriate: U.S. history
Approximate Grade Levels: 5, 6, 7, 8 **EL, JH**
Cost: $15 (cassette), $20 (disk)
Type of Program: Drill and practice, game
System(s) on Which It Will Run: TRS-80 Color Computer with 32K
Description: A "Jeopardy"-style game to test students on twenty-five questions per game. Two hundred and fifty questions are possible and are randomly selected.

History of Asia and Africa Democomp

Source(s): Focus Media
Course(s) for Which Appropriate: Geography, world history
Approximate Grade Levels: 7, 8, 9, 10, 11, 12 **JH, HS**
Cost: $70
Type of Program: Tutorial, tool
System(s) on Which It Will Run: Apple II family
Description: Allows students to see political, social, and economic changes in Africa and Asia and
to create maps from different time periods in these continents. Includes an eighty-page student
workbook with a variety of activities and worksheets. Three disks and backups are included.

History of Europe Democomp

Source(s): Focus Media
Course(s) for Which Appropriate: Geography, world history
Approximate Grade Levels: 7, 8, 9, 10, 11, 12 **JH, HS**
Cost: $70
Type of Program: Tool
System(s) on Which It Will Run: Apple II family
Description: The three-program set allows the teacher or student to utilize colorful maps and
graphs that demonstrate the political and social changes in Europe. Programs include: The
Drive to Unify: Italy and Germany; World War I: Europe in Chaos; and The Soviet Union:
A Changing Nation.

History of Japan

Source(s): Intellectual Software
Course(s) for Which Appropriate: World history, comparative cultures
Approximate Grade Levels: 10, 11, 12 **HS**
Cost: $35
Type of Program: Tutorial
System(s) on Which It Will Run: Apple II family
Description: Covers the entire history of Japan in an interactive tutorial.

History of the U.S. Democomp Package

Source(s): Focus Media
Course(s) for Which Appropriate: U.S. history
Approximate Grade Levels: 5, 6, 7, 8, 9, 10, 11, 12 **EL, JH, HS**
Cost: $130
Type of Program: Tutorial
System(s) on Which It Will Run: Apple II family
Description: Using an eighty-page student workbook and extensive graphic displays this program
builds map, chart, and graph interpretation skills and critical thinking. Includes six programs
ranging from explorers, colonization, expansion, and immigration. Workbook and six disks
and backups are included.

History of Western Civilization

Source(s): COMpress
Course(s) for Which Appropriate: World history
Approximate Grade Levels: 9, 10, 11, 12 **HS**
Cost: $50 each, $500 set
Type of Program: Drill and practice
System(s) on Which It Will Run: IBM PC
Description: A series of twelve programs covering the entire span of Western civilization from
Ancient Greece to The Nuclear Age. Each reviews students on geography, chronology, and
identification of people and events. Teachers can add or delete material, and hints are
provided to students.

History Study Center

Source(s): Teach Yourself by Computer Software
Course(s) for Which Appropriate: U.S. history
Approximate Grade Levels: 6, 7, 8, 9, 10, 11, 12 **EL, JH, HS**
Cost: $40
Type of Program: Drill and practice, game
System(s) on Which It Will Run: Apple II family
Description: A variety of activities from games to multiple-choice tests let students review over 400 questions covering a variety of topics. A mini-authoring system allows teachers to add their own questions and answers.

Holidays and Festivals

Source(s): Right On Programs
Course(s) for Which Appropriate: Elementary social studies
Approximate Grade Levels: 2, 3 **EL**
Cost: $25
Type of Program: Tutorial
System(s) on Which It Will Run: Apple II family; Commodore 64
Description: Describes holidays celebrated in the U.S. and other countries. Vocabulary, games, customs, and gifts are included. Reproducible worksheets and a teacher's manual are a part of the program.

Hometown: A Local Area Study

Source(s): Active Learning Systems
Course(s) for Which Appropriate: Government, sociology
Approximate Grade Levels: 6, 7, 8, 9, 10, 11, 12 **EL, JH, HS**
Cost: $148
Type of Program: Database
System(s) on Which It Will Run: Apple II family; IBM PC
Description: An open database designed around a questionnaire that contains basic demographic questions. Nine open fields allow users to define questions of special interest. Students can then interview a sample of individuals, enter the data, and use the database to provide an analysis of the sample.

How a Bill Becomes a Law

Source(s): Intellectual Software
Course(s) for Which Appropriate: Government, U.S. history
Approximate Grade Levels: 7, 8, 9 **JH**
Cost: $60
Type of Program: Simulation
System(s) on Which It Will Run: IBM PC; Apple II family
Description: Covers a wide variety of topics, including lobbying, committees and subcommittees, quorums, parliamentary procedures, seniority, and vetos.

IFs: International Futures Simulation

Source(s): Conduit
Course(s) for Which Appropriate: Government, economics, sociology
Approximate Grade Levels: 11, 12+ **HS, CO**
Cost: $95
Type of Program: Simulation
System(s) on Which It Will Run: IBM PC
Description: This package introduces students to the key issues of global development, its data and trends, and the connections among issues and regions.

I Love America Series

Source(s): K-12 MicroMedia
Course(s) for Which Appropriate: Geography, U.S. history, elementary social studies
Approximate Grade Levels: 4, 5, 6, 7, 8 **EL, JH**
Cost: $70 (cassette), $85 (disk)
Type of Program: Game, tutorial, drill and practice
System(s) on Which It Will Run: Apple II family
Description: Four programs—two teach map skills and two are drill and practice programs for history facts and states and their capitals.

Incredible But True

Source(s): Orange Cherry Media
Course(s) for Which Appropriate: U.S. history, world history
Approximate Grade Levels: 7, 8, 9, 10, 11 **JH, HS**
Cost: $78
Type of Program: Tutorial
System(s) on Which It Will Run: Apple II family; Commodore 64; TRS-80 Models III and 4
Description: This high-interest series explores the amazing facts and events surrounding some of the most outstanding disasters in history.

Indians, Indians Computer Kit

Source(s): Orange Cherry Media
Course(s) for Which Appropriate: Elementary social studies
Approximate Grade Levels: 2, 3, 4, 5 **EL**
Cost: $39
Type of Program: Tutorial
System(s) on Which It Will Run: Apple II family; Commodore 64
Description: This kit illustrates the rich culture of the American Indian for elementary grades. Colorful computer graphics bring the history of the native American to life for students.

Indians of North America

Source(s): Frontier Software
Course(s) for Which Appropriate: U.S. history
Approximate Grade Levels: 3, 4, 5, 6 **EL**
Cost: $40
Type of Program: Tutorial
System(s) on Which It Will Run: Apple II family
Description: The program presents information on major North American Indian tribes and their groupings. Emphasis is placed on the culture, habits, location, and accomplishments of each tribe.

Industrialism in America

Source(s): Focus Media
Course(s) for Which Appropriate: U.S. history, economics
Approximate Grade Levels: 9, 10, 11, 12 **HS**
Cost: $99
Type of Program: Tutorial
System(s) on Which It Will Run: Apple II family
Description: Covers American industrialism from the birth of the factory system to the present. Three programs are included: The Industrial Revolution Comes to America, The Age of Big Business, and Industrial America in the 20th Century.

Inner City

Source(s): Computer Island
Course(s) for Which Appropriate: U.S. history, sociology, psychology
Approximate Grade Levels: 7, 8, 9, 10, 11, 12 **JH, HS**
Cost: $50
Type of Program: Simulation
System(s) on Which It Will Run: TRS-80 Color Computer with 32K and disk drive
Description: A role-play simulation in which students experience the challenges and frustrations
of inner city life. Teacher's and students' guides included.

Interviews with History

Source(s): Educational Publishing Concepts
Course(s) for Which Appropriate: U.S. history
Approximate Grade Levels: 4, 5, 6, 7, 8 **EL, JH**
Cost: $200
Type of Program: Game, tutorial
System(s) on Which It Will Run: Apple II family
Description: The student assumes the role of a reporter and interviews twelve historical figures
who helped shape the country's past. The student is tested on the knowledge gained after
each interview and tutored on the points missed. This program won a 1988 *Classroom Computer
Learning* Software Award of Excellence.

Into the Unknown: A Voyage Simulation

Source(s): Focus Media
Course(s) for Which Appropriate: World history
Approximate Grade Levels: 4, 5, 6, 7, 8 **EL, JH**
Cost: $99
Type of Program: Simulation
System(s) on Which It Will Run: Apple II family; Commodore 64
Description: Students simulate a sea voyage in the fifteenth century to seek wealth and discover
lands in Africa. The program simulates problems such as storms, disease, hunger, mutiny,
shipwreck, and native attacks. Information sheets and grid sheets are included with teacher's
materials.

Introduction to Economics

Source(s): Queue
Course(s) for Which Appropriate: Economics
Approximate Grade Levels: 9, 10, 11, 12 **HS**
Cost: $110
Type of Program: Tutorial
System(s) on Which It Will Run: Apple II family
Description: Introduces basic concepts in economics, including scarcity; allocation of resources;
goods and services; natural, capital, and human resources; market value; and opportunity
costs. This is a two-disk program.

Introduction to Geography

Source(s): Orange Cherry Media
Course(s) for Which Appropriate: Geography
Approximate Grade Levels: 5, 6, 7, 8 **EL, JH**
Cost: $55
Type of Program: Drill and practice, maps
System(s) on Which It Will Run: Apple II family
Description: The first part reviews and tests students' knowledge about the fifty states. The
second, Mapping the World, uses color graphics to introduce map- and globe-reading skills.

Inventions That Affect Our Lives

Source(s): Orange Cherry Media
Course(s) for Which Appropriate: Elementary social studies, U.S. history
Approximate Grade Levels: 3, 4, 5, 6, 7 **EL, JH**
Cost: $39
Type of Program: Tutorial
System(s) on Which It Will Run: Apple II family; Commodore 64; TRS-80 Models III and 4
Description: Inventions result from man's curiosity about the world and from the desire to improve the quality of life. This two-part program looks at important inventions that have shaped twentieth century life.

Jamestown, an Early Settlement

Source(s): Aquarius
Course(s) for Which Appropriate: U.S. history
Approximate Grade Levels: 7, 8, 9, 10, 11 **JH, HS**
Cost: $35 (backup included)
Type of Program: Tutorial, simulation
System(s) on Which It Will Run: Apple II family; IBM PC; TRS-80 Models III and 4
Description: Part of the series America, an Early History which gives the student insight into social, religious, economic, and political aspects of early America. Historical figures are used to "speak" to the student.

Jenny's Journeys

Source(s): MECC
Course(s) for Which Appropriate: Elementary social studies
Approximate Grade Levels: 4, 5, 6 **EL**
Cost: $55
Type of Program: Tutorial
System(s) on Which It Will Run: Apple II family; IBM PC
Description: Students learn geographic concepts in "real-life" situations. Skills developed include using a map index, finding locations, and planning routes. Three levels of difficulty allow students to progress at their own pace.

Jury Trial II

Source(s): NAVIC Software
Course(s) for Which Appropriate: Government
Approximate Grade Levels: 7, 8, 9, 10, 11, 12 **JH, HS**
Cost: $49
Type of Program: Simulation
System(s) on Which It Will Run: IBM PC; Apple II family; Commodore 64
Description: Introduces students to the adversary system of justice. Two students play the roles of prosecutor and defense attorney to question witnesses, played by the computer.

Know Your State

Source(s): Right On Programs
Course(s) for Which Appropriate: Geography
Approximate Grade Levels: 3, 4, 5, 6 **EL**
Cost: $25
Type of Program: Tutorial
System(s) on Which It Will Run: Apple II family; Commodore 64
Description: A different program for each of the fifty states. Each contains a disk, large road map of the state, reproducible masters, suggested activities, and additional pamphlets. The program can be used to develop research skills, map skills, and inquiry skills.

Know Your States

Source(s): Computer Island
Course(s) for Which Appropriate: Social studies
Approximate Grade Levels: 4, 5, 6 **EL**
Cost: $20 (tape), $25 (disk)
Type of Program: Drill and practice
System(s) on Which It Will Run: TRS-80 Color Computer with at least 32K
Description: Graphics portray each state for the student to identify. "Help" command provides a picture of the state within the U.S. Students can choose the number of states they will try to identify.

Labor

Source(s): Queue
Course(s) for Which Appropriate: Economics
Approximate Grade Levels: 9, 10, 11, 12 **HS**
Cost: $110
Type of Program: Tutorial
System(s) on Which It Will Run: Apple II family
Description: A two-disk program that enables students to examine the history of the labor movement and the functions of unions today. Covers skilled vs. unskilled labor, the effect of unions on wages, and discrimination, and includes a case study of the United Auto Workers and the Ford Motor Company.

Language of Maps

Source(s): Focus Media
Course(s) for Which Appropriate: Geography, elementary social studies
Approximate Grade Levels: 4, 5, 6, 7, 8 **EL, JH**
Cost: Two sets, $99 each
Type of Program: Tutorial
System(s) on Which It Will Run: Apple II family
Description: Teaches students to ask and answer questions regarding maps. The first set deals with the surface of the earth, the second with location and distance. Each set includes a free backup disk and teacher support materials.

Law in American History I and II

Source(s): Queue
Course(s) for Which Appropriate: U.S. history
Approximate Grade Levels: 7, 8, 9, 10, 11, 12 **JH, HS**
Cost: $45 each
Type of Program: Simulation
System(s) on Which It Will Run: TRS-80 Models III and 4; IBM PC; Commodore 64
Description: Seven programs provide simulations of legal cases in American history. Students can work in teams to "question" witnesses and "try" the cases. A database on the Bill of Rights is included. Paper copy printouts of student work can be made.

Learning about Geography, Maps, and Globes

Source(s): Educational Activities
Course(s) for Which Appropriate: Geography
Approximate Grade Levels: 4, 5, 6 **EL**
Cost: $159 set
Type of Program: Tutorial
System(s) on Which It Will Run: Apple II family
Description: Set includes three programs (available separately for $60): Introduction to Geography, Maps, and Globes; Making Use of Maps; and Maps in Your Life. Advanced graphics are used to show political, product, time, and population maps. Backups, management, and masters included.

Lessons in American History

Source(s): COMpress
Course(s) for Which Appropriate: U.S. history
Approximate Grade Levels: 9, 10, 11, 12 **HS**
Cost: $50 each, $240 set
Type of Program: Drill and practice
System(s) on Which It Will Run: IBM PC
Description: Contains drills on people, places, events, chronology, and geography of each period. Teachers can add or delete material. Includes: History to 1763, American Revolutionary Era, Early National Era, Jacksonian Era, Antebellum Era, and the Civil War Era.

Lewis and Clark Expedition

Source(s): MicroEd
Course(s) for Which Appropriate: U.S. history
Approximate Grade Levels: 5, 6, 7, 8, 9, 10, 11, 12 **EL, JH, HS**
Cost: $50
Type of Program: Simulation
System(s) on Which It Will Run: Commodore 64
Description: Provides accurate historical information about the Lewis and Clark expedition. Students try to duplicate the journey to the Pacific Ocean. Decisions as to when to receive information, when to answer questions, and when to travel determine success or failure.

Lincoln's Decisions

Source(s): Educational Activities
Course(s) for Which Appropriate: U.S. history
Approximate Grade Levels: 8, 9, 10, 11 **JH, HS**
Cost: $63
Type of Program: Tutorial
System(s) on Which It Will Run: Apple II family; TRS-80; IBM PC
Description: Students are presented with crucial decisions that faced Lincoln. They may get help from a variety of clues, if necessary, before making a decision. An explanation follows each decision, right or wrong. A teacher's guide is included.

Location and Distance

Source(s): Edu-Tron, Focus Media
Course(s) for Which Appropriate: Geography, elementary social studies
Approximate Grade Levels: 3, 4, 5, 6, 7, 8 **EL, JH**
Cost: $99
Type of Program: Tutorial
System(s) on Which It Will Run: Apple II family
Description: Students learn about the poles, equator, prime meridian, International Date Line, cardinal directions, the compass rose, meridians, and map scales in this interactive format.

Lollipop Dragon's World of Maps and Globes

Source(s): SVE
Course(s) for Which Appropriate: Elementary social studies
Approximate Grade Levels: K, 1, 2, 3 **EL**
Cost: $189/$49
Type of Program: Drill and practice
System(s) on Which It Will Run: Apple II family
Description: Unique program uses four filmstrips and a cartoon dragon to introduce maps and globes. Students learn directions, how to use different types of maps, and how to make their own map. The computer disk gives activities to practice the skills—helping a dragon move furniture using directions. Disk only costs $49.

Macroeconomics

Source(s): Queue
Course(s) for Which Appropriate: Economics
Approximate Grade Levels: 10, 11, 12 **HS**
Cost: $40
Type of Program: Tutorial
System(s) on Which It Will Run: Apple II family; IBM PC; Macintosh
Description: Includes basic principles of economics such as computation of GNP, consumer demand, propensity of demand schedule, savings, the multiplier, monetary policy, inflation, and depression.

Map Reading

Source(s): SVE, Micro Power and Light
Course(s) for Which Appropriate: Geography
Approximate Grade Levels: 5, 6, 7, 8, 9, 10, 11, 12 **EL, JH, HS**
Cost: $25 ($35 with backup)
Type of Program: Tutorial
System(s) on Which It Will Run: Apple II family
Description: Three programs provide an introduction to distance and direction—The Compass, The Concept of Scale, and The Notation.

Maps and Globes

Source(s): SVE, MicroEd
Course(s) for Which Appropriate: Geography
Approximate Grade Levels: 5, 6, 7, 8, 9, 10, 11, 12 **EL, JH, HS**
Cost: $136
Type of Program: Drill and practice
System(s) on Which It Will Run: Apple II family; Commodore 64; TRS-80 Model III
Description: Nineteen programs which provide immediate feedback and track the user's progress. Some of those included are A Map Is Made, How Far Is It? The Earth's Land Masses, Flat Maps of a Round Earth, The World's Climates, What Grows on the Land, and Finding Cities and Countries.

Map Skills

Source(s): Learning Arts
Course(s) for Which Appropriate: Elementary social studies
Approximate Grade Levels: 2, 3 **EL**
Cost: $30
Type of Program: Tutorial
System(s) on Which It Will Run: Apple II family
Description: Very early map-reading skills are presented in a question/response format. Includes distinguishing between pictures and maps, map symbols and keys, neighborhood and route maps, cardinal and intermediate directions. Management system included.

Market Economy

Source(s): Queue
Course(s) for Which Appropriate: Economics
Approximate Grade Levels: 9, 10, 11, 12 **HS**
Cost: $110
Type of Program: Tutorial
System(s) on Which It Will Run: Apple II family
Description: This two-disk program helps students understand how different economic systems work in terms of production and distribution in command, market, and mixed economies. A case study of the 1973 oil crisis is included.

Marketplace

Source(s): Learning Arts
Course(s) for Which Appropriate: Economics
Approximate Grade Levels: 7, 8, 9, 10, 11, 12 **JH, HS**
Cost: $40 (backup included)
Type of Program: Tutorial, drill and practice
System(s) on Which It Will Run: Apple II family
Description: Introduces the concepts of supply and demand, provides drill in recognizing the impact of varying curves on market price and quantity. Teacher's guide included.

Market Place

Source(s): MECC
Course(s) for Which Appropriate: Elementary social studies, economics
Approximate Grade Levels: 3, 4, 5, 6, 7, 8 **EL, JH**
Cost: $55
Type of Program: Simulation
System(s) on Which It Will Run: Apple II family; IBM PC; Commodore 64; Radio Shack Color Computer
Description: Simulations involve students in learning economic concepts, such as supply and demand. Students operate businesses selling apples, tomato plants, and lemonade.

Maxi Taxi

Source(s): MicroEd
Course(s) for Which Appropriate: Elementary social studies, economics
Approximate Grade Levels: 4, 5, 6, 7, 8, 9 **EL, JH, HS**
Cost: $30
Type of Program: Drill and practice, tutorial
System(s) on Which It Will Run: Commodore 64
Description: The objective of this program is to determine maximum earnings in a work situation by relating time to money.

Measuring Economic Activity

Source(s): Focus Media
Course(s) for Which Appropriate: Economics
Approximate Grade Levels: 9, 10, 11, 12 **HS**
Cost: $55
Type of Program: Tutorial
System(s) on Which It Will Run: Apple II family
Description: Introduces important economic indicators, allows students to enter data relating to them, and creates graphs and charts to represent the data. Printouts of these graphs and charts are available. A student reference booklet is included.

MECC Dataquest: The Fifty States

Source(s): MECC
Course(s) for Which Appropriate: Geography, elementary social studies
Approximate Grade Levels: 5, 6, 7, 8, 9, 10 **EL, JH, HS**
Cost: $55
Type of Program: Database
System(s) on Which It Will Run: Apple II family
Description: Database includes information on geography, climate, demographics, economics, and the history of each state. Students create their own questions or hypotheses and the database provides the information.

MECC Dataquest: The Presidents

Source(s): MECC
Course(s) for Which Appropriate: U.S. history
Approximate Grade Levels: 9, 10, 11, 12 **HS**
Cost: $55
Type of Program: Database
System(s) on Which It Will Run: Apple II family
Description: Provides a database on the presidents, their administrations, and events that took place during their terms. Students create their own questions or hypotheses and use the database to provide evidence.

MECC Dataquest: The World Community

Source(s): MECC
Course(s) for Which Appropriate: Geography, economics
Approximate Grade Levels: 7, 8, 9, 10, 11, 12 **JH, HS**
Cost: $55
Type of Program: Database
System(s) on Which It Will Run: Apple II family
Description: The database includes twenty-seven categories of information about ninety-five countries around the world. Students can explore a storehouse of data about geography, demographics, and economics.

Medalists Series

Source(s): Learning Arts, Hartley
Course(s) for Which Appropriate: U.S. history, geography
Approximate Grade Levels: 4, 5, 6, 7, 8, 9 **EL, JH**
Cost: $50 each
Type of Program: Drill and practice
System(s) on Which It Will Run: Apple II family; IBM PC
Description: Encourages students to learn about five areas in programs entitled Black Americans, Continents, Presidents, States, and Women in History. The student "buys" clues to help guess the individual or place the computer has chosen. The teacher may change clues and point values. Scores are automatically recorded.

Microeconomics

Source(s): Queue
Course(s) for Which Appropriate: Economics
Approximate Grade Levels: 10, 11, 12 **HS**
Cost: $40
Type of Program: Tutorial
System(s) on Which It Will Run: Apple II family; IBM PC; Macintosh
Description: Includes sections on supply and demand, price, demand schedule and curve, elasticity of demand, tax, government interference, law of diminishing returns, monopoly, antitrust legislation, and factor pricing.

The Middle Ages

Source(s): Right On Programs
Course(s) for Which Appropriate: World history
Approximate Grade Levels: 6, 7, 8 **EL, JH**
Cost: $25
Type of Program: Tutorial
System(s) on Which It Will Run: Apple II family; Commodore 64
Description: Introduces basic historical information regarding this time period. A teacher's guide and reproducible worksheets are included.

Modern Eurasia

Source(s): Focus Media
Course(s) for Which Appropriate: World history
Approximate Grade Levels: 4, 5, 6, 7, 8 **EL, JH**
Cost: $99 (backup included)
Type of Program: Tutorial
System(s) on Which It Will Run: Apple II family
Description: Presents information on the Middle East, Europe, and Russia and Asia. Help is provided for incorrect answers. Includes information on politics, cultures, and economics. Maps are used, too.

Monarch

Source(s): Dynacomp
Course(s) for Which Appropriate: Government, world history, economics
Approximate Grade Levels: 7, 8, 9, 10, 11, 12 **JH, HS**
Cost: $19
Type of Program: Simulation
System(s) on Which It Will Run: IBM PC
Description: Allows students to simulate being ruler of a country. Decisions must be made regarding how to manage the country's resources and distribute wealth among the population.

Money and Financial Institutions

Source(s): Queue
Course(s) for Which Appropriate: Economics
Approximate Grade Levels: 9, 10, 11, 12 **HS**
Cost: $110
Type of Program: Tutorial
System(s) on Which It Will Run: Apple II family
Description: Describes the process by which money is created; the difference between money, value, and money supply; and the importance of trade in our economy. Simple models also show how a checking account works, explain the role of the Federal Reserve, and discuss the discount rate.

National Economic Policy

Source(s): Queue
Course(s) for Which Appropriate: Economics
Approximate Grade Levels: 9, 10, 11, 12 **HS**
Cost: $110
Type of Program: Tutorial
System(s) on Which It Will Run: Apple II family
Description: Views the workings of the economy as the government attempts to manipulate supply and demand. Covers components of aggregate demand; the relationship between GNP, unemployment, and inflation; budget deficits; supply and demand curves; government controls; and obstacles to stability.

National Economy

Source(s): Queue
Course(s) for Which Appropriate: Economics
Approximate Grade Levels: 9, 10, 11, 12 **HS**
Cost: $110
Type of Program: Tutorial
System(s) on Which It Will Run: Apple II family
Description: The interrelationship between inflation, recession, employment, and unemployment are examined in this macroeconomic two-disk tutorial. A case study of the 1981/1982 recession is used to demonstrate some of these relationships.

National Inspirer

Source(s): Tom Snyder Productions
Course(s) for Which Appropriate: Geography
Approximate Grade Levels: 5, 6, 7, 8 **EL, JH**
Cost: $70
Type of Program: Game
System(s) on Which It Will Run: Apple II family; IBM PC; Tandy 1000
Description: Students compete to plan strategic moves from state to state to acquire commodities and resources. Students, working in small groups, learn how these resources are distributed throughout the country, sharpen skills in state identification and map reading, and learn state statistics.

Nationalism: Past & Present

Source(s): Focus Media
Course(s) for Which Appropriate: U.S. history, world history
Approximate Grade Levels: 9, 10, 11, 12 **HS**
Cost: $169 (backup included)
Type of Program: Tutorial, simulation, problem solving
System(s) on Which It Will Run: Apple II family
Description: Five programs on five disks—Nationalism: Its European Roots; Nation-Building; Graphing the Nation-Building Process; Destructive Nationalism; and Nationalism Today: The Soviet Union. Involves simulation, case study, and using the computer as a tool. Integrates classroom research with CAI.

New World

Source(s): K-12 MicroMedia
Course(s) for Which Appropriate: U.S. history
Approximate Grade Levels: 4, 5, 6, 7, 8 **EL, JH**
Cost: $30
Type of Program: Simulation
System(s) on Which It Will Run: Apple II family
Description: Students lead an expedition for England, France, or Spain in 1495. Colonists must be recruited, supplies and soldiers raised, and transportation arranged.

Non-Western Cultures

Source(s): Focus Media
Course(s) for Which Appropriate: World history
Approximate Grade Levels: 7, 8, 9, 10 **JH, HS**
Cost: $99 (backup included)
Type of Program: Drill and practice, game, review
System(s) on Which It Will Run: Apple II family; TRS-80 Models III and 4; Commodore 64
Description: Three programs on two disks: Africa & The Middle East, China & Japan, and India & Latin America. Using game formats, students review material relating to the non-Western world. Support materials are provided for the teacher.

North America Databases

Source(s): Sunburst
Course(s) for Which Appropriate: Geography, government
Approximate Grade Levels: 5, 6, 7, 8, 9, 10, 11, 12 **EL, JH, HS**
Cost: $59
Type of Program: Database
System(s) on Which It Will Run: Apple II family; Commodore 64
Description: Includes data on people, climate, demography, culture, economy, and government of each North American nation. Must be used with the **Bank Street School Filer**.

Oceans and Continents

Source(s): MicroEd
Course(s) for Which Appropriate: Elementary social studies
Approximate Grade Levels: 2, 3, 4, 5 **EL**
Cost: $30
Type of Program: Drill and practice
System(s) on Which It Will Run: Commodore 64
Description: The program is designed to help students locate and identify oceans and continents.

Old Ironsides

Source(s): Edu-Tron
Course(s) for Which Appropriate: Elementary social studies
Approximate Grade Levels: 1, 2, 3, 4 **EL**
Cost: $40
Type of Program: Simulation
System(s) on Which It Will Run: Apple II family
Description: A two-player game of naval strategy and skill that recreates engagements of sailing ships. Using a variety of tactics and contending with wind direction and cloud cover, students attempt to out-gun the opponent.

One World: A Countries Database

Source(s): Active Learning Systems
Course(s) for Which Appropriate: Geography, world history
Approximate Grade Levels: 5, 6, 7, 8, 9, 10, 11, 12 **EL, JH, HS**
Cost: $148
Type of Program: Database
System(s) on Which It Will Run: Apple II family; IBM PC
Description: Contains information on 30 categories regarding 178 countries of the world. The program will sort and print information using up to three fields as criteria. Students can find information or check hypotheses in a very short time using the database.

Oregon Trail

Source(s): MECC
Course(s) for Which Appropriate: U.S. history
Approximate Grade Levels: 4, 5, 6, 7, 8, 9, 10, 11, 12 **EL, JH, HS**
Cost: $55/$59
Type of Program: Simulation
System(s) on Which It Will Run: Apple II family
Description: Simulation of a wagon train crossing of the West, including a variety of events such as illness, bad weather, Indian and animal attacks, and other events that could befall a group going West. The goal is to try to make it to Oregon. The higher price is for a 3½-inch disk. This is a revised and improved version of the program.

The Other Side

Source(s): Tom Snyder Productions
Course(s) for Which Appropriate: U.S. history, government
Approximate Grade Levels: 7, 8, 9, 10, 11, 12 **JH, HS**
Cost: $70
Type of Program: Simulation
System(s) on Which It Will Run: Apple II family; IBM PC
Description: Teams of students represent countries as they make choices regarding their economies and international affairs. Teams may choose collaboration or competition as they make these decisions and attempt to win the game. Game board and other materials are provided.

Our Town Meeting

Source(s): Tom Snyder Productions
Course(s) for Which Appropriate: Government, economics
Approximate Grade Levels: 5, 6, 7, 8, 9, 10, 11, 12 **EL, JH, HS**
Cost: $100
Type of Program: Simulation
System(s) on Which It Will Run: Apple II family; IBM PC; Tandy 1000
Description: The challenge is to enhance the town's image and popularity without bankrupting the treasury. As members of the town's agencies, students must propose civic projects to meet this goal. In the process they must negotiate with other agencies. An understanding of municipal budgeting is developed.

Parking Lot

Source(s): MicroEd
Course(s) for Which Appropriate: Elementary social studies, economics
Approximate Grade Levels: 4, 5, 6, 7, 8, 9 **EL, JH**
Cost: $30
Type of Program: Simulation
System(s) on Which It Will Run: Commodore 64
Description: The objective of this program is to help make the greatest business profit by applying the law of supply and demand.

Political Genie: House Version

Source(s): Boring Software Company
Course(s) for Which Appropriate: Government
Approximate Grade Levels: 7, 8, 9, 10, 11, 12 **JH, HS**
Cost: $75
Type of Program: Database
System(s) on Which It Will Run: Apple II family; IBM PC
Description: Students select a House member to be evaluated and 25 issues from a list of 100. Students discuss the issues and vote on them. Then the program provides information on how the House member voted, how the House voted, how the Senate voted, and gives the president's position.

Political Genie: Senate Version

Source(s): Boring Software Company
Course(s) for Which Appropriate: Government, economics
Approximate Grade Levels: 7, 8, 9, 10, 11, 12 **JH, HS**
Cost: $75
Type of Program: Database
System(s) on Which It Will Run: Apple II family; IBM PC
Description: Students select a senator to be evaluated. Then they select up to 25 issues from 100 available. Students then discuss the issues and vote among themselves. The program provides information about how the senator voted, how the Senate voted, how the House voted, and gives the president's position.

Polls and Politics

Source(s): MECC
Course(s) for Which Appropriate: Government
Approximate Grade Levels: 7, 8, 9, 10, 11, 12 **JH, HS**
Cost: $35
Type of Program: Tutorial, simulation
System(s) on Which It Will Run: IBM PC; Apple II family
Description: The concept of political polling is presented. Then students use three of the programs included to create and analyze survey data.

Presidency Series

Source(s): Focus Media
Course(s) for Which Appropriate: Government
Approximate Grade Levels: 7, 8, 9, 10, 11, 12 **JH, HS**
Cost: $99
Type of Program: Tutorial, simulation
System(s) on Which It Will Run: Apple II family
Description: Five-part series: The Nature of the Office, Presidential Roles and Uses of Power, Organization of the Presidency, Who Can Be President, and Evaluating Presidential Leadership. Extensive program with backups and lesson planners.

Presidential Profiles

Source(s): Opportunities for Learning
Course(s) for Which Appropriate: U.S. history, elementary social studies
Approximate Grade Levels: 5, 6, 7, 8, 9, 10, 11, 12 **EL, JH, HS**
Cost: $50
Type of Program: Tutorial
System(s) on Which It Will Run: Apple II family
Description: Four interactive programs allow each president to "introduce" himself to the students. Three games are included to determine what students have learned.

President's Choice

Source(s): Edu-Tron
Course(s) for Which Appropriate: U.S. history, economics
Approximate Grade Levels: 8, 9, 10, 11, 12 **JH, HS**
Cost: $40
Type of Program: Simulation
System(s) on Which It Will Run: IBM PC
Description: The student simulates being the President of the U.S. Working with economic advisers, the student makes decisions regarding the economy. If the student maintains popularity based on these decisions, reelection is assured.

Property

Source(s): Queue
Course(s) for Which Appropriate: Government
Approximate Grade Levels: 9, 10, 11, 12+ **HS, CO**
Cost: $55/$85
Type of Program: Tutorial
System(s) on Which It Will Run: Apple II family
Description: A three-disk tutorial covering the legal aspects of property for high school and college. The higher-priced program contains a student management system which records data on individual student performance.

Quest for Files: Social Studies

Source(s): Mindscape
Course(s) for Which Appropriate: U.S. history
Approximate Grade Levels: 9, 10, 11, 12 **HS**
Cost: $50 each
Type of Program: Database
System(s) on Which It Will Run: Apple II family; IBM PC
Description: Three database programs with questions that require students to analyze the information and support hypotheses. Each is sold separately: The Melting Plot (profiles of immigrant families), Hail to the Chief (twenty-four fields of information on presidents), and Dawn's Early Light (the first Congress).

Rails West

Source(s): Strategic Simulations
Course(s) for Which Appropriate: Economics
Approximate Grade Levels: 9, 10, 11, 12 **HS**
Cost: $40
Type of Program: Simulation
System(s) on Which It Will Run: Apple II family; Atari
Description: A historically-based simulation set in 1870. Players make choices which affect the course of the simulation. Choices include starting a corporation, buying and selling stock, securing a loan, and other business decisions. The country's economic cycles are a factor.

Reading a Map

Source(s): Aquarius
Course(s) for Which Appropriate: Elementary social studies
Approximate Grade Levels: 2, 3, 4 **EL**
Cost: $45 (backup included)
Type of Program: Drill and practice
System(s) on Which It Will Run: Apple II family
Description: Students learn to read maps through practice and testing provided step by step. Graphics are used to illustrate content and for test items. A management system is a part of the program.

Regions of the United States

Source(s): Educational Activities
Course(s) for Which Appropriate: Geography
Approximate Grade Levels: 5, 6, 7, 8, 9, 10, 11, 12 **EL, JH, HS**
Cost: $60 (backup included)
Type of Program: Drill and practice
System(s) on Which It Will Run: Apple II family; Commodore 64; Atari; TRS-80 Models III and 4
Description: Students review states by regions. They then have to identify states, in the beginner level, and identify and spell the names of the states correctly in the Super Quiz. Major cities, landforms, products, and climates are also described.

Renaissance

Source(s): Right On Programs
Course(s) for Which Appropriate: World history, elementary social studies
Approximate Grade Levels: 6, 7, 8 **EL, JH**
Cost: $25
Type of Program: Tutorial
System(s) on Which It Will Run: Apple II family; Commodore 64
Description: Describes science, inventions, medicine, painting, sculpture, architecture, exploration, and religion during the Renaissance. A teacher's manual and reproducible worksheets are included.

Review Questions in American History

Source(s): Queue
Course(s) for Which Appropriate: U.S. history
Approximate Grade Levels: 9, 10, 11, 12 **HS**
Cost: $50 (two disks)
Type of Program: Game
System(s) on Which It Will Run: Apple II family
Description: Four hundred questions covering the entire span of U.S. history. Each wrong answer branches to an explanation.

Review Questions in World History

Source(s): Queue
Course(s) for Which Appropriate: World history
Approximate Grade Levels: 9, 10, 11, 12 **HS**
Cost: $50
Type of Program: Drill/practice
System(s) on Which It Will Run: Apple II family; IBM PC
Description: Disk 1 covers to 1500 and Disk 2 covers since that time. Each contains over 200 questions. Students receive feedback and are branched to an explanation. The Apple program has an optional student management program for an additional $10.

Revolutions: Past, Present, and Future

Source(s): Focus Media
Course(s) for Which Appropriate: World history
Approximate Grade Levels: 9, 10, 11, 12 **HS**
Cost: $169
Type of Program: Tutorial
System(s) on Which It Will Run: Apple II family; TRS-80 Models III and 4
Description: Leads students through the process of historical analysis as they perform a comparative study of the revolutionary process in different countries. The computer is also used to provide a visual comparison of the results of their quantitative study.

Ripple That Changed American History

Source(s): Tom Snyder Productions
Course(s) for Which Appropriate: U.S. history
Approximate Grade Levels: 5, 6, 7, 8, 9, 10, 11, 12 **EL, JH, HS**
Cost: $70
Type of Program: Game
System(s) on Which It Will Run: Apple II family; IBM PC; Tandy 1000
Description: A dangerous disturbance (called The Ripple) is destroying America's past and may destroy the present! Using clues given in the form of historical conversations students must determine where The Ripple is and destroy it.

Rivers and Ancient Cultures

Source(s): Teach Yourself by Computer Software
Course(s) for Which Appropriate: Elementary social studies
Approximate Grade Levels: 4, 5, 6, 7 **EL, JH**
Cost: $40
Type of Program: Tutorial
System(s) on Which It Will Run: Apple II family
Description: The development of the Egyptian and Sumerian civilizations are explored, including the discovery of the wheel and the development of the calendar. The influence of the Nile, Tigris, and Euphrates rivers on the cultures is shown. Branching texts, animated graphics, and tests are included.

Road Rally U.S.A.

Source(s): Edu-Tron
Course(s) for Which Appropriate: Geography, elementary social studies
Approximate Grade Levels: 5, 6, 7, 8 **EL, JH**
Cost: $40
Type of Program: Simulation
System(s) on Which It Will Run: Apple II family; Commodore 64; IBM PC
Description: Simulates driving in a cross-country road rally through real roads and cities. The three difficulty levels develop a knowledge of geography and problem-solving skills.

Run for President

Source(s): Edu-Tron
Course(s) for Which Appropriate: Geography
Approximate Grade Levels: 6, 7, 8, 9, 10, 11, 12 **EL, JH, HS**
Cost: $40
Type of Program: Game
System(s) on Which It Will Run: Apple II family
Description: A review of American geography is set within a mock election for the presidency. Votes are based on a knowledge of capitals, major cities, industries, and famous features and sites of the fifty states.

Russian Revolution

Source(s): Frontier Software
Course(s) for Which Appropriate: World history
Approximate Grade Levels: 6, 7, 8, 9, 10 **EL, JH, HS**
Cost: $40
Type of Program: Tutorial
System(s) on Which It Will Run: Apple II family
Description: Includes the causes, events, battles, and people of the Russian Revolution.

Sailing Ships Game

Source(s): Queue
Course(s) for Which Appropriate: U.S. history, world history, geography
Approximate Grade Levels: 7, 8, 9, 10, 11 **JH, HS**
Cost: $45
Type of Program: Simulation
System(s) on Which It Will Run: Apple II family
Description: Simulates navigating a large sailing ship around the world's oceans. The program accounts for atmospheric circulation and students must apply their knowledge of wind belts in order to be successful. It is possible to reconstruct famous voyages of discovery.

SAMP: Survey Sampling

Source(s): Conduit
Course(s) for Which Appropriate: Sociology
Approximate Grade Levels: 11, 12+ **HS, CO**
Cost: $70
Type of Program: Simulation
System(s) on Which It Will Run: Apple II family; IBM PC
Description: This program offers a choice of four sampling designs: simple random, cluster sampling, stratified sampling, and quota sampling. Using one of these designs, students draw samples and explore the effects of various factors on the precision of the results.

Santa Fe Trail

Source(s): Educational Activities
Course(s) for Which Appropriate: U.S. history
Approximate Grade Levels: 7, 8, 9, 10, 11, 12 **JH, HS**
Cost: $60
Type of Program: Simulation
System(s) on Which It Will Run: Apple II family
Description: The student is a trader between 1820 and 1829 traveling between Independence, Missouri, and Santa Fe. Decisions must be made relating to a variety of issues. Each year the situations change. Geographical and political conditions and random factors also interject themselves.

Satellite Down

Source(s): Focus Media
Course(s) for Which Appropriate: Geography
Approximate Grade Levels: 7, 8, 9, 10, 11, 12 **JH, HS**
Cost: $85 each edition
Type of Program: Game
System(s) on Which It Will Run: Apple II family
Description: A U.S. satellite is down. The student, acting as a government agent, must find the location quickly. A series of clues is available from the satellite about its location. Students must piece together the evidence. A world edition and a U.S. edition are available and a map is included.

Save the !Kung

Source(s): Micro Power and Light Co., Edu-Tron
Course(s) for Which Appropriate: World history, sociology, anthropology
Approximate Grade Levels: 9, 10, 11, 12+ **HS, CO**
Cost: $35 ($45 with backup)
Type of Program: Simulation
System(s) on Which It Will Run: Apple II family
Description: Students use nine variables to prolong the reign of a tribe. If students do not manipulate these essential variables the tribe will either die or overpopulate.

Scare City Motel

Source(s): MicroEd
Course(s) for Which Appropriate: Elementary social studies, economics
Approximate Grade Levels: 4, 5, 6, 7, 8, 9 **EL, JH**
Cost: $30
Type of Program: Tutorial
System(s) on Which It Will Run: Commodore 64
Description: The objective of this program is to teach the student how to maximize business earnings by equating supply with demand.

Scholastic pfs: World Geography Database

Source(s): Scholastic
Course(s) for Which Appropriate: Geography, economics
Approximate Grade Levels: 5, 6, 7, 8, 9, 10, 11, 12 **EL, JH, HS**
Cost: $80
Type of Program: Database
System(s) on Which It Will Run: Apple II family
Description: Databases included relate to world geography, economics, and world cultures. A copy of **pfs:FILE/REPORT** is included for the development of student-made databases to create and test hypotheses. Also included are backup disks, a user's manual, and a teacher's guide. Winner of the *Classroom Computer Learning* software award.

Scholastic pfs: U.S. Government Database

Source(s): Scholastic
Course(s) for Which Appropriate: Government, U.S. history
Approximate Grade Levels: 5, 6, 7, 8, 9, 10, 11, 12 **EL, JH, HS**
Cost: $80
Type of Program: Database
System(s) on Which It Will Run: Apple II family
Description: Five activity units, including three prepared databases, help students learn to develop databases using data they collect. Then, hypotheses can be tested. The program contains **pfs:FILE/REPORT** for creation of additional databases, a user's manual, and a teacher's guide.

Scholastic pfs: U.S. History Database

Source(s): Scholastic
Course(s) for Which Appropriate: U.S. history
Approximate Grade Levels: 5, 6, 7, 8, 9, 10, 11, 12 **EL, JH, HS**
Cost: $80
Type of Program: Database
System(s) on Which It Will Run: Apple II family; IBM PC
Description: Three databases (Expanding Frontier, Inventions and Technology, and Twentieth Century America) and three units to help students create their own databases are included. Program includes **pfs:FILE/RECORD** for creation of additional databases, a user's manual and a teacher's guide.

Search and Rescue: Geography Skills

Source(s): Learning Arts
Course(s) for Which Appropriate: Geography, elementary social studies
Approximate Grade Levels: 4, 5, 6, 7, 8 **EL, JH**
Cost: $59
Type of Program: Game
System(s) on Which It Will Run: Apple II family
Description: Students apply knowledge of directions, latitude, and longitude as they play a game. They must locate cities and countries in which a stolen object is being held. Then they travel to various points to collect the items using either compass directions or latitude and longitude. Three levels.

Sea Voyagers

Source(s): Edu-Tron, Mindscape
Course(s) for Which Appropriate: Elementary social studies, U.S. history
Approximate Grade Levels: 3, 4, 5, 6, 7, 8 **EL, JH**
Cost: $50
Type of Program: Game
System(s) on Which It Will Run: Apple II family; Commodore 64; IBM PC
Description: The game includes information about thirty New World explorers. Interactive activities help students learn facts so that they can match the explorers with their country, routes, and accomplishments.

Settling America

Source(s): Edu-Tron
Course(s) for Which Appropriate: U.S. history
Approximate Grade Levels: 6, 7, 8, 9, 10, 11, 12 **EL, JH, HS**
Cost: $40
Type of Program: Simulation
System(s) on Which It Will Run: Apple II family
Description: A simulation that requires decision making regarding which crops to plant, buildings to build, and other decisions relating to settling in the Ohio River Valley between 1789 and 1793.

Seven Cities of Gold

Source(s): Edu-Tron
Course(s) for Which Appropriate: U.S. history
Approximate Grade Levels: 4, 5, 6, 7, 8, 9, 10, 11, 12 **EL, JH, HS**
Cost: $40
Type of Program: Simulation
System(s) on Which It Will Run: Apple II family; Commodore 64; IBM PC; Amiga
Description: An interactive program that centers on exploring the New World, establishing missions, discovering gold, and dealing with the Indians.

Shore Features

Source(s): Teach Yourself by Computer Software
Course(s) for Which Appropriate: Geography
Approximate Grade Levels: 7, 8, 9, 10, 11, 12 **JH, HS**
Cost: $25
Type of Program: Tutorial
System(s) on Which It Will Run: Apple II family
Description: Familiarizes students with geographical features of shores and beaches. Graded tests, review options, and a manual are included in the program.

Simplicon

Source(s): Cross Cultural Software
Course(s) for Which Appropriate: Government, economics, sociology
Approximate Grade Levels: 9, 10, 11, 12 **HS**
Cost: $120 (two disks, backup included)
Type of Program: Simulation
System(s) on Which It Will Run: Apple II family
Description: A complex simulation involving a nation's goals, economic needs, interest group pressures, political needs, and other events. Students must develop an understanding of these concepts and are required to integrate them in the course of the simulation.

Simulation Construction Kit

Source(s): Hartley
Course(s) for Which Appropriate: U.S. history, government, sociology, world history
Approximate Grade Levels: 7, 8, 9, 10, 11, 12 **JH, HS**
Cost: $80
Type of Program: Simulation, tool
System(s) on Which It Will Run: Apple II family
Description: This program includes a simulation, but its biggest use is for teachers and students to create their own simulations. Complete documentation in manuals and a tutorial disk. Disks are copyable. This program won the Classroom Computer Learning Software Excellence Award in 1987.

Social Studies Explorer: American History

Source(s): SVE, Mindscape
Course(s) for Which Appropriate: U.S. history
Approximate Grade Levels: 5, 6, 7, 8 **EL, JH**
Cost: $40 each, $150 set
Type of Program: Game, problem solving
System(s) on Which It Will Run: Apple II family; IBM PC; Commodore 64
Description: Students must identify an event by using clues and deductive reasoning. They must also give facts to support their conclusion. A student management system is included. Programs include: Revolution/Constitution, Discovery/Exploration, Westward Expansion, and Civil War.

Social Studies Explorer: World Geography

Source(s): SVE, Mindscape
Course(s) for Which Appropriate: Geography, world history
Approximate Grade Levels: 5, 6, 7, 8 **EL, JH**
Cost: $40 each, $150 set
Type of Program: Drill and practice, problem solving
System(s) on Which It Will Run: Apple II family; IBM PC
Description: Students find themselves in an unidentified location. By answering questions and using deductive thinking, students are to name their location. Two levels of difficulty and a student management program are included. Set includes: Central U.S., Western Europe, Eastern U.S., Asia/Australia.

Social Studies Skill Builder

Source(s): Queue
Course(s) for Which Appropriate: Elementary social studies
Approximate Grade Levels: 6, 7, 8, 9 **EL, JH**
Cost: $60, on-site reproduction license $180
Type of Program: Tutorial
System(s) on Which It Will Run: Apple II family
Description: Contains four reading skills lessons and nine writing skills lessons using drill and tutorial elements. Culminating writing activities center on a number of social studies topics.

Social Studies Regions

Source(s): MicroEd
Course(s) for Which Appropriate: Elementary social studies
Approximate Grade Levels: 4, 5, 6 **EL**
Cost: $50
Type of Program: Tutorial
System(s) on Which It Will Run: Commodore 64
Description: Helps develop vocabulary that relates to regions, including forest, desert, farming, ocean, manufacturing, trading, and political regions.

SOCTERMS: Sociological Definitions

Source(s): Conduit
Course(s) for Which Appropriate: Sociology
Approximate Grade Levels: 10, 11, 12+ **HS, CO**
Cost: $60
Type of Program: Drill and practice
System(s) on Which It Will Run: IBM PC
Description: By helping students to learn the meanings of sociological terms on their own, **SOCTERMS** frees class time for more stimulating use. The eighty-eight terms covered include the majority of those needed for introductory sociology courses in college.

South American Geography

Source(s): Sunshine Computer Company
Course(s) for Which Appropriate: Geography
Approximate Grade Levels: 7, 8, 9, 10, 11, 12 **JH, HS**
Cost: $29
Type of Program: Drill and practice
System(s) on Which It Will Run: IBM PC
Description: A map of South America is presented on the screen. Using the cursor control keys, the student selects a country. The student is asked to name the country, its capital, and the largest city. Correct answers produce the country's anthem. Help is provided if needed.

Space Commander: States and Capitals Game

Source(s): Gameco
Course(s) for Which Appropriate: Elementary social studies, geography
Approximate Grade Levels: 3, 4, 5, 6 **EL**
Cost: $55 (backup included)
Type of Program: Drill and practice, game
System(s) on Which It Will Run: Apple II family; TRS-80 Models III and 4; Commodore 64/128
Description: A strategy game for two players; it includes a drill in which students must locate the states on a map, spell the names of the states and capitals correctly, and abbreviate state names. A management system for up to 200 students is built into the program.

Spell M-O-N-E-Y

Source(s): MicroEd
Course(s) for Which Appropriate: Elementary social studies, economics
Approximate Grade Levels: 5, 6, 7, 8, 9 **EL, JH**
Cost: $30
Type of Program: Tutorial
System(s) on Which It Will Run: Commodore 64
Description: The objective of this program is to help the student identify the definitions of basic economic terms.

Standing Room Only

Source(s): Sunburst
Course(s) for Which Appropriate: World history, economics, sociology
Approximate Grade Levels: 8, 9, 10, 11, 12 **JH, HS**
Cost: $65
Type of Program: Tool
System(s) on Which It Will Run: Apple II family
Description: An interactive model that can be used to study population and hypotheses about population growth. By manipulating migration, family composition, and life expectancy for seven countries, students can see the effects of these factors.

States

Source(s): Queue
Course(s) for Which Appropriate: Geography
Approximate Grade Levels: 3, 4, 5, 6 **EL**
Cost: $40
Type of Program: Drill and practice
System(s) on Which It Will Run: Apple II family; Commodore 64
Description: Use graphics to teach the recognition of states by shape and by neighboring states. Also presents interesting facts about each state.

States and Capitals

Source(s): Gameco
Course(s) for Which Appropriate: Elementary social studies, geography
Approximate Grade Levels: 3, 4, 5, 6 **EL**
Cost: $55 (backup included)
Type of Program: Drill and practice, game
System(s) on Which It Will Run: Apple II family; TRS-80 Models III and 4; Commodore 64/128
Description: Arcade-style game allows students to choose from eight levels involving locating states, identifying capitals, and identifying principal cities. Questions are randomly generated and after three errors the correct answer is given. Student management system accommodates up to 200 students.

States and Capitals

Source(s): MicroEd
Course(s) for Which Appropriate: Geography, elementary social studies
Approximate Grade Levels: 3, 4, 5 **EL**
Cost: $30
Type of Program: Drill and practice
System(s) on Which It Will Run: Commodore 64
Description: Helps students link the names of states with their capitals.

States and Traits

Source(s): Britannica Software
Course(s) for Which Appropriate: Geography, U.S. history
Approximate Grade Levels: 9, 10, 11, 12 **HS**
Cost: $30/$40
Type of Program: Drill and practice, game
System(s) on Which It Will Run: Apple II family; Commodore 64; IBM PC
Description: The student moves outlines of states to their correct location on a U.S. map. Then they answer questions about the states. The faster they answer the higher their score. The lower price is for the Commodore 64 version.

Stickybear Town Builder

Source(s): SVE
Course(s) for Which Appropriate: Elementary social studies
Approximate Grade Levels: 1, 2, 3 **EL**
Cost: $40
Type of Program: Game, tool
System(s) on Which It Will Run: Apple II family; Commodore 64
Description: Students build a town from the ground up, including roads, parks, bridges, and buildings. Then they can drive around the town using a compass and directions to locate the mystery keys.

Stock Market Simulation

Source(s): Queue
Course(s) for Which Appropriate: Economics
Approximate Grade Levels: 7, 8, 9, 10, 11, 12 **JH, HS**
Cost: $60
Type of Program: Simulation
System(s) on Which It Will Run: Apple II family; TRS-80 Models III and 4
Description: Students learn the basics of stock market trading through buying and selling stocks. Concepts of inflation and deflation should be developed. The program gives each team/individual $5,000 and adds proceeds to savings, compounds interest, and pays commissions.

Strange Encounters

Source(s): Orange Cherry Media
Course(s) for Which Appropriate: Geography, elementary social studies
Approximate Grade Levels: 4, 5, 6, 7, 8 **EL, JH**
Cost: $67
Type of Program: Problem solving
System(s) on Which It Will Run: Apple II family; TRS-80; Atari
Description: Students read and review evidence on both sides of mythical/controversial issues—Bigfoot, the Bermuda Triangle, the Loch Ness Monster, and the Snowman of the Himalayas.

Street Map

Source(s): Micro Power and Light Co.
Course(s) for Which Appropriate: Geography, elementary social studies
Approximate Grade Levels: 4, 5, 6, 7, 8 **EL, JH**
Cost: $35 ($45 with backup)
Type of Program: Game
System(s) on Which It Will Run: Apple II family
Description: Students maneuver their car around computer-mapped streets of Washington, D.C., Paris, London, and Tokyo. Students choose the best routes from one landmark to another using an overview or a detailed map. Students compete against each other or against the clock.

Street Map

Source(s): Computer Island
Course(s) for Which Appropriate: Social studies
Approximate Grade Levels: 2, 3, 4 **EL**
Cost: $20 (tape), $25 (disk)
Type of Program: Simulation
System(s) on Which It Will Run: TRS-80 Color Computer with at least 32K
Description: Graphics portray a typical section of a street map including homes, school, park, etc. Questions are asked about how to get from one place to another. Footsteps appear on the screen to show the route.

Struggle for Independence

Source(s): Aquarius
Course(s) for Which Appropriate: U.S. history
Approximate Grade Levels: 7, 8, 9, 10, 11 **JH, HS**
Cost: $35 (backup included)
Type of Program: Tutorial, simulation
System(s) on Which It Will Run: Apple II family; IBM PC; TRS-80 Models III and 4
Description: Part of the series America, an Early History, which gives the student insight into social, religious, economic, and political aspects of early America. Historical figures are used to "speak" to the student.

Super Quiz Computer Game

Source(s): Queue
Course(s) for Which Appropriate: U.S. history, world history
Approximate Grade Levels: 4, 5, 6 **EL**
Cost: $67
Type of Program: Game
System(s) on Which It Will Run: Apple II family; TRS-80
Description: Questions relate to five categories: Famous Leaders, Past and Present, Historical and News Events, World Geography, and Presidents of the U.S. One or two players can play at a time. Each student starts with $300. After a category is selected, a bet is made. Questions vary in difficulty.

Supreme Court Decision

Source(s): Intellectual Software
Course(s) for Which Appropriate: Government
Approximate Grade Levels: 9, 10, 11, 12 **HS**
Cost: $80
Type of Program: Simulation
System(s) on Which It Will Run: Apple II family; IBM PC
Description: Students become an attorney preparing and arguing a civil or criminal law case from the pretrial level all the way to the Supreme Court. The program teaches constitutional law and how the judicial system works.

Surface of the Earth

Source(s): Edu-Tron, Focus Media
Course(s) for Which Appropriate: Geography, elementary social studies
Approximate Grade Levels: 3, 4, 5, 6, 7, 8 **EL, JH**
Cost: $99
Type of Program: Tutorial
System(s) on Which It Will Run: Apple II family
Description: A tutorial with interactive exercises helps students learn the "language of maps" by interpreting legends regarding location, elevation, water depth, and land forms.

Survey Taker

Source(s): Scholastic Inc.
Course(s) for Which Appropriate: Elementary social studies, math
Approximate Grade Levels: 4, 5, 6, 7, 8 **EL, JH**
Cost: $29.95
Type of Program: Tool
System(s) on Which It Will Run: Apple 48K and IIGS
Description: Teaches students statistical methods, bar graphs, and how to compile and print data.

Taxes and Government

Source(s): Queue
Course(s) for Which Appropriate: Economics, government
Approximate Grade Levels: 9, 10, 11, 12 **HS**
Cost: $110
Type of Program: Tutorial
System(s) on Which It Will Run: Apple II family
Description: Provides an overview of the types and range of taxes and shows how revenues are
    spent. A case study presents personal income taxes as the fairest way to pay for the services
    we all use, in varying degrees. Two disks.

Teddytronic

Source(s): Queue
Course(s) for Which Appropriate: Economics
Approximate Grade Levels: 9, 10, 11, 12 **HS**
Cost: $60
Type of Program: Simulation
System(s) on Which It Will Run: Apple II family
Description: Students run a teddy bear factory and attempt to solve randomly generated
    problems. Trends in the industry, seasonal sales, prices, advertising, wages, cash flow and
    other real problems affect the output of Teddytronic. A period of eighteen months is
    simulated.

Texas History

Source(s): Frontier Software
Course(s) for Which Appropriate: U.S. history, geography
Approximate Grade Levels: 3, 4, 5, 6, 7, 8 **EL, JH**
Cost: $40 each
Type of Program: Tutorial
System(s) on Which It Will Run: Apple II family
Description: Covers famous people who molded Texas (Part I) and important cities of Texas
    (Part II).

The Other Side

Source(s): Tom Snyder Productions
Course(s) for Which Appropriate: Government, economics, sociology
Approximate Grade Levels: 5, 6, 7, 8, 9, 10, 11, 12 **EL, JH, HS**
Cost: $70
Type of Program: Simulation, game
System(s) on Which It Will Run: Apple II family; IBM PC; Tandy 1000
Description: Simulates global conflict resolution in a game format. Students form two teams,
    each representing an independent nation with limited resources. The teams must develop
    strategies for maintaining a stable economy, military responsibility, and national security.

Thirteen Colonies

Source(s): Aquarius
Course(s) for Which Appropriate: U.S. history
Approximate Grade Levels: 7, 8, 9, 10, 11 **JH, HS**
Cost: $35 (backup included)
Type of Program: Tutorial, simulation
System(s) on Which It Will Run: Apple II family; IBM PC; TRS-80 Models III and 4
Description: Part of the series America, an Early History, which gives the student insight into social, religious, economic, and political aspects of early America. Historical figures are used to "speak" to the student.

Time-Line

Source(s): Intellectual Software
Course(s) for Which Appropriate: World history, U.S. history
Approximate Grade Levels: 9, 10, 11, 12 **HS**
Cost: $50 each
Type of Program: Tool
System(s) on Which It Will Run: Apple II family
Description: Allows the teacher or students to use or add to the database in the program to create timelines or quizzes. Programs include Ancient History, World History, Non-Western Cultures, and American History.

Time-Lines in History

Source(s): Queue
Course(s) for Which Appropriate: World history
Approximate Grade Levels: 7, 8, 9, 10, 11, 12 **JH, HS**
Cost: $50 each
Type of Program: Database
System(s) on Which It Will Run: Apple II family
Description: Each program contains a database of hundreds of important events and people. Timelines can be created for any period or category of events in the database. Separate programs include Ancient History, World History, and Non-Western Cultures.

TimeLiner

Source(s): Tom Snyder Productions
Course(s) for Which Appropriate: U.S. history
Approximate Grade Levels: 5, 6, 7, 8, 9, 10, 11, 12 **EL, JH, HS**
Cost: $60
Type of Program: Tool
System(s) on Which It Will Run: Apple II family
Description: Includes several historical timelines that can be added to, merged, or printed as is in large letters for display. Additional data disks for American history, science and technology, and the 1970s and 1980s contain ten researched timelines each; the cost is $20 for each timeline.

Time Machine Traveler

Source(s): Queue
Course(s) for Which Appropriate: U.S. history
Approximate Grade Levels: 3, 4, 5, 6 **EL**
Cost: $67
Type of Program: Problem solving
System(s) on Which It Will Run: Apple II family
Description: Students are presented with four historical events and asked how they would have handled situations that arose in them. Magellan's travels, Washington at Valley Forge, Lincoln at Gettysburg, and Custer's last stand are the episodes covered.

Time Tunnel: American History Series 2

Source(s): Focus Media
Course(s) for Which Appropriate: U.S. history
Approximate Grade Levels: 7, 8, 9, 10, 11, 12 **JH, HS**
Cost: $99
Type of Program: Game, drill and practice
System(s) on Which It Will Run: Apple II family
Description: Students go back in time to meet a mystery American. Based on clues, the student must determine who the person is. Three programs included cover 1760-1860, 1860-1920, and 1920-1985.

Time Tunnel: American History Series 1

Source(s): Focus Media
Course(s) for Which Appropriate: U.S. history
Approximate Grade Levels: 5, 6, 7, 8, 9, 10, 11, 12 **EL, JH, HS**
Cost: $99
Type of Program: Game
System(s) on Which It Will Run: Apple II family; Commodore 64; IBM PC; TRS-80 Models III and 4
Description: Includes three programs in American history: 1760-1860, 1860-1917, and 1917-1970. The student journeys back in time and is given clues to the identity of a famous person. The student is to use the clues to solve the mystery of the person's identity. Two levels of difficulty are available.

Time Tunnel: America Series

Source(s): Focus Media
Course(s) for Which Appropriate: U.S. history
Approximate Grade Levels: 4, 5, 6, 7, 8 **EL, JH**
Cost: $75 each, $179 set
Type of Program: Game, drill and practice
System(s) on Which It Will Run: Apple II family; Commodore 64; IBM PC; Tandy 1000
Description: Students go back into time and encounter famous persons. Given a variety of clues, the student must determine who the historical figure is. Three series, two programs each; can be purchased as a set or separately: Series 1, Early America; Series 2, A Nation Emerges; and Series 3, the Presidents. Backups included.

Time Tunnel: European History

Source(s): Focus Media
Course(s) for Which Appropriate: World history
Approximate Grade Levels: 7, 8, 9, 10, 11, 12 **JH, HS**
Cost: $89 (backup included)
Type of Program: Game, problem solving
System(s) on Which It Will Run: Apple II family; IBM PC
Description: Students are given clues from which they attempt to identify famous persons in world history. There are two difficulty levels, and three programs are included: pre-1500, 1500-1815, and 1815-present.

Time Tunnel: The Presidents

Source(s): Focus Media
Course(s) for Which Appropriate: U.S. history
Approximate Grade Levels: 4, 5, 6, 7, 8 **EL, JH**
Cost: $69 (backup included)
Type of Program: Game, problem solving
System(s) on Which It Will Run: Apple II family; IBM PC
Description: Students are given clues. From these they try to determine to which president the clues refer. There are two difficulty levels. A poster of the presidents is included.

Torts

Source(s): Queue
Course(s) for Which Appropriate: Government
Approximate Grade Levels: 9, 10, 11, 12+ **HS, CO**
Cost: $45/$65
Type of Program: Tutorial
System(s) on Which It Will Run: Apple II family
Description: A two-disk tutorial program on torts for high school and college. The higher-priced program includes a student management program that records data on individual student performance.

Tragedy of War: A Simulation

Source(s): Focus Media
Course(s) for Which Appropriate: World history
Approximate Grade Levels: 7, 8, 9, 10, 11, 12 **JH, HS**
Cost: $99
Type of Program: Simulation
System(s) on Which It Will Run: Apple II family
Description: Introduces students to the decisions, strategies, and feelings associated with war through a simulation of the Western Front during World War I. Information is provided as students use an interactive attack simulation. A wide variety of supplementary materials is included.

Trail West

Source(s): MicroEd
Course(s) for Which Appropriate: Elementary social studies
Approximate Grade Levels: 3, 4, 5, 6 **EL**
Cost: $30
Type of Program: Tutorial
System(s) on Which It Will Run: Commodore 64
Description: Gives students practice in allocating resources to achieve a goal.

Transcontinental Railroad

Source(s): MicroEd
Course(s) for Which Appropriate: U.S. history
Approximate Grade Levels: 5, 6, 7, 8, 9, 10, 11, 12 **EL, JH, HS**
Cost: $30
Type of Program: Tutorial
System(s) on Which It Will Run: Commodore 64
Description: Provides information about the building of the first transcontinental railroad.

Transportation

Source(s): Right On Programs
Course(s) for Which Appropriate: Elementary social studies
Approximate Grade Levels: 2, 3, 4 **EL**
Cost: $25
Type of Program: Tutorial
System(s) on Which It Will Run: Apple II family; Commodore 64
Description: The history of transportation, as well as modern transportation, are explained. The importance of transportation to each individual is stressed. Reproducible worksheets and a teacher's guide are included.

Travels with Za-Zoom

Source(s): Focus Media
Course(s) for Which Appropriate: Geography
Approximate Grade Levels: 4, 5, 6, 7, 8 **EL, JH**
Cost: $85 each edition
Type of Program: Game
System(s) on Which It Will Run: Apple II family; Commodore 64; IBM PC
Description: Za-Zoom the Geography Genie takes students to unknown places. Students must piece together data about latitude, longitude, food, lifestyles, etc. to determine their location. A U.S. and a world version are available. Each includes a wall map and reward stickers.

Tut, a Boy King

Source(s): MicroEd
Course(s) for Which Appropriate: Elementary social studies, world history
Approximate Grade Levels: 5, 6, 7, 8 **EL, JH**
Cost: $30
Type of Program: Tutorial
System(s) on Which It Will Run: Commodore 64
Description: Acquaints students with the life of King Tutankhamun of ancient Egypt.

Understanding Contracts

Source(s): MCE
Course(s) for Which Appropriate: Economics
Approximate Grade Levels: 7, 8, 9, 10, 11, 12 **JH, HS**
Cost: $60
Type of Program: Tutorial
System(s) on Which It Will Run: Apple II family
Description: Using familiar situations the program guides students through an understanding of their rights and responsibilities regarding contracts. Buying a car and renting an apartment are just two of the situations used. A backup disk and an instructional guide are included.

Understanding the United States Constitution

Source(s): Mindscape
Course(s) for Which Appropriate: Government, U.S. history
Approximate Grade Levels: 7, 8, 9, 10, 11, 12 **JH, HS**
Cost: $50
Type of Program: Tutorial
System(s) on Which It Will Run: Apple II family
Description: The program, developed by a team of constitutional experts, leads students through the Constitution in a step-by-step manner. Questions are interspersed with text, and scoring is automatic with printouts for the teacher.

United States Geography Series

Source(s): Intellectual Software
Course(s) for Which Appropriate: Geography
Approximate Grade Levels: 7, 8, 9, 10 **JH, HS**
Cost: $30 each, $195 set
Type of Program: Tutorial, drill and practice
System(s) on Which It Will Run: Apple II family; IBM PC
Description: Programs present tutorial and drills covering the important geographic, economic, and demographic features of sections of the country. Programs include: New England, Middle Atlantic, Southeast, Midwest, Deep South, Central, and Far West. Management for Apple at extra cost.

United States Regional Studies

Source(s): Orange Cherry Media
Course(s) for Which Appropriate: Elementary social studies, geography
Approximate Grade Levels: 3, 4, 5, 6, 7, 8 **EL, JH**
Cost: $78
Type of Program: Tutorial
System(s) on Which It Will Run: Apple II family; Commodore 64; IBM PC
Description: This series illustrates how geography, natural resources, and other related factors led to the present day makeup of the United States. Students learn how and why the nation's commercial, transportation, and cultural centers developed as they did.

Unlocking the Map Code

Source(s): Rand McNally
Course(s) for Which Appropriate: Geography, elementary social studies
Approximate Grade Levels: 5, 6, 7, 8, 9 **EL, JH**
Cost: $111
Type of Program: Tutorial
System(s) on Which It Will Run: Apple II family
Description: Develops maps and globe skills related to land and water forms, map symbols, direction, location, time, and scale. A simulation game serves as the culminating activity. A teacher's guide and workbook masters are included.

USA in Profile

Source(s): Active Learning Systems
Course(s) for Which Appropriate: U.S. history, geography, economics, sociology
Approximate Grade Levels: 6, 7, 8, 9, 10, 11, 12 **EL, JH, HS**
Cost: $148
Type of Program: Database
System(s) on Which It Will Run: Apple II family; IBM PC
Description: Contains information divided into twenty-nine categories for each state and the District of Columbia. Has analyze, sort, and print functions for providing information based on up to three criteria.

U.S. Atlas Action

Source(s): Edu-Tron, SVE
Course(s) for Which Appropriate: Geography, elementary social studies
Approximate Grade Levels: 3, 4, 5, 6, 7, 8 **EL, JH**
Cost: $44
Type of Program: Drill and practice, game
System(s) on Which It Will Run: Apple II family
Description: Colorful maps are used to help students learn locations and facts about each state. A student management system is included.

U.S. Constitution

Source(s): Classroom Consortia Media
Course(s) for Which Appropriate: U.S. history, government
Approximate Grade Levels: 8, 9, 10, 11, 12 **JH, HS**
Cost: $70 IBM, $35 Apple
Type of Program: Tutorial
System(s) on Which It Will Run: Apple II family; IBM PC
Description: A study of the Constitution and the Bill of Rights with explanations of major points. A crossword puzzle and multiple-choice questions serve as a review. A case study of a trial based on a Bill of Rights issue is presented and the student is the "judge."

U.S. Constitution

Source(s): Queue
Course(s) for Which Appropriate: Government, U.S. history
Approximate Grade Levels: 8, 9, 10, 11, 12 **JH, HS**
Cost: $50
Type of Program: Tutorial
System(s) on Which It Will Run: Apple II family; IBM PC
Description: The Constitution and Bill of Rights are covered in this program. Using graphics and animation to maintain interest, the program attempts to attain comprehension and mastery of the material.

U.S. Constitution: Nationalism and Federalism

Source(s): Focus Media
Course(s) for Which Appropriate: U.S. history
Approximate Grade Levels: 7, 8, 9, 10, 11, 12 **JH, HS**
Cost: $99 (backup included)
Type of Program: Tutorial
System(s) on Which It Will Run: Apple II family
Description: Three programs in a game show format are included—Development of the Constitution, Creation of the Constitution, and Testing Your Knowledge. Covers British colonial government, Articles of Confederation, and the creation of the Constitution and its contents. Includes charts, graphs, and role playing.

U.S. Constitution Then and Now

Source(s): Scholastic
Course(s) for Which Appropriate: U.S. history, government
Approximate Grade Levels: 7, 8, 9, 10, 11, 12 **JH, HS**
Cost: $60
Type of Program: Database
System(s) on Which It Will Run: Apple II family and a copy of **AppleWorks**
Description: Consists of data files, plus activities to involve the students in analyzing information using spreadsheets, creating charts and tables, and using word processing. Students play roles of delegates to the Constitutional Convention. Step-by-step lessons are provided for the teacher.

U.S. Databases

Source(s): Sunburst
Course(s) for Which Appropriate: U.S. history, geography, government, elementary social studies
Approximate Grade Levels: 5, 6, 7, 8, 9, 10, 11, 12 **EL, JH, HS**
Cost: $59
Type of Program: Database
System(s) on Which It Will Run: Apple II family; Commodore 64
Description: The database contains geographic, political, and historical information about each state. A travel database provides a format for students to create their own database by entering additional information about the states. This program must be used with the **Bank Street School Filer.**

U.S. Geography Adventure

Source(s): Intellectual Software
Course(s) for Which Appropriate: Geography
Approximate Grade Levels: 5, 6, 7, 8, 9, 10, 11, 12 **EL, JH, HS**
Cost: $60
Type of Program: Game, drill and practice
System(s) on Which It Will Run: IBM PC; Apple II family
Description: Students travel through the fifty states, D.C., and the possessions. Identification of capitals, large cities, rivers, and other features is necessary to proceed. Hints are available but lead to point reductions. The program also helps students learn states' locations in relationship to one another.

U.S. Geography Series

Source(s): Intellectual Software
Course(s) for Which Appropriate: Geography
Approximate Grade Levels: 5, 6, 7, 8, 9 **EL, JH**
Cost: $30 each, $195 set
Type of Program: Tutorial, drill and practice
System(s) on Which It Will Run: Apple II family; IBM PC (both with disk drive)
Description: Covers important geographic, economic, and demographic features of the following groups of states: New England, Middle Atlantic, Southeast, Midwest, Deep South, Central, and Far West. A disk for each group is available separately.

U.S. History: Growth of a Nation

Source(s): Focus Media
Course(s) for Which Appropriate: U.S. history
Approximate Grade Levels: 5, 6, 7, 8, 9, 10, 11, 12 **EL, JH, HS**
Cost: $99 (backup included)
Type of Program: Game, drill and practice
System(s) on Which It Will Run: Apple II family; Commodore 64
Description: Three programs on two disks—Constitution to Civil War, Civil War to World Power, Modern America. Using game formats, students review facts related to these periods of American history.

U.S. History Series

Source(s): Queue
Course(s) for Which Appropriate: U.S. history
Approximate Grade Levels: 6, 7, 8, 9, 10, 11, 12 **EL, JH, HS**
Cost: $55 each, $225 entire series
Type of Program: Tutorial
System(s) on Which It Will Run: Apple II family
Description: Each of the five programs contains 80-100 excerpts from primary source materials. Overviews, vocabulary development and questions checking literal and inferential comprehension are included. Each program covers a major section of American history.

U.S. History: The Young Republic

Source(s): Focus Media
Course(s) for Which Appropriate: U.S. history
Approximate Grade Levels: 7, 8, 9, 10, 11, 12 **JH, HS**
Cost: $99 (backup included)
Type of Program: Game, drill and practice
System(s) on Which It Will Run: Apple II family; TRS-80 Models III and 4; Commodore 64
Description: Three programs (two disks) cover the thirteen colonies, colonial life, and the American Revolution. Students compete in a shooting gallery, Grand Prix race, and as mountain climbers by answering questions. Review is provided for incorrect answers.

U.S. Time Zones

Source(s): MicroEd
Course(s) for Which Appropriate: Elementary social studies
Approximate Grade Levels: 4, 5, 6 **EL**
Cost: $30
Type of Program: Tutorial
System(s) on Which It Will Run: Commodore 64
Description: Teaches students to tell time from one time zone to another.

Valdez

Source(s): K-12 MicroMedia
Course(s) for Which Appropriate: U.S. history, geography
Approximate Grade Levels: 9, 10, 11, 12 **HS**
Cost: $24
Type of Program: Simulation
System(s) on Which It Will Run: Apple II; Atari; TRS-80
Description: Navigation of a supertanker is simulated in this program. A radar display and a detailed map help students develop map-reading and navigational skills.

Voyages of Discovery

Source(s): Learning Arts
Course(s) for Which Appropriate: U.S. history, elementary social studies
Approximate Grade Levels: 4, 5, 6, 7, 8 **EL, JH**
Cost: $69
Type of Program: Simulation
System(s) on Which It Will Run: Apple II family
Description: Students simulate being either Columbus or Lewis and Clark as they make voyages of discovery. They select supplies and routes, and face a wide range of decisions.

Wagons West

Source(s): Focus Media
Course(s) for Which Appropriate: U.S. history
Approximate Grade Levels: 5, 6, 7, 8 **EL, JH**
Cost: $99
Type of Program: Simulation
System(s) on Which It Will Run: Apple II family
Description: A simulation of a wagon train journey to the West. Includes not only familiar features of popular simulations but also student history guides, journey record sheets, and posters.

War Simulations

Source(s): Hartley
Course(s) for Which Appropriate: U.S. history, world history
Approximate Grade Levels: 8, 9, 10, 11, 12 **JH, HS**
Cost: $80 each
Type of Program: Simulation
System(s) on Which It Will Run: Apple II family (64K); IBM PC (256K)
Description: Four strategy simulations that enable students to learn more about history. The programs and grade levels are: Pacific Theater (10-12), Civil War (8-10), European Theatre (10-12), and Indian Wars (8-12).

Washington's Decisions

Source(s): Educational Activities
Course(s) for Which Appropriate: U.S. history
Approximate Grade Levels: 7, 8, 9, 10, 11, 12 **JH, HS**
Cost: $63
Type of Program: Tutorial
System(s) on Which It Will Run: Apple II family
Description: Students are presented with crucial decisions that faced Washington. They may get
help from a variety of clues, if necessary, before making a decision. An explanation follows
each decision, right or wrong. A teacher's guide is included.

Water Pollution

Source(s): EME Corporation
Course(s) for Which Appropriate: Economics
Approximate Grade Levels: 9, 10, 11, 12 **HS**
Cost: $49
Type of Program: Simulation
System(s) on Which It Will Run: Apple II family; TRS-80; IBM PC; Tandy 1000
Description: This interactive simulation investigates the impact of pollution on aquatic life.
Students solve realistic problems on different water environments by varying temperature,
type of waste, dumping rate, and the method of treatment. Student lab booklets and study
guide are included.

Weather Fronts

Source(s): Teach Yourself by Computer Software
Course(s) for Which Appropriate: Geography
Approximate Grade Levels: 7, 8, 9, 10, 11, 12 **JH, HS**
Cost: $25
Type of Program: Tutorial
System(s) on Which It Will Run: Apple II family
Description: Covers the structure and characteristics of weather activity. *Creative Computing*
called the graphics "excellent." Graded tests, review options, and a manual are included.

Western Civilization

Source(s): Focus Media
Course(s) for Which Appropriate: World history
Approximate Grade Levels: 8, 9, 10, 11 **JH, HS**
Cost: $99 (backup included)
Type of Program: Drill and practice, review
System(s) on Which It Will Run: Apple II family; TRS-80 Models III and 4; Commodore 64
Description: Three programs on three disks—The Ancient World & Middle Ages, Reformation to
Nationalism, and The Twentieth Century. Game format is used to review concepts and facts
from these time periods. Graphics are used to present maps and histograms.

Western Europe

Source(s): MicroEd
Course(s) for Which Appropriate: World history, geography
Approximate Grade Levels: 5, 6, 7, 8, 9, 10, 11 **EL, JH, HS**
Cost: $30
Type of Program: Drill and practice
System(s) on Which It Will Run: Commodore 64
Description: Teaches students to identify western European countries on the map.

Western Expansion

Source(s): Aquarius
Course(s) for Which Appropriate: U.S. history
Approximate Grade Levels: 7, 8, 9, 10, 11 **JH, HS**
Cost: $35 (backup included)
Type of Program: Tutorial, simulation
System(s) on Which It Will Run: Apple II; TRS-80; IBM/MS-DOS
Description: Part of the series America, an Early History, which gives the student insight into social, religious, economic, and political aspects of early America. Historical figures are used to "speak" to the student.

Whatsit Corporation

Source(s): Sunburst
Course(s) for Which Appropriate: Economics, free enterprise
Approximate Grade Levels: 5, 6, 7, 8, 9 **EL, JH**
Cost: $65 (backup included)
Type of Program: Simulation
System(s) on Which It Will Run: Apple II family; IBM PC; Commodore 64
Description: Students make decisions regarding market surveys, economic forecasts, inventory, and advertising. Results are based on these decisions and changing economic conditions. Can be performed as a small group activity as well as by individuals.

Where in the USA Is Carmen Sandiego?

Source(s): SVE
Course(s) for Which Appropriate: Geography
Approximate Grade Levels: 5, 6, 7, 8, 9 **EL, JH**
Cost: $45
Type of Program: Game, drill and practice
System(s) on Which It Will Run: Apple II family; IBM PC; Commodore 64
Description: The student is a detective tracking Carmen Sandiego and her gang of thieves, following clues about geography, economics, and history. A copy of Fodor's USA travel guide is included for help.

Where in the World Is Carmen Sandiego?

Source(s): SVE
Course(s) for Which Appropriate: Geography
Approximate Grade Levels: 8, 9, 10, 11, 12 **JH, HS**
Cost: $40
Type of Program: Game, drill and practice
System(s) on Which It Will Run: Apple II family; IBM PC; Commodore 64
Description: The student is a detective following master thieves by following clues. A copy of the *World Almanac of Facts* is included for help. Ten suspects, thirty cities, and nearly 1,000 clues make the game interesting.

Who Built America?

Source(s): Right On Programs
Course(s) for Which Appropriate: Elementary social studies, U.S. history
Approximate Grade Levels: 4, 5 **EL**
Cost: $25
Type of Program: Tutorial
System(s) on Which It Will Run: Apple II family; Commodore 64
Description: The program discusses the reasons why immigrants came to America, what they have contributed, and why they are welcome. Reproducible worksheets and a teacher's guide are included.

Who Can Be President?

Source(s): Focus Media
Course(s) for Which Appropriate: U.S. history, government
Approximate Grade Levels: 7, 8, 9, 10, 11, 12 **JH, HS**
Cost: $39 (backup included)
Type of Program: Tutorial
System(s) on Which It Will Run: Apple II family
Description: Presents information on the backgrounds of presidents. Then students input information about their own actual and intended experience. The computer compares them to persons who actually became presidents.

Who'll Save Abacaxi?

Source(s): Focus Media
Course(s) for Which Appropriate: World history, global studies
Approximate Grade Levels: 7, 8, 9, 10, 11, 12 **JH, HS**
Cost: $65
Type of Program: Simulation
System(s) on Which It Will Run: Apple II family
Description: Students role play being the new president and staff of Abacaxi. Overpopulation, high unemployment, low literacy, and increasing infant mortality are a few of the challenges that face the new president. A student workbook helps students understand these problems and the alternatives.

Women in History Series

Source(s): MicroEd
Course(s) for Which Appropriate: U.S. history, world history
Approximate Grade Levels: 9, 10, 11, 12 **HS**
Cost: $79.95 each
Type of Program: Tutorial
System(s) on Which It Will Run: Commodore 64; Apple II family
Description: Each program includes a disk and a book relating the history of women in their cultures, past and present. Available are (Women in) Ancient Greece and Rome, Medieval/ Renaissance Europe, Africa (ancient), Africa (present), Traditional China, Modern China, Latin America (ancient and present).

World Atlas Action

Source(s): Edu-Tron, SVE
Course(s) for Which Appropriate: Geography
Approximate Grade Levels: 3, 4, 5, 6, 7, 8 **EL, JH**
Cost: $44
Type of Program: Drill and practice, game
System(s) on Which It Will Run: Apple II family
Description: Using colorful maps of the world, students learn locations and facts about countries. The program contains a student management system and reproducible worksheets.

World Desert Regions

Source(s): Right On Programs
Course(s) for Which Appropriate: Elementary social studies
Approximate Grade Levels: 3, 4, 5 **EL**
Cost: $25
Type of Program: Tutorial
System(s) on Which It Will Run: Apple II family; Commodore 64
Description: Background information on the animals and plant life in desert regions is given. Reproducible worksheets and a teacher's manual are included.

World Geography Adventure I-IV

Source(s): Intellectual Software, Queue
Course(s) for Which Appropriate: Geography, world history
Approximate Grade Levels: 7, 8, 9, 10, 11, 12 **JH, HS**
Cost: $60 each
Type of Program: Game, drill and practice
System(s) on Which It Will Run: Apple II family; Macintosh; IBM PC
Description: Four programs to help students learn the locations of countries, cities, and physical features in relationship to one another. Programs include: The Americas, Europe, Africa, and Asia.

World Geography Series

Source(s): Intellectual Software
Course(s) for Which Appropriate: Geography
Approximate Grade Levels: 9, 10, 11, 12 **HS**
Cost: $30 each, $240 set
Type of Program: Drill and practice
System(s) on Which It Will Run: Apple II family; IBM PC
Description: Covers countries and features of each area. For an additional $90 Apple users receive a student management system. Programs include: Africa, Asia, Europe, Central America/Caribbean, Middle East, South America, Canada, Mexico, and Australia/New Zealand. A wall map is included with each.

World History Adventure

Source(s): Queue
Course(s) for Which Appropriate: World history
Approximate Grade Levels: 9, 10, 11, 12 **HS**
Cost: $60
Type of Program: Problem solving
System(s) on Which It Will Run: Apple II family; IBM PC
Description: Students must locate events in history and identify the important personalities connected with these events.

World History on Computer

Source(s): Opportunities for Learning
Course(s) for Which Appropriate: World history
Approximate Grade Levels: 6, 7, 8, 9, 10 **EL, JH, HS**
Cost: $119
Type of Program: Tutorial
System(s) on Which It Will Run: Apple II family
Description: Maps and text help students learn about major events that occurred between the beginning of history and the Age of Exploration. Students trace the rise of ancient civilizations of Egypt, Phoenecia, Greece, Rome, and Europe in the Middle Ages.

World Mountain Regions

Source(s): Right On Programs
Course(s) for Which Appropriate: Elementary social studies
Approximate Grade Levels: 3, 4, 5 **EL**
Cost: $25
Type of Program: Tutorial
System(s) on Which It Will Run: Apple II family; Commodore 64
Description: Information on the animals and plant life is given. Reproducible worksheets and a teacher's manual are included.

World of Economics

Source(s): South-Western Publishing Co.
Course(s) for Which Appropriate: Economics, free enterprise, consumer economics
Approximate Grade Levels: 9, 10, 11, 12 **HS**
Cost: $70 for three disks
Type of Program: Tutorial
System(s) on Which It Will Run: Apple II family; IBM PC; Tandy 1000
Description: Introduces economic concepts identified by the Joint Council on Economic Education. Disks include a teacher's manual. Student workbooks are $5.25 each. Can be used by individuals or in small groups. Disk titles are Introduction to Economic Concepts, Microeconomics, and Macroeconomics.

World Polar Regions

Source(s): Right On Programs
Course(s) for Which Appropriate: Elementary social studies
Approximate Grade Levels: 3, 4, 5 **EL**
Cost: $25
Type of Program: Tutorial
System(s) on Which It Will Run: Apple II family; Commodore 64
Description: Information on the animals and plant life that live in polar areas is given. Reproducible worksheets and a teacher's manual are provided.

World Time Zones

Source(s): MicroEd
Course(s) for Which Appropriate: Elementary social studies
Approximate Grade Levels: 4, 5, 6, 7, 8 **EL, JH**
Cost: $30
Type of Program: Tutorial
System(s) on Which It Will Run: Commodore 64
Description: Teaches students to identify the day and hour from one time zone to another on a world map of time zones.

Yesterday's Explorers

Source(s): Orange Cherry Media
Course(s) for Which Appropriate: Elementary social studies, U.S. history
Approximate Grade Levels: 4, 5, 6, 7 **EL, JH**
Cost: $39
Type of Program: Tutorial
System(s) on Which It Will Run: Apple II family; Commodore 64
Description: This two-part series gives a vivid and colorful account of the Spanish, French, and English explorers.

You and the Law

Source(s): Queue
Course(s) for Which Appropriate: Government
Approximate Grade Levels: 7, 8, 9, 10, 11, 12 **JH, HS**
Cost: $190
Type of Program: Tutorial
System(s) on Which It Will Run: Apple II family; IBM PC
Description: Interactive tutorial covers eight individual programs, available separately for $35: Our Legal System, Introduction to Criminal Law, Civil Law, Introduction to Contract Law, Consumer Law, Cars and the Law, Housing Law, and Law and the Family. Reading level grades 6-8.

Zendar

Source(s): K-12 MicroMedia
Course(s) for Which Appropriate: World history, economics
Approximate Grade Levels: 9, 10, 11, 12 **HS**
Cost: $30
Type of Program: Simulation
System(s) on Which It Will Run: Apple II family
Description: Students discover the problems of running a developing country in this game which focuses on economic problems.

Programs Listed by Subject Matter and Grade Level

The following lists represent the programs previously described, arranged by subject matter and subdivided by grade level. The grade levels reflect the recommendations of the producers. We have not tried out all the programs and cannot guarantee that they are appropriate for any specific grade level. In any event, students differ, and a program that is appropriate for one fifth-grade class might not be appropriate for another. Any teacher who buys a program should try it with his or her class. If the program is not effective, it can be sent back to the company. In some cases a program may be appropriate for two different levels. In such instances, the title is listed under both grade levels.

U.S. History

Elementary Level

All about America
America Moves West
American History Adventures
American History
American Indians
American People
Around and about the Civil War
Around and about the Revolutionary War
Bank Street School Filer
Decisions, Decisions: Colonization
Decisions, Decisions: Revolutionary War
Democomp
Discover the World
Easy Search: American Studies
Explorers and Settlers
Famous American Women
Famous Blacks in U.S. History
Famous Women in U.S. History
Geography Search
Great Depression
The Golden Spike: Building America's First
    Transcontinental Railroad
Growth of the United States
History and Geography
History Game
History of the U.S. Democomp Package
History Study Center
I Love America Series

Indians of North America
Interviews with History
Inventions That Affect Our Lives
Lewis and Clark Expedition
Medalist Series
New World
Oregon Trail
Presidential Profiles
Ripple That Changed American History
Scholastic pfs: U.S. Government Database
Scholastic pfs: U.S. History Database
Sea Voyagers
Settling America
Seven Cities of Gold
Social Studies Explorer: American
    History
Super Quiz Computer Game
Texas History
TimeLiner
Time Machine Traveler
Time Tunnel: America Series
Time Tunnel: American History Series
Time Tunnel: The Presidents
Transcontinental Railroad
USA in Profile
U.S. Databases
U.S. History: Growth of a Nation
U.S. History Series
Voyages of Discovery
Wagons West
Who Built America?
Yesterday's Explorers

Junior High Level

A New Continent Is Discovered
Amendments to the Constitution
America Moves West
American History: 1865-1912
American History Adventure
American History Adventures
American History Games
American History Keyword Series
American People
Around and about the Civil War
Around and about the Revolutionary War
Bank Street School Filer
Choice or Chance?
Congress
Constitution of the United States
Creating the U.S. Constitution
Day to Find Out
Decades Game 1, 2, and 3
Decisions, Decisions: Colonization
Decisions, Decisions: Revolutionary Wars
Democomp
Discover the World
Easy Search: American Studies
Exploration to the Jeffersonian Era
Explorers and Settlers
Famous American Women
Famous Blacks in U.S. History
Famous Women in U.S. History
Game of Presidents
Geography Search
The Golden Spike: Building America's First
    Transcontinental Railroad
Government Keyword Series
Great Depression
Great Knowledge Race: U.S. History Series
Hail to the Chief
History and Geography
History Game
History of the U.S. Democomp Package
History Study Center
I Love America Series
Incredible But True
Interviews with History
Inventions That Affect Our Lives
Law in American History I and II
Lewis and Clark Expedition
Lincoln's Decisions
Medalist Series
New World
Oregon Trail
President's Choice
Presidential Profiles
Ripple That Changed American History

Sailing Ships Game
Santa Fe Trail
Scholastic pfs: U.S. Government Database
Scholastic pfs: U.S. History Database
Sea Voyagers
Settling America
Seven Cities of Gold
Simulation Construction Kit
Social Studies Explorer: American History
Texas History
TimeLiner
Time Tunnel: America Series
Time Tunnel: American History
Time Tunnel: American History Series
Time Tunnel: The Presidents
Transcontinental Railroad
Understanding the United States Constitution
USA in Profile
U.S. Constitution
U.S. Constitution: Nationalism and
    Federalism
U.S. Constitution Then and Now
U.S. Databases
U.S. History: Growth of a Nation
U.S. History Series
U.S. History: The Young Republic
Voyages of Discovery
Wagons West
War Simulations
Washington's Decisions
Who Can Be President?
Yesterday's Explorers

Senior High Level

Amendments to the Constitution
American Foreign Policy
American History Keyword Series
American History Achievement I: To 1860
American History Achievement II: 1860-1890
American History Adventure
American History Games
American History: 1865-1912
American People
America's Presidents
A New Continent Is Discovered
Bank Street School Filer
Choice or Chance?
Congress
Constitutional Amendments
Constitution of the United States
Creating the U.S. Constitution
Decades Game 1, 2, and 3
Decisions, Decisions: Colonization

Decisions, Decisions: Revolutionary Wars
Democomp
Diffusion Game
Discover the World
Easy Search: American Studies
Evaluating Presidential Leadership
Exploration to the Jeffersonian Era
Game of Presidents
Government Keyword Series
Great American History Knowledge Race
Great Knowledge Race: U.S. History Series
Hail to the Chief
History of the U.S. Democomp Package
History Study Center
Incredible But True
Industrialism in America
Law in American History I and II
Lessons in American History
Lewis and Clark Expedition
Lincoln's Decisions
MECC Dataquest: The Presidents
Oregon Trail
Presidential Profiles
President's Choice
Quest for Files: Social Studies
Review Questions in American History
Ripple That Changed American History
Sailing Ships Game
Santa Fe Trail
Scholastic pfs: U.S. Government Database
Scholastic pfs: U.S. History Database
Settling America
Seven Cities of Gold
Simulation Construction Kit
States and Traits
Time-Line
TimeLiner
Time Tunnel: American History
Time Tunnel: American History Series
Transcontinental Railroad
Understanding the United States Constitution
USA in Profile
U.S. Constitution
U.S. Constitution
U.S. Constitution: Nationalism and
    Federalism
U.S. Constitution Then and Now
U.S. Databases
U.S. History: Growth of a Nation
U.S. History Series
U.S. History: The Young Republic
Valdez
War Simulations
Washington's Decisions
Who Can Be President?

World History

Elementary Level

Alexander the Great
Ancient Civilizations
Ancient Civilizations and the Middle Ages
Ancient Rome
Annam: A Developing Country
Bank Street School Filer
Caravan: The Adventures of Marco Polo
Communication
Community Search
Early Humans
Eastern Europe
European Nations and Locations
Expedition to Saqqara
French Revolution
Into the Unknown: A Voyage Simulation
Middle Ages
Modern Eurasia
One World: A Countries Database
Renaissance
Russian Revolution
Social Studies Explorer: World Geography
Super Quiz Computer Game
Tut, a Boy King
Western Europe
World History on Computer

Junior High Level

Africa
Alexander the Great
Ancient Civilizations
Ancient Civilizations and the Middle Ages
Ancient Civilizations Keyword
Ancient Rome
Annam: A Developing Country
Bank Street School Filer
Beyond the Rising Sun: Discovering Japan
Caravan: The Adventures of Marco Polo
Communication
Community Search
Early Humans
Eastern Europe
Eurographics
European Nations and Locations
Expedition to Saqqara
French Revolution
(The) Grand Tour of Western Europe
Great World History Knowledge Race
Greek Mythology
History of Europe Democomp

History of Asia and Africa Democomp
Incredible But True
Into the Unknown: A Voyage Simulation
Middle Ages
Modern Eurasia
Non-Western Cultures
One World: A Countries Database
Renaissance
Russian Revolution
Sailing Ships Game
Simulation Construction Kit
Social Studies Explorer: World Geography
Standing Room Only
Time-Lines in History
Time Tunnel: European History
Time Tunnel: European History Series
Tragedy of War: A Simulation
Tut, a Boy King
War Simulations
Western Civilization
Western Europe
Who'll Save Abacaxi?
World Geography Adventure I-IV
World History on Computer

Senior High Level

Africa
Ancient Civilizations and the Middle Ages
Ancient Civilizations Keyword
Ancient Rome
Annam: A Developing Country
Bank Street School Filer
Beyond the Rising Sun: Discovering Japan
Campaign
Canada
Caravan: The Adventures of Marco Polo
Disraeli and the Eastern Question
Eastern Europe
Eurographics
European States and Traits
Expedition to Saqqara
French Revolution
(The) Grand Tour of Western Europe
Great World History Knowledge Race
Greek Mythology
History of Asia and Africa Democomp
History of Europe Democomp
History of Japan
History of Western Civilization
Incredible But True
Nationalism: Past and Present
Non-Western Cultures
One World: A Countries Database

Review Questions in World History
Revolutions: Past, Present, and Future
Russian Revolution
Sailing Ships Game
Save the !Kung
Simulation Construction Kit
Standing Room Only
Time-Line
Time-Lines in History
Time Tunnel: European History
Time Tunnel: European History Series
Tragedy of War: A Simulation
War Simulations
Western Civilization
Western Europe
Who'll Save Abacaxi?
World Geography Adventure I-IV
World History Adventure
World History on Computer
Zendar

Geography

Elementary Level

Adventure Island
Agent U.S.A.
All about America
America Coast to Coast
Bank Street School Filer
Coast-to-Coast America
Community Search
Continents and Countries
Crosscountry California
Crosscountry Canada
Crosscountry Texas
Crosscountry USA
Dr. Know's Geography
Eastern Europe
Easy Search
Easy Search: American Studies
Geography Games
Geography Search
Geo World
Globe Master II
Great States Race
Heart of Africa
History and Geography
I Love America Series
Introduction to Geography
Know Your State
Language of Maps
Learning about Geography, Maps, and
     Globes

Location and Distance
Map Reading
Maps and Globes
MECC Dataquest: The Fifty States
Medalist Series
National Inspirer
North America Databases
One World: A Countries Database
Regions of the United States
Road Rally U.S.A.
Run for President
Scholastic pfs: World Geography Database
Search and Rescue: Geography Skills
Social Studies Explorer: World Geography
Space Commander: States and Capitals Game
States
States and Capitals
Strange Encounters
Street Map
Surface of the Earth
Texas History
Travels with Za-Zoom
United States Regional Studies
Unlocking the Map Code
USA in Profile
U.S. Atlas Action
U.S. Databases
U.S. Geography Adventure
U.S. Geography Series
Western Europe
Where in the USA Is Carmen Sandiego?
World Atlas Action

Junior High Level

Adventure Island
Africa
African Geography
Agent U.S.A.
America Coast to Coast
Bank Street School Filer
Choice or Chance?
Coast-to-Coast America
Community Search
Continents and Countries
Crosscountry California
Crosscountry Canada
Crosscountry Texas
Crosscountry USA
Dr. Know's Geography
Eastern Europe
Easy Search
Easy Search: American Studies
Eurographics

Geographics
Geography Games
Geography Keyword
Geography Quiz Series
Geography Search
Geo World
Globe Master II
(The) Grand Tour of Western Europe
Heart of Africa
Hill Railway
History and Geography
History of Asia and Africa Democomp
History of Europe Democomp
I Love America Series
Introduction to Geography
Language of Maps
Location and Distance
Map Reading
Maps and Globes
MECC Dataquest: The Fifty States
MECC Dataquest: The World Community
Medalist Series
National Inspirer
North America Databases
One World: A Countries Database
Regions of the United States
Road Rally U.S.A.
Run for President
Sailing Ships Game
Satellite Down
Scholastic pfs: World Geography Database
Search and Rescue: Geography Skills
Shore Features
Social Studies Explorer: World Geography
Strange Encounters
Street Map
Surface of the Earth
Texas History
Travels with Za-Zoom
United States Geography Series
United States Regional Studies
Unlocking the Map Code
USA in Profile
U.S. Atlas Action
U.S. Databases
U.S. Geography Adventure
U.S. Geography Series
Weather Fronts
Western Europe
Where in the USA Is Carmen Sandiego?
Where in the World Is Carmen Sandiego?
World Atlas Action
World Geography Adventure I-IV

Senior High Level

Africa
African Geography
Bank Street School Filer
Choice or Chance?
Continents and Countries
Demo-graphics: Populations and Projections
Eastern Europe
Easy Search
Easy Search: American Studies
Eurographics
European States and Traits
Geographics
Geography Keyword
Geography Quiz Series
Geo World
Globe Master II
(The) Grand Tour of Western Europe
Heart of Africa
Hill Railway
History of Asia and Africa Democomp
History of Europe Democomp
Maps and Globes
MECC Dataquest: The Fifty States
MECC Dataquest: The World Community
North America Databases
One World: A Countries Database
Regions of the United States
Run for President
Sailing Ships Game
Satellite Down
Scholastic pfs: World Geography Database
Shore Features
States and Traits
United States Geography Series
USA in Profile
U.S. Databases
U.S. Geography Adventure
Valdez
Weather Fronts
Western Europe
Where in the World Is Carmen Sandiego?
World Geography Adventure I-IV
World Geography Series

Government

Elementary Level

Bank Street School Filer
Hometown: A Local Area Study
North America Databases
Our Town Meeting

Polls and Politics
Scholastic pfs: U.S. Government Database
The Other Side
U.S. Databases

Junior High Level

Amendments to the Constitution
American Government
Bank Street School Filer
Congress
Congressional Bill Simulator
Constitution and the Government of the U.S.
Constitution of the United States
Consumers and the Law
Creating the U.S. Constitution
Government Keyword Series
Hail to the Chief
Hometown: A Local Area Study
How a Bill Becomes a Law
Law in American History I and II
Monarch
North America Databases
Our Town Meeting
Political Genie: House Version
Political Genie: Senate Version
Polls and Politics
Presidency Series
Scholastic pfs: U.S. Government Database
Simulation Construction Kit
The Other Side
Understanding the United States Constitution
U.S. Constitution
U.S. Constitution Then and Now
U.S. Databases
Who Can Be President?
You and the Law

Senior High Level

Amendments to the Constitution
American Government
American Government I-V
ASK: A Survey Kit
Balance of Power
Bank Street School Filer
BIFs: Basics in Forecasting
Congress
Congressional Bill Simulator
Constitutional Amendments
Constitutional Law
Constitution and the Government of the U.S.
Constitution of the United States

Consumers and the Law
Contracts Law
Creating the U.S. Constitution
Criminal Law
Criminal Procedure
Demo-graphics: Populations and Projections
Evaluating Presidential Leadership
Evidence
Government and the Market
Government Keyword Series
Hail to the Chief
Hometown: A Local Area Study
IFs: International Futures Simulation
Jury Trial II
Law in American History I and II
Monarch
North America Databases
Our Town Meeting
Political Genie: House Version
Political Genie: Senate Version
Polls and Politics
Presidency Series
Property
Scholastic pfs: U.S. Government Database
Simpolicon
Simulation Construction Kit
Supreme Court Decision
Taxes and Government
The Other Side
Torts
Understanding the United States Constitution
U.S. Constitution
U.S. Constitution
U.S. Constitution Then and Now
U.S. Databases
Who Can Be President?
You and the Law

Economics

Elementary Level

Bank Street School Filer
Factory
Market Place
Maxi Taxi
Our Town Meeting
Parking Lot
Scare City Motel
Scholastic pfs: World Geography Database
Spell M-O-N-E-Y
The Other Side
USA in Profile
Whatsit Corporation

Junior High Level

Bank Street School Filer
Consumers and the Law
Factory
Market Place
Maxi Taxi
MECC Dataquest: The World Community
Monarch
Our Town Meeting
Parking Lot
Political Genie: Senate Version
President's Choice
Scare City Motel
Scholastic pfs: World Geography Database
Spell M-O-N-E-Y
Standing Room Only
Stock Market Simulation
The Other Side
Understanding Contracts
USA in Profile
Whatsit Corporation

Senior High Level

Air Pollution
Bank Street School Filer
BIFs: Basics in Forecasting
Business Organization
Business Simulations Package
Consumers and the Law
Credit and Banking
Credit: The First Steps
Decisions
Diffusion Game
Economics Keyword
Economics: What, How & For Whom?
Elements of Economics
Financial Cookbook and Consumer's Guide
Government and the Market
IFs: International Futures Simulation
Industrialism in America
Introduction to Economics
Labor
Market Economy
Measuring Economic Activity
MECC Dataquest: The World Community
Microeconomics
Monarch
Money and Financial Institutions
National Economic Policy
National Economy
Our Town Meeting
Political Genie: Senate Version

President's Choice
Rails West
Scholastic pfs: World Geography Database
Simpolicon
Standing Room Only
Stock Market Simulation
Taxes and Government
Teddytronic
The Other Side
Understanding Contracts
USA in Profile
Water Pollution
World of Economics
Zendar

Sociology

Junior High Level

Bank Street School Filer
Expedition to Saqqara
Hometown: A Local Area Study
Simulation Construction Kit
Standing Room Only
The Other Side
USA in Profile

Senior High Level

ASK: A Survey Kit
Bank Street School Filer
BIFs: Basics in Forecasting
Demo-graphics: Populations and Projections
Diffusion Game
Expedition to Saqqara
Hometown: A Local Area Study
IFs: International Futures Simulation
SAMP: Survey Sampling
Save the !Kung
Simpolicon
Simulation Construction Kit
SOCTERMS: Sociological Definitions
Standing Room Only
The Other Side
USA in Profile

Elementary Social Studies (General)

Ad Game
All about America
America Coast to Coast
Beginning Geography
Caravan: The Adventures of Marco Polo
Choices, Choices: On the Playground
Choices, Choices: Taking Responsibility
Community Helpers
Crosscountry California
Crosscountry Canada
Crosscountry Texas
Crosscountry USA
Dinosaur Days
European Nations and Locations
Farm Life
Great States Race
Holidays and Festivals
I Love America Series
Location and Distance
Maxi Taxi
MECC Dataquest: The Fifty States
Old Ironsides
Presidential Profiles
Renaissance
Rivers and Ancient Cultures
Road Rally U.S.A.
Scare City Motel
Search and Rescue: Geography Skills
Space Commander: States and Capitals
     Game
States and Capitals
States and Capitals
Strange Encounters
Street Map
Surface of the Earth
Survey Taker
Transportation
Treasure Hunter
U.S. Atlas Action
U.S. Databases
Unlocking the Map Code
Voyages of Discovery
Who Built America?

APPENDIX—SOURCES OF SOFTWARE IN SOCIAL STUDIES

The creation of educational software is truly part of the new information age. It can be produced by anyone with imagination and programming skills, with little capital investment. Thus, software is produced both by large publishing companies and small companies operated out of homes. Smaller companies usually have their products sold by software distributors. The source of software may be the company that produces programs or one that distributes the software created by others. The following list contains large and small companies of both these types. Each sells one or more of the programs included in this book.

Active Learning Systems
5365 Avenida Encinas, Suite J
Carlsbad, CA 92008

Addison-Wesley Publishing Co., Inc.
1 Jacob Way
Reading, MA 01867

Advanced Ideas
2902 San Pablo Avenue
Berkeley, CA 94702

Aldus Corporation
411 First Avenue South, Suite 200
Seattle, WA 98104

Apple Computer, Inc.
20525 Marianni Avenue
Cupertino, CA 95014

Aquarius
P.O. Box 128
Indian Rocks Beach, FL 33535

Baudville
5380 52nd Street SE
Grand Rapids, MI 49508

Beard Sales Company
P.O. Box 27931
Houston, TX 77227

Boring Software Company
P.O. Box 568
Boring, OR 97009

Britannica Software
345 Fourth Street
San Francisco, CA 94107

Broderbund Software
345 Fourth St.
San Francisco, CA 94107

BRS
1200 Route 7
Latham, NY 12110

Career Aids
Division of Opportunities for Learning, Inc.
20417 Nordhoff St.
Chatsworth, CA 91311

Classroom Consortia Media
One Edgewater Plaza, Suite 209
Staten Island, NY 10305

COMpress
P.O. Box 102
Wentworth, NH 03282

CompuServe Consumer Information Service
P.O. Box 20212
Columbus, OH 43220

Computer Island
227 Hampton Green
Staten Island, NY 10312

Concept Educational Software
P.O. Box 6184
Allentown, PA 18001

Conduit
The University of Iowa
Iowa City, IA 52242

Cross Cultural Software
5385 Elrose Avenue
San Jose, CA 95124

D.C. Heath and Company
125 Spring Street
Lexington, MA 02173

Dialog Information Services, Inc.
Subsidiary of Lockheed Corp.
3460 Hillview Ave.
Palo Alto, CA 94304

Didatech Software Ltd.
3812 William Street
Burnaby, B.C. V5C 3H9
Canada

Dilithium Software
921 S.W. Washington St. Suite 870
Portland, OR 97250

Dow Jones News Retrieval
P.O. Box 300
Princeton, NJ 08540

Dynacomp
178 Phillips Road
Webster, NY 14580

Earthware Computer Services
P.O. Box 30039
2386 Spring Blvd.
Eugene, OR 97403

Educational Activities
1937 Grand Avenue
Baldwin, NY 11510

Educational Publishing Concepts
P.O. Box 715
St. Charles, IL 60174

Educational Testing Service
Rosedale Road
Princeton, NJ 08541

Edu-Tron
3112 Waits Avenue
Fort Worth, TX 76109

EMC Publishing
300 York Avenue
St. Paul, MN 55101

EME Corporation
P.O. Box 2805
Danbury, CT 06813

Field Publications
Division of Field Corp.
245 Long Hill Rd.
Middletown, CT 06457

Focus Media
839 Stewart Avenue
Garden City, NY 11530

Frontier Software
P.O. Box 56505
Houston, TX 77227

Gameco Industries
P.O. Box 1862W1
Big Spring, TX 79721

Grolier Electronic Publishing
Sherman Turnpike
Danbury, CT 06816

Hartley Courseware
133 Bridge Street
Diamondale, MI 48821

Intellectual Software
798 North Avenue
Bridgeport, CT 06606

Interlearn, Inc.
Box 342
Cardiff by the Sea, CA 92007

K-12 Micromedia
6 Arrow Road
Ramsey, NJ 07446

Learning Arts
P.O. Box 179
Wichita, KS 67201

Letraset USA
40 Eisenhower Drive
Paramus, NJ 07653

Living Videotext, Inc.
Division of Symantec Corp.
117 Easy St.
Mountain View, CA 94043

Logic eXetension Resources
9651 Business Center Drive, Suite C
Rancho Cucamonga, CA 91730

Macmillan Publishing Company
866 Third Avenue
New York, NY 10022

MCE, Inc.
57 S. Kalamazoo Mall, #250
Kalamazoo, MI 49007

McGraw-Hill School Division
P.O. Box 25308
Oklahoma City, OK 73125

MECC
3490 Lexington Avenue North
St. Paul, MN 55126

Microcomputer Workshops
225 Westchester Avenue
Port Chester, NY 10573

MicroEd
P.O. Box 24750
Edina, MN 55424

Micro Power and Light
12820 Hillcrest Road, Suite 120
Dallas, TX 75230

Micromedia Software
Division of Oakland Group
276 Oakland Street
Wellesley, MA 02181

Microsoft Company
P.O. Box 25308
Redmond, WA 98073

Milliken
1100 Research Boulevard
St. Louis, MO 63132

Mindplay
100 Conifer Hill Road
Building 3, Suite 301
Danvers, MA 01923

Mindscape, Inc.
3444 Dundee Road, Dept. C
Northbrook, IL 60062

National Geographic Society
17th and M Streets N.W.
Washington, DC 20036

NAVIC Software
P.O. Box 30277
Palm Beach Gardens, FL 33410

Nystrom
Division of Herff Jones
3333 Elston Avenue
Chicago, IL 60618

Opportunities for Learning
8950 Lurline Avenue
Chatsworth, CA 91311

Orange Cherry Media
P.O. Box 390
Pound Ridge, NY 10576

Polarware
P.O. Box 311
Geneva, IL 60134

Queue
562 Boston Avenue
Bridgeport, CT 06610

Rand McNally
P.O. Box 7600
Chicago, IL 60680

Right On Programs
1737 Veterans Highway
Central Islip, NY 11722

Rightsof
20033 Wood St.
Suite 218
Sarasota, FL 34237

Scandura Training Systems
12149 Greentree Line
Narberth, PA 19072

Scholastic, Inc.
730 Broadway
New York, NY 10003

Scott, Foresman & Co.
1900 East Lake Avenue
Glenview, IL 60025-9969

SDC/Orbit
2500 Colorado Avenue
Santa Monica, CA 90406

Sensible Software
210 South Woodward, Suite 229
Birmingham, MI 48011

Silicon Beach Software, Inc.
9580 Black Mountain Road, Suite E
P.O. Box 261430
San Diego, CA 92126

Simon & Shuster
Gulf & Western Building
1 Gulf & Western Plaza
New York, NY 10023

Software Publishing Corp.
1901 Landings Drive, P.O. Box 7210
Mountain View, Ca 94043

The Learning Company
6493 Kaiser Drive
Freemont, CA 94555

The Source
Source Telecomputing Corp.
1616 Anderson Road
McLean, VA 22102

South-Western Publishing
5101 Madison Road
Cincinnati, OH 45227

Spinnaker Software Corp.
One Kendall Square
Cambridge, MA 02139

Springboard Software, Inc.
7808 Creekridge Circle
Minneapolis, MN 55435

Strategic Simulations
883 Stierlin Road, #A-200
Mountain View, Ca 94043

Sunburst Communications
39 Washington Avenue
Pleasantville, NY 10570

Sunshine Computer Software
1101 Post Oak Boulevard, #9-493
Houston, TX 77056

SVE
1345 Diversey Parkway
Chicago, IL 60614

Tandy/Radio Shack
1800 One Tandy Center
Fort Worth, TX 76102

Teach Yourself By Computer
2128 Jefferson Road
Pittsford, NY 14534

Tom Snyder Productions
90 Sherman Street
Cambridge, MA 02140

Touch Technologies
9990 Mesa Rim Road, Suite 220
San Diego, Ca 92121

Unicorn Software
2950 E. Flamingo Road
Greenview Park, Suite B
Las Vegas, NV 89121

Vernier Software
2920 S.W. 89th Street
Portland, OR 97225

INDEX